Memory, War and Trauma

Nigel C. Hunt

CAMBRIDGE
UNIVERSITY PRESS

CAMBRIDGE UNIVERSITY PRESS
Cambridge, New York, Melbourne, Madrid, Cape Town, Singapore,
São Paulo, Delhi, Tokyo, Mexico City

Cambridge University Press
The Edinburgh Building, Cambridge CB2 8RU, UK

Published in the United States of America by
Cambridge University Press, New York

www.cambridge.org
Information on this title: www.cambridge.org/9780521716253

First published 2010
Reprinted 2011

Printed in the United Kingdom at the University Press, Cambridge

A catalogue record for this publication is available from the British Library

Library of Congress Cataloging-in-Publication Data
Hunt, Nigel C., 1963–
   Memory, war and trauma / Nigel C. Hunt.
      p.   cm.
Includes bibliographical references and index.
   ISBN 978-0-521-88784-7 – ISBN 978-0-521-71625-3 (pbk.)
   1. War and society.   2. War–Psychological aspects.
3. Post-traumatic stress disorder.   I. Title.
HM554.H88 2010
303.6'6–dc22
                                                                    2010001104

ISBN 978-0-521-88784-7 Hardback
ISBN 978-0-521-71625-3 Paperback

Memory, War and Trauma

Many millions of people are affected by the trauma of war. Psychologists have a good understanding of how experiences of war impact on memory, but the significance of external environmental influences is often disregarded. *Memory, War and Trauma* focuses on our understanding of the psychosocial impact of war in its broadest sense. Nigel C. Hunt argues that, in order to understand war trauma, it is critical to develop an understanding not only of the individual perspective but also of how societal and cultural factors impact on the outcome of an individual's experience. This is a compelling book which helps to demonstrate why some people suffer from post-traumatic stress while other people don't, and how narrative understanding is important to the healing process. Its multidisciplinary perspective will enable a deeper understanding of both individual traumatic stress and the structures of memory.

NIGEL C. HUNT is Associate Professor in the Institute of Work, Health and Organisations at the University of Nottingham.

For Sue

Contents

Preface

I first became interested in the different ways people interpret war and the memory of war when I was a child, when I saw how my parents looked back on the Second World War with very different views. My father, who, in the RAF, was a participant throughout, tended to be neutral, not indifferent, but saw those 6 years with a mixture of positive, negative and inevitably fading memories; my mother, who was a child and adolescent, looked back with anger, seeing the war as a period which disrupted and destroyed her childhood; so I knew from an early age that people thought about the same events very differently.

This book is a culmination of my thinking over the last few years: from a recognition that much of what I was taught about memory as an undergraduate student was simplistic, focusing largely on a narrow individualistic view of memory as some kind of input–storage–output device which lacked explanatory value in terms of the way memory really works; to a growing recognition that in order to understand people and their thought processes psychologists such as myself should draw on the knowledge and understanding from other disciplines, such as history and sociology, in order to develop a fuller understanding of the ways in which people think. Furthermore, psychologists can learn as much, or more, from reading a good novel as from reading the scientific literature. A narrow disciplinary focus does not lead to good science, just restricted understanding. In the same way, modularisation has had many negative effects in higher education by artificially separating our subjects into discrete areas that are perceived as having little overlap; the 'modularisation' of disciplines restricts the development of knowledge and understanding about whatever aspect of the world one is interested in.

The title of the book gives away the foci. If we are to understand memory we must explore the influence of culture and society, and how memories are affected by the stories we tell ourselves and others – the narratives. At this level there is also a complex association between memory and history, and the ways in which memory becomes history over generations. War and trauma are unfortunately closely interlinked.

Many people who experience war are traumatised by its effects (though many more are not). Most previous research into war trauma has focused on the individual effects. In this book I attempt to integrate material across disciplines (e.g. history) and across methods (not only standard quantitative and qualitative methods, but also literature and a battlefield tour) to develop a more rounded understanding of what war does to people.

I would like to thank the people who, in one way or another, have contributed to the making of this book. In the first place the veterans of war. I have talked to many of these over the years – veterans of wars going back to the Second World War and sometimes back even further to the First World War – and coming forward to the wars that are still being fought. In one sense all these people share common experiences, from the boredom, excitement, fun and comradeship on one side, to the terror, horror and grief on the other. In another sense they differ greatly. People who fight in wars in different times and places are not treated the same, and the psychological outcomes are not the same. Prior to the twentieth century, few people took any interest in what happened to soldiers. Those who fought in the British armed forces in the Second World War were treated as heroes; those who fought in the German armed forces at the same time were forgotten, as were the experiences of many British troops during the final colonial period in the 1950s, 1960s and 1970s. In the USA, troops returning from Vietnam were often seen as murderers. In terms of treatment for war trauma, that has changed dramatically throughout the twentieth century, as indicated by the front cover of this book, which represents the men who were shot at dawn by the British authorities in the First World War. In modern times many would have been treated for post-traumatic stress disorder.

I would also like to thank those people who have personally helped me through the long process of writing this book. Many of them were probably unaware that they were doing so, because the writing of a book is a lonely business, and getting on with real life with family and friends is very important to me, even if it does delay the completion of the book. I would like to thank my parents for inspiring me in the first place, and for being there when I have needed them; the rest of my family and the children (both now adults) Jack and Conor; my friends, including everyone in the 'Yew Tree', South Wingfield, and the 'footballers' at Lea Green on a Monday night. I would also like to thank those who have helped me along with my thoughts over the years, particularly Ian Robbins and Peter Coleman. My employer, the University of Nottingham, by enabling me to take slightly longer than usual holidays in the summer has inadvertently granted me short sabbaticals during which I write.

I am also grateful to the University of Helsinki, particularly Airi Hautamaki, for allowing me several weeks of space during which I wrote a significant part of the book.

Most of all I would like to thank my wife, Sue, for putting up with me while writing this book, for commenting on earlier drafts of certain chapters that were unclear to me until she told me how to put the material in the right order, for being dragged to famous and obscure battlefields from the Russian Front and Leningrad to the Ebro, Bull Run to Sarajevo (though, with her love of France, such places as Normandy, the Vercors, Verdun and the Somme were 'easier' destinations), and for putting up with me writing the book when we were on 'holiday' in Spain. I would like to dedicate the book to her.

1 Background and purpose

I was recently asked to write about the health consequences of war (Hunt, 2008). I started by trying to trace the number of casualties in the wars of the twentieth century, but quickly gave up trying to obtain any sort of accurate account; records were often not kept, or were lost during wars, were deliberately manipulated by the winners or by the losers, or the records are still (presumably) in secret files. I then tried counting the number of wars during the century; this too became very difficult, as so many of them are relatively minor in terms of casualties (unless you are a participant). In the end I gave up trying to look at every war. I ended up focusing on those wars where there were more than 1 million dead. Accounting for the wounded and sick, and those with psychological problems, these are wars with possibly 5 million casualties – and then there is the impact on surviving family members and friends. The twentieth century had around 26 such wars – if we count episodes such as Stalin's campaign against the Kulaks and Chairman Mao's killing of the Chinese, which were not strictly wars, but were internal actions that still led to millions of deaths. On the basis of the figures available, I calculated that, overall, around 240 million people (give or take 50 million) had died as a result of these large wars in the twentieth century – not counting the victims of smaller wars. Adding the injured, that makes possibly 1 billion casualties. And that does not include all those psychologically damaged people, many of them civilians, who have had to live with their memories for the rest of their lives – memories of torture, massacres, death of family members, starvation, exile and rape. There are also the thousands or millions of perpetrators who carried out these acts, but whose voices are rarely heard. They are still people who have had to live with their memories of what they did. They are still, in some ways, victims.

These numbers are too large to comprehend. They are also probably widely inaccurate, but they do serve to show the scale of modern warfare, and how it impacts on so many people across the world, either directly or indirectly. This book is about the psychological casualties of war. Casualties are not just those who are killed or wounded, or civilians who are caught up in the fighting or just happened to get in the way of marching troops; they are ordinary people who cannot bear their memories of what has happened – the traumatised. We cannot accurately estimate the number of victims of war who are psychologically damaged by their experiences.

This book is an account of the psychosocial impact of war in its broadest sense – that of understanding memory not just as individual memory, but also as the ways in which other people, society and culture, and history, all affect how we remember. It considers the relationship between memory, war and traumatic stress. Many people have psychological problems as a direct consequence of war; many have terrible memories of these experiences that they find difficult to deal with; and many never do learn to deal with these memories. How can you come to terms with killing people, the loss of a child, or being raped multiple times, or remembering that you have killed civilians, or that you have had to permanently leave your home and your family?

On the other hand, we also know that the majority of people who go through these experiences do not have serious long-term problems, and that they are able to handle their memories and emotions and get on with their lives, more or less successfully. Many may still experience intense emotion when they think of what they have been through, but that does not mean they are traumatised. There is ample evidence to show that many of the psychosocial responses that we observe within a culture are not universal, that in some historical periods more people are likely to have problems, and in different cultures and historical periods they have different kinds of problems. Why is this so? What is it about memory, war and traumatic stress that make it so difficult to fully comprehend? Psychologists have studied memory for well over a century. We have studied the impact of war for just about as long. We have developed good theories and effective ways of treating people traumatised by war, yet still our understanding has serious limitations. It is argued here that some of these limitations are due to focusing too much on the individual, and not enough on the social and cultural world in which we live.

While there is a lot of good research – fascinating, detailed and useful theories about traumatic stress, and, perhaps most importantly, therapies that help people to cope with the overwhelming response – our understanding of memory and trauma still has something missing. Memory is not objective; it is not some kind of computer-like registration, storage and retrieval system. Memory is flexible, permeable, changeable, and – critically – affected by the social and cultural world in which people live. We live in the world as social beings; we do not and cannot live in isolation. No matter what the Zeitgeist says – that we live in an increasingly individualistic society – in the end we depend on culture and we depend on each other. These are essential to psychological health. This is why social support consistently comes out as being the most important factor concerning how people deal with stress and difficulties in their lives.

The other key concept that is used throughout the book is that of narrative. We constantly narrate our lives, creating and telling stories about who and what we are, and why we exist. We are natural storytellers and natural audiences (you can see the link to social support). Narrative is an essential function. We use and manipulate our memories, consciously and unconsciously, in order to present ourselves to the world in a particular way. Our life stories are constantly changing according to our circumstances. We do not have any choice in the matter. We are compelled to narrate.

Low perceived social support is seen as a predictor of traumatic stress. If a person experiences a traumatic event and they do not perceive that they have good social support, then they are more likely to be traumatised than if they perceive that they have good social support. Our fundamental need for narrative is met by interacting with others, by being able to narrate their problems, work them through, with someone who will listen appropriately. Social support is used to help people resolve their issues through discussion.

While narration is about storytelling and the construction of narratives that may relate closely to how events actually happened, or they may be largely fabricated, the argument is not that we fabricate our lives, but that psychological reality is more fluid, social and malleable than we usually think. In the context of the response to war then, this must be taken into account when we are building our theories, when we are trying to treat people with war-related psychological problems, and when we are just listening to war stories.

We must include the social and narrated worlds in our psychological theories. In order to do this effectively, psychological research is not enough. If we are to understand the nature of war, and the impact it has on people, then we must examine other approaches to understanding, through, for example, literature, history and the media. This book weaves together the story of memory, war and trauma by drawing on these different elements to increase our understanding of the lived experience and impact of war. Any psychologist who tells you that they can only learn about human nature from reading a psychology journal article or textbook, without considering the contribution of a good novel, play or poem, is naïve. We are studying behaviour, in all its shapes and forms, and good literature is part of that tapestry of understanding, along with historical accounts, sociology and politics.

Narrative, social discourse and collective memory

These concepts are central to the arguments presented in this book. Individual narratives are what we all have as explanations of our selves, our immediate environment and the world. Our narratives provide us with memories and with the sets of beliefs by which we conduct our lives. They are more or less coherent, more or less individual, and more or less meaningful, depending on the characteristics of the person and their situation.

These narratives must have origins, and there are a number of sources for them. Narratives, life stories or autobiographies[1] depend on social discourse – the main themes and threads of argument that are the social world. This is everything from common notions of the representation of the sexes, race or homosexuality, through to the use of particular terms that have ambiguous and changing meanings, such as 'cripple', 'lady' or 'queer'.

The importance of social discourse – the way people interpret events – should not be underestimated. The example below is contentious, and is intended as such, because it illustrates how our personal narratives, our ways of thinking, are affected by social discourse. 'Holocaust' is a term that most people agree pertains only or mainly to the killing of Jews in the Nazi era. Indeed, denial of this is a crime in some countries, as David Irving found to his cost in Austria when he was imprisoned for this offence. The recognised social discourse is that the Holocaust was the most terrible, evil series of events known to mankind. This is the social discourse that – not surprisingly – began to be created immediately after the war by the surviving Jews. They wanted people to remember. They knew it was important to tell people about what had happened, to inform future generations, to try and keep it as a living memory, in order that it would not happen again. The stories of the extermination camps, the brutality and the cold-blooded murder are unquestionably horrific. Few would argue that what happened to the Jews in the Second World War was utterly abhorrent, a crime against humanity, and something that is very difficult to comprehend by those who were not there. But there is an alternative social discourse – that there have been many

---

[1] Interestingly, mainstream psychologists only started to talk about autobiographical memory about 20 years ago. It was then thought of as a novel concept, rather than something that people in all societies have understood the need for and purpose of for millennia. It was the same with the concept of consciousness around the same time.

periods in history that have been just as bad as the Holocaust – for example, the Stalinist era of the USSR, the Maoist massacres in China, Pol Pot's regime in Cambodia or the ethnic cleansing in Bosnia. This is not about scale (though some were on a greater scale than the Holocaust); it is about the depth of human tragedy.

Another example where the term 'holocaust' may apply is the destruction of the native people of North America. Many of the terms that generally applied to Nazi Germany are at least as applicable in the nineteenth-century USA context. For instance, *Lebensraum* represents the idea that the white man wanted the whole of North America for himself, and that there was no room for the *untermensch* (the native people). This was genocide (the natives of North America were destroyed in the same way Hitler intended for the Jews) and, to use a more modern term, 'ethnic cleansing'. The term 'holocaust' may be even more appropriate to nineteenth-century USA than to twentieth-century Germany because the state – the USA – deliberately set out to cleanse a continent of its indigenous people and replace them with Europeans. They succeeded almost completely, while Hitler tried to remove one tribe from Europe, and only partially succeeded. We now see that tribe thriving in Palestine (the Holy Land, Israel – take your pick of social constructs), while the few survivors of the North American tribes live mainly in reservations, perhaps better described as concentration camps.

It is not that the destruction of native North Americans was conducted in the same way as the destruction of the Jews in Hitler's Germany, nor that the intentions of the perpetrators were necessarily the same; it is that the nature of the social discourse – the ways in which the events are interpreted – plays a crucial part in people's individual and collective memories of those events.

If we are to understand our narratives of war – or of anything else – we must understand the power of the social constructions we use when describing our behaviours and our thoughts and feelings. The examples above are not wrong; it is just that society – at least Western society – accepts a particular social construct. If the allies, including the USA, had lost the war against Germany in 1945, then the situation – the social construct – would be very different. The history books, which contain the social constructs of a society, would contain very different stories.

There is a relationship between individual narrative and social discourse, with one impacting on the other, but there are other key variables that must be included in the equation: the first is 'collective memory'. Collective memory is information about society that is accumulated over the years and develops into a kind of 'social fund', and is drawn upon in the development of social discourses and individual narratives.

Collective memory is important for the notion of commemoration and memorialisation – so important to many societies, and individuals, when remembering war.

A second key area is that of the relationship between memory and history. There is an increasing need to define these terms clearly and consider their interaction. The link between psychology and history is central to this book. Traditionally, memory studies have focused on the memory of the individual person, or sometimes on the notion of a collective memory, but still focused on actual memories. History has been the systematic and relatively objective study of the past, whether that is concerned with individuals, societies or politics. There is now a blurring of the edges – as is to be expected from the increasing interdisciplinarity we are finding throughout academia – and the distinction between memory and history has become blurred. For example, the growing field of oral history – loved and hated by both psychologists (hated for not being the scientific study of memory, loved because it focuses on real remembered memories) and by historians (hated for not being sufficiently objective and relying on unreliable eye-witness accounts, loved because it is personal and social) – exemplifies the strength of an interdisciplinary approach, drawing on the resources of the historian and the detailed memories of individuals who lived through the times of interest. Psychologists are increasingly interested in the study of individual detailed memories outside the narrow confines of the laboratory, as it is only through this approach that they can begin to understand the complexities of the mind. These are explored in later chapters.

Thus narrative is central to our understanding of self and identities. These narratives depend on the social context, including the audience they are designed for, as well as individual motivation and desires. Memory itself is constructed partly through narrative and the social context. If we wish to understand war trauma, we need to take into account these narratives and the socio-cultural situation the person lives in. At the same time, there are also fundamental underlying universals regarding memory, the stress and fear response and other variables which also determine the response to traumatic experiences such as war, and through which psychologists have developed a good understanding via laboratory and other research.

War trauma

An agreed definition of the central concept of war trauma is difficult to obtain, as there is disagreement over the terms that should be used when discussing the psychological effects of traumatic situations such as war.

The distinction between stress and trauma is critical; while most authors would agree there is a distinction, this is not always made clear. The term 'stress' was used by Cannon, an early pioneer in the area, to describe a stimulus – physical or emotional – that disturbs a person's internal homeostasis or balance, and that may be pathological if it reaches a critical level (Cannon, 1929). Selye (1956) defined stress as changes within a biological system that occur as a response to 'stressors', environmental stimuli that evoke such internal changes. Mason (1975), building on the work of Selye, argued that whether or not a stress response occurs depends on a range of individual variables such as appraisal, coping style and – critically for our discussion – the social world. Levine and Ursin (1991) define stress as a situation where the body anticipates or determines that there is some threat to the organism, and organises the body's defences against that threat in order to restore homeostasis. The stress response is a normal and predictable response to environmental threats. It only becomes a problem when the threat is sufficiently prolonged or intense that it overwhelms the body's resources.

Traumatic stress is fundamentally different to 'ordinary' stress, in the sense that there is a fundamental rift or breakdown of psychological functioning (memory, behaviour, emotion) which occurs as a result of an unbearably intense experience that is life threatening to the self or others. It is usually a time-limited experience (even within the context of war, traumatic experiences usually occur relatively rarely) of such intensity that the resources of the person are overwhelmed. There are a set of symptoms associated with these changes, including intrusive recollections, avoidance and emotional numbing, and hyperarousal. The overwhelming nature of the event is such that it leads to important and often permanent changes in the physiology and mental state of the individual. A traumatic memory is formed, a memory that is at once cognitive, emotional and possibly behavioural. The traumatic memory does not exist in normal 'stress'. The traumatic memory relates to the person's initial unconscious response to the traumatic event. As the person survived the event, the memory is indelibly fixed within the mind. This is adaptive. The person experienced a life-threatening situation and survived, and so if the same traumatic situation arose in the future, they should behave in the same manner again, hence increasing their chances of survival. So in this way, the traumatic response can be an evolutionary useful process. Unfortunately, owing to the mechanisms involved (which will be explained later), that response contains memorised bodily and psychological responses that are potentially damaging to the psyche.

This traumatic response can recur in different ways. For some people, the memories of the event are overwhelming and continuous, and they are traumatised. They find it difficult to cope with ordinary living, because their memories are emotionally unbearable. In response to this they may withdraw emotionally to help them cope, and so find themselves withdrawing from their family and friends – their key social support. This can lead to a range of clinical problems. Other people manage to suppress their memories, whether through conscious or unconscious mechanisms. They are able to avoid thinking about them. They may need to avoid reminders such as the place where the event took place, or the people involved, but they successfully manage to get on with their lives. When they do think about what happened, they manage to deal with the memory. Another group of people actively think about what happened – their memories, their emotions, their bodily responses – and they 'work through' or cognitively process their responses, change their narratives of the time, and perhaps even learn from what happened, maybe becoming a better person. The final group of people, perhaps the majority, who live through a traumatic event are not traumatised at all. They have no difficult emotional memories or problems. They can probably look back at the event and perhaps they get emotional, but it does not really bother them unduly or in a prolonged manner.

The details of the traumatic response will be discussed later in the book; suffice to say now that war trauma is concerned with the responses of people to their war experiences. We are concerned not only with those for whom the experiences are genuinely traumatic, but also those who live through these events and are not traumatised. By understanding the individual factors that determine whether or not someone is traumatised, we can perhaps learn to help those who do have difficulties.

But what is a traumatic stressor? The clinical classification of a trauma has changed throughout the years in which it has been represented in the classification systems DSM and ICD. When post-traumatic stress disorder (PTSD) was first introduced in 1980, as described in the *Diagnostic and Statistical Manual of Mental Disorders*, 3rd edn (DSM-III, American Psychiatric Association, 1980), there was an attempt to objectify the stressor, to say that the event must in some way be extraordinary, outside the range of normal human existence. The attempt was to include things such as war, disaster or rape, but to exclude events such as the death of a loved one. In later editions (DSM-IV, American Psychiatric Association (APA), 1994), a more subjective interpretation has been accepted; the interpretation of the individual was then considered to be more important. Rather than closely define the traumatic event, there was a greater emphasis on the person's response (fear, horror, helplessness) to the event. If there was an event and a response of fear, helplessness or horror, then it was considered satisfactory for a person to have that diagnostic criterion.

This change came about because there was no acceptable answer to the question regarding which kinds of events could be traumatic. The argument is that an event is traumatic if it traumatises the person. What is traumatic for one person may not be for another. The argument is circular, which is why understanding both the psychological and bodily response to the event is critical. The event, to be traumatic, must cause changes in bodily coping mechanisms that effect possibly permanent changes to the individual. These should, in principle, be measurable both physiologically and psychologically.

Researchers have studied a range of phenomena that have been classified as traumatic. These include short-term, usually isolated events such as rape or armed robbery, man-made disasters such as the sinking of ferries, natural disasters such as earthquakes or floods, and often longer term, chronic conditions such as war and child abuse. The negative psychological effects of these disparate traumatic events are very similar, though Herman (1992) and others have drawn a useful distinction between simple and complex PTSD. Simple PTSD usually, but not necessarily, relates to a single event. Complex PTSD refers to the response to complex events such as war or chronic child abuse. We will, of course, be mainly concerned with the more complex forms of the disorder. Though the general symptoms are similar, there are complicating factors, which will emerge in our discussion of war trauma.

Post-traumatic stress disorder

War trauma is not the same as PTSD, as the range of symptoms is much broader in the former, but the construct is in many ways a useful one. This will be discussed in more detail in Chapter 4, but it is helpful to have an outline of the disorder here.

The *Diagnostic and Statistical Manual of Mental Disorders*, 3rd edn (DSM-III) (American Psychiatric Association, APA, 1980) provided the initial diagnostic criteria for PTSD. These criteria have since been revised several times (DSM-III-R, APA, 1987; DSM-IV, APA, 1994; DSM-IV-TR, APA, 2000). The key criteria, apart from the event itself, now include intrusive re-experiencing, avoidance, emotional numbing and hyperarousal. In order to be classified with PTSD there must also be a significant impact on social, occupational or family functioning. Finally, there is a temporal component, to include acute (over 30 days), chronic (longer than 3 months) and delayed-onset (symptoms appear after more than 6 months) PTSD.

The main symptoms are, in themselves, often normal responses when the situation is normally stressful. Someone distressed by everyday events, whether students sitting exams or someone going for a job interview, will experience intrusion and avoidance. If a person has to sit an exam, then they may spend hours worrying about it unduly. They may also spend hours in avoidance – perhaps visiting the pub or going for a long walk in the country. These symptoms are normal. It is only when someone is devastated by a terrible, overwhelming event that these normal responses – or coping strategies – become abnormal, the memories become unbearable, emotions run riot, and it is impossible to live one's life in a normal manner.

A traumatic event, by definition, breaks down the accepted social and personal structures and belief systems of the individual. If you believe in the essential goodness of other people, then your experience of trauma will demonstrate that belief to be false. If you believe that terrible events will not happen to you – perhaps because it is statistically unlikely – and you are on a ferry that sinks, then in the future you may not want to go near a ferry because you now believe that it is likely to sink. This can make life very difficult for the traumatised person, and any treatment must try and rebuild their belief system, not one that is identical to the pre-trauma system, but one that includes the new knowledge provided by the traumatic event. In the end, as argued in Chapter 6, this can lead to someone knowing that they have psychologically benefited (or experienced positive growth) because of their experiences and that they are in some way wiser, more knowledgeable and more caring than they were before.

Trauma and identity

War experiences can fundamentally change one's sense of self or identity. Our identity consists of the beliefs we hold about ourselves, the world and the future. A person may grow up thinking that on the whole people are good, that the world is a safe place and that one is safe in the world. War can change that. Witnessing and taking part in battle, being involved in killing, being captured and perhaps subjected to torture, taking part in being a victim of or witnessing atrocities against other soldiers or against civilians, destroying artefacts – all of these can lead to a breakdown in one's belief systems and have an impact on one's identity. The traumatised soldier's positive beliefs about the world break down, and with those beliefs can go everything which the soldier considers important – love of family and friends, concern about the future, concern about protecting one's life. This is war trauma, though a host of other names have been applied to essentially the same condition: shellshock, battle neurosis, war neurosis, battle fatigue and combat fatigue, though many of these terms have been applied specifically to soldiers rather than to all people traumatised by war. Whatever name is applied, the results are the same. In combat, many soldiers experience a total physical, psychological and emotional breakdown that can have a long-term or permanent effect on their sense of identity. It is similar for civilians traumatised by war, though in many ways it is worse, because while the soldier has some limited control over his actions, the civilian has no such control; and the traumatic response is linked to the degree of control one has over a situation.

After the war: soldiers leaving the armed forces

Soldiers leaving the armed forces always have problems. They have to learn to adapt to civilian life, and they leave the 'family' they may have known for many years. For some, this may be the only family they have, one which has provided them with effective support, or comradeship. Whatever the circumstances, the ex-soldier has to adapt to a new identity. For some, this is a difficult time, which may lead to them experiencing a form of war trauma, resulting not necessarily from particular combat experiences, but from the novel experience of being a civilian and being unable to adapt.

The effects may initially be subtle, only becoming serious over time: they get bored, they get aggressive, they drink, and they have difficulty holding down a job. When a soldier's identity is destroyed they cannot cope in the world. There is often a whole series of psychological symptoms of anxiety and depression, what we recognise as PTSD, and problems relating to drugs, violence or suicidal tendencies. Initially there is a slow deterioration in their psychological health. At first it is not really a problem; it is only over months or years that it becomes clinically significant.

Civilians

The concern in this book is not just with traumatised soldiers, but also with all those, including civilians, who are caught up in the trauma of war. Throughout the twentieth century, an ever-increasing proportion of the victims of war were civilians. The proportion of civilians affected by war in the twentieth century rose from around 10% of casualties in World War One, to 50% of casualties in World War Two, to 90% in Bosnia. Of course, this is not a linear increase, and it is not that civilians did not in the past suffer greatly because of war. In the English Civil War, from 1642 to1648, it has been estimated that around 3% of the population died, from soldiers in battle to civilians from famine and disease.

Civilians experience war differently to soldiers. With significant exceptions, they do not have guns; they are not trained to kill. They are often women, children or older people, and there are many psychological issues specific to these groups. Children who experience war trauma have their beliefs shattered before those beliefs have even been fully formed. That can affect the rest of their lives. The same goes for women who are raped by soldiers. Civilians are generally powerless to protect themselves. They have not been trained in, and prepared for, the brutalities of war.

Finally

This opening chapter has looked at the background to the book, and has begun to define what we mean by war trauma. We will return to this theme in later chapters. After one further introductory chapter exploring the historical background to our understanding of trauma (Chapter 3), the book is split into three main sections.

The first section explores our current perspectives on trauma and memory. We cannot function as scientists without clear methods, so Chapter 3 focuses on methods and ethics. Trauma psychologists use methods that are similar to other psychologists – experiments, interviews, surveys and so on – but they are adapted to the practice of applied trauma research. That is, the methods may not always be applied in a pure manner; compromises are made according to the sometimes difficult circumstances in which researchers find themselves. The ethical issues in trauma research are potentially serious, as there is the potential to cause distress to participants, for example by making them relive their experiences, and harm to researchers, particularly if they collect data in a war zone, but also just through interviewing traumatised people, some of whom can be angry and violent. Chapter 4 focuses on PTSD, describing the construct, and its validity and limitations with regard to war trauma. For a full description of the symptoms associated with war trauma, we need to look at comorbid disorders such as depression and substance abuse. Chapter 5 focuses on our broader understanding of war trauma, drawing on research from a number of fields to describe current theory. It also looks at ideas about how we manage to cope with these memories. Chapter 6 takes a different angle, looking at research on post-traumatic growth, a relatively recent area within psychology which focuses on how many people go through traumatic experiences and emerge having experienced positive life changes, for example a better understanding of the meaning of life or relationships.

The next section is concerned with the centrality of narrative to the understanding of trauma, and is the heart of the book. Up to this point, the main focus of the discussion has been the individual; it now moves out to the socio-cultural perspective and the relationship between the individual and the social world. Chapter 7 looks at the relationship between memory and history – a contentious relationship – ignored by psychologists though discussed extensively by sociologists. Chapter 8 builds on this and considers narrative and social discourse – the key link between the understanding of the personal narrative and memory, and how they interact with the social world.

There is little point in building theory that does not relate to practice, particularly in the area of traumatic stress, where the final aim is always to help people improve their lives, though we also hope to advance our theoretical understanding, so the last section focuses on practical examples, beginning with Chapter 9, on how narrative can be used scientifically to explore war trauma. Chapter 10, on ageing and trauma, draws on my research and others' to explore the specific areas relevant to people who are ageing: how traumatic events can have a permanent effect on life, and how old age can change the nature of the trauma. In Chapter 11 there is an account of how psychologists can draw on literature in order to understand traumatic stress. Many people who have experienced war have written about it in detail, and as Shay (1994) argued, some of this literature can extend our understanding of traumatic stress by going further than, say, an account of PTSD. Chapter 12 goes back to the relationship between the individual and society, exploring the role of memorialisation and commemoration, and how societal and cultural memories change and develop over time, changing the ways in which individuals remember. Chapter 13 is a slightly unusual chapter for a psychology book, extends the previous chapter and describes battlefield tours and their importance, showing how people who have not experienced battle wish to participate in remembrance activities on the battlefield itself. There are examples of such tours provided, along with some ideas about how to build such a tour. This is an example of practical collaboration between individual and societal memory. Finally, Chapter 14 draws the material together and suggests how psychologists and others can benefit from this broader interdisciplinary and practical perspective, not only to advance theory and understanding about the psychology of war trauma, but also to help in the treatment of those who have been affected by war.

2   Historical perspective

The effects of traumatic war experience have been recorded throughout history (Trimble, 1985), particularly through literature. Evidence of flashbacks, dissociation and startle response might be seen as witchcraft (Rosen, 1960) or acts of God (Ellenberger, 1970). In the western world the evidence can be traced back at least as far as the Bible, though it was not until the nineteenth century that the scientific study of the psychological responses to war experience was considered in any detail. Furthermore, the terminology used to describe trauma is very recent, so we have to be cautious about interpreting what authors from the past were saying. We should try to avoid over- or under-interpreting information. People in previous eras did not only describe things differently – they *were* different. They were brought up to behave in particular ways, they were used to death in a way that few people in the West are now used to it, and they had different attitudes and beliefs. The past is another world.

The Bible describes the siege of Jericho, where all the soldiers of Israel marched around the city walls for six days, and where on the seventh day trumpeters blew their rams' horns as the army marched around the walls seven times, then all the people shouted, and this led to the walls of the city falling down. The story is not meant to be taken literally, but is an illustration of how traumatic loud noises can be. One can imagine the people inside the besieged city getting increasingly distressed as this went on, and finally flinging open the gates when they could stand it no more. This is a tactic used more recently, such as the rock music played at the siege of Waco or by the US forces attacking General Noriega in Panama.

Nearly 3,000 years ago Homer[1] described in the *Iliad* the experiences of Achilles and his comrades in the last stages of the siege of Troy. Achilles, after the death of Patroclus – his friend, mentor and possible homosexual partner – experiences psychological symptoms that we

---

[1] Assuming he existed as a single person, which appears unlikely.

would now describe as PTSD: bad dreams, withdrawal, social isolation, guilt, etc. This has been described very well by Jonathan Shay (1991), who likened the experiences of Achilles to the symptoms of PTSD experienced by Vietnam veterans. Around 400 years later, at the Battle of Marathon, Herodotus described how an Athenian soldier collapsed in the midst of battle. He was found afterwards, unwounded, but unable to see or to move his legs. This may have been a hysterical reaction to an unbearable situation, as was recorded in World War One. The soldier could not cope with the fear of being in the midst of flashing swords, jabbing spears and maniacal (but equally terrified) enemies, so he refused to see it, and refused to take part in it. This was not a conscious decision, but his body reacting to the trauma. According to Herodotus the man never recovered his sight. Of course, Herodotus is considered to be one of the West's most unreliable historians, but the point is valid whether or not the event took place. Some situations are so unbearable our bodies find many ways of shutting down in order to cope, to stay alive.

Shakespeare, writing at the cusp of the seventeenth century, describes several scenes reminiscent of modern-day conceptions of trauma. Macbeth is a tale of trauma, but perhaps the best relating to war trauma is in *Henry IV, Part 1*:

> Tell me, sweet lord, what is't that takes from thee
> Thy stomach, pleasure and golden sleep?
> Why dost though bend thine eyes upon the earth,
> And start so often when thou sit'st alone?
> Why hast thou lost the fresh blood in thy cheeks,
> And given my treasures and my rights of thee
> To thick-eyed musing and cursed melancholy?

This piece illustrates that the fundamental symptoms of traumatic stress were present in Shakespeare's time. Henry had just been to war, and may now have been classified as traumatised. But see how the language has changed? A modern Shakespeare might write:

> Why, Henry, do you have an eating disorder and sleep disturbance?
> Why are you depressed, experiencing symptoms of hyperarousal and
>   social anxiety?
> Why are you anaemic, and why have you lost your sex drive,
> And why do you experience intrusive thoughts and depression?

Perhaps we will leave it to Shakespeare.

Half a century later, in 1666, Samuel Pepys recorded in his diary that, after the Great Fire of London, he had nightmares for some months, nightmares that are now considered to be one of the key representations of traumatic memories. Along with the nightmares, he experienced the range of symptoms: intrusive images, feelings of detachment, memory impairment and survivor's guilt (Daly, 1983). The fire must have been a terrifying sight, eventually burning down a large proportion of London's mainly wooden houses in the old city, destroying St Paul's cathedral and killing an unknown number of people – unknown because there was no accurate census of the people living in the city at the time, and a fire of that heat would have entirely obliterated bodies caught up in it. At one point the fire threatened Pepys' house. He kept his gold in the cellar and a cynic might argue that his nightmares were more about the possibility of losing his gold than his house or his life.

Nightmares were also described by Charles Dickens after he helped the victims of one of the earliest train crashes in England. The problems associated with railway injury, including psychological symptoms, were acknowledged in law, through 'railway spine', a disorder recognised in people who had been through train crashes (Erichsen, 1866). Railway spine was noted for the shaking or jarring of the spine, and initially people might not have noticed they were injured because they felt confused, but once they got home, 'he bursts into tears, becomes unusually talkative, and is excited. He cannot sleep, or if he does, he wakes suddenly with a feeling of alarm.' As a reminder that there is nothing new, litigation against railway companies during the Victorian era often used railway spine as evidence.

The essentially random nature of battle – you cannot predict with any accuracy where the bullets and shell components will be travelling – has led many soldiers to acknowledge the instability of life. This affected soldiers in different ways. Those best able to cope were those who could accept that life and death in battle has a lot to do with chance and one may as well be fatalistic about it. Those who failed to cope may well have developed psychological problems. The difficulty we have from this distance is understanding these problems, as the language of trauma has changed. We may read of soldiers committing suicide and assume that they were traumatised. William Surtees, a British sergeant during the Napoleonic wars, described feeling sick in heart and body when he witnessed the mass shooting of prisoners. He called his feelings 'unpleasant sensations'; that is how much language has changed in 200 years. French soldiers of the same era who displayed symptoms that resembled what we now might call PTSD were labelled as having 'nostalgia'. It was thought that their symptoms – far from being related to the fear of being shelled, shot at or stabbed by a bayonet or hacked by a sword – resulted from the soldiers missing their mothers and sweethearts!

Reid (2000) describes traumatic stress reactions during the Crimean War. Sergeant-Major Smith describes the aftermath of the Charge of the

Light Brigade, and how a round shot had taken off the arm of one of his comrades, leaving his own arm splattered with blood. The descriptions are quite detached, and Reid describes how this indicates a numbing of responsiveness, linking it to the PTSD criteria of diminished interest, restricted range of affect and feelings of estrangement. Bombardment often plays a key role. Major Henry Clifford described how shelling made a great impression on soldiers' nerves, and that it was a 'trying thing' to sit idly by while being bombarded. Again, note the use of language. Major Clifford also noticed how bombardments could affect sleep patterns, how his tent-mate developed restlessness under night bombardment and shooting. The Russian view of the Crimean War was well described by Tolstoy in his recollections of the time he fought against the British. As a novelist, Tolstoy spent time describing the impact of a shell landing close to an officer, and how the soldier's spirit went from life through death to utter oblivion (Reid, 2000). Another example provided by Reid is that of Colin Campbell, who developed symptoms of PTSD during the Crimean War. His letters showed that he became destroyed emotionally as he was experiencing traumatic events on a daily basis. He became desensitised to the death around him, and he failed to experience a great deal of feeling even when he heard about his sister's death. This is a classic case of emotional numbing. Campbell described the different reactions of the soldiers, highlighting that during one of the attacks, 'a good many of the men did not behave well'; this looks euphemistic to modern eyes. Interestingly, Campbell explored substance abuse, distinguishing between those who drank steadily all night and performed their duty during the day and those who got very drunk whenever they could and spent a lot of time in the guardhouse. The latter tended to survive longer than the former; though perhaps that was because they spent a lot of time in the guardhouse.

During the US Civil War in the 1860s, soldiers experienced psychological symptoms in and after battle. Oliver Wendell Holmes described suffering the 'most intense anxiety' during the early days. The psychological problems experienced by the common soldier were described some years later by Da Costa (1871), who coined the term 'soldier's heart', and explained the symptoms as resulting from soldiers having a weak heart, that is they had a physiological problem underlying the psychological symptoms. The idea that there must be a physiological explanation for traumatic symptoms was usual in the nineteenth century. Disorders were thought to be physiological, with physical causes (and physical cures). It was not until the 1880s that people such as Charcot, Freud, Breuer and Janet would open up the debate regarding the psychological genesis of mental disorders. These authors produced seminal works based on their clinical experiences. During the last years of the nineteenth century and into the early years of the twentieth, they fundamentally changed our understanding of traumatic stress, moving from the physiological origin to the psychological one, recognising that psychological and physical symptoms could arise from psychological causes.

It was not until World War One that the psychological genesis of trauma was at least partially recognised by the military authorities in the West, particularly through the work of people such as Rivers, who treated Wilfred Owen and Siegfried Sassoon. It was recognised much later than this in countries such as Germany and Russia, both of which regularly shot soldiers who displayed symptoms of war trauma up until the end of World War Two. In the UK we stopped shooting them after World War One.

There was, of course, a long period where it was not clear whether there were physiological or psychological causes of war trauma. During the Russo-Japanese war of 1904–5, psychiatrists served near the front. The Russians had learned from their experiences in the Crimean War, where they had lost significant numbers of men to psychiatric problems. The Russians had a psychiatric hospital at Harbin where they treated 2,000 psychiatric casualties. Unfortunately the Russians wrongly attributed psychological symptoms to physiological injury – a problem to be repeated in the First World War. Nevertheless, this was the first war in which psychological reactions to the heat of battle were recognised (Baker, 1975). The symptoms formed the basis for the classification systems used in the First World War.

Hesnard (1914) reported psychological effects resulting from the sinking of the French ships Liberté and léna at Toulon in 1911 and 1907. These conformed to PTSD-type symptomatology: intrusive images, nightmares, anxiety, avoidance, somnambulism, hypervigilance, lack of concentration, and amnesia. It was becoming clear by this stage that there were a number of symptoms that tended to co-occur after a traumatic event.

Throughout the historical periods discussed there was never a wide recognition that men could experience psychological problems in battle; apart from the letters sent home (and these were only written by the educated and the literate) it was rare to recognise the reality of psychological trauma. There would have been many examples of psychological breakdown; it is just that few people wrote about it. Generally, if someone experienced symptoms in battle they were usually seen as cowards, and would often be executed. This applies across cultures and across historical time periods. Breaking down in battle has always been seen as a weakness on the part of an individual rather than as a sensible reaction to extraordinarily frightening events. It was not until after World War One that people wrote about war trauma openly. The poems of Wilfred Owen, or Remarque's *All Quiet on the Western Front,* are classics. Even now, when we have a hundred years of psychological theory which conclusively proves the general nature of the traumatic response, breaking down in battle is still seen as a weakness. This is perhaps inevitable given that soldiers have to be trained to fight in very dangerous conditions. Without this training, without the macho culture, it would be impossible for anyone to go to battle – a classic paradox for the armed forces.

In World War One the British Army authorities executed over 300 soldiers who were accused of cowardice in the face of the enemy or desertion. The case for these men was expounded in detail by Babington (1983), a lawyer who claimed that the men were suffering from psychological trauma in the face of overwhelming circumstances in battle. These men have now been pardoned. This is an excellent example of how modern ideas have been imposed historically to change history. These men were sentenced at a time when the law clearly stated that the sentence for cowardice or desertion was death. War trauma or PTSD was not recognised in law, and was not considered a defence. To be frightened so much that you could not face the enemy was cowardice, and that was it, according to the authorities. It does remain questionable whether decisions made in one era should be overturned nearly a century later, when conditions are very different. Look at the spate of apologies issued by countries' leaders in the last few years. What is the point of apologising for something carried out by different people in an era largely unconnected with our own – despite our still living with the consequences of the events of history? It is agreed by most people that Tony Blair acted illegally in sending troops to war in Iraq in 2003, and there is a good case for him being tried as a war criminal under international law, but he is not responsible for African slavery in the seventeenth century.

Nevertheless, it is a difficult decision, perhaps with no right answer, illustrating the interlinked nature of cultures. With respect to the First World War, the opinions and attitudes of the first decades of the century were very different to those of today.

At the outbreak of the First World War psychiatric services in the UK were very limited, but the war led to major advances (Lipgar and Pines, 2003). Before the war there were very few psychiatrists attached to the military. There was an asylum at Netley for troops who had mental disorders such as depression or psychosis. Generally speaking, the less serious mental disorders were treated by non-specialist doctors. Once war broke out there were people who did not believe there would be a problem.

Dr Albert Wilson stated that 'I do not think psychologists will get many cases' (quoted in Jones, 2004, p. 92). But it quickly became clear that soldiers who were repeatedly exposed to bombardment could experience an emotional breakdown, and it was debated whether this was caused by microscopic damage to the central nervous system (literally, shellshock), or whether it was a psychological problem. The term 'shellshock' was popular during the First World War (Salmon, 1921). Charles Myers, a doctor in the Royal Army Medical Corps, described the condition of emotionally disturbed troops arriving back from France in 1914 as shell-shock. It was thought at the time that soldiers' brains had been damaged by exploding shells, that the forces of compression and decompression led to microscopic brain haemorrhage. It was also thought that carbon monoxide from the blast might contribute to cerebral poisoning (Jones, 2004). Articles began to be published on the subject. These were summarised by Salmon (1921) in his post-war report on shellshock, by which time it was widely recognised that shellshock was a psychological disorder, not a physiological one.

In order to best understand the traumatic response of the soldiers of World War One, it may be most appropriate to turn to the poetry and literature of the time. Both Wilfred Owen and Siegfried Sassoon experienced shellshock during World War One and were sent to Craiglockhart hospital outside Edinburgh for treatment, though Sassoon was actually sent there for criticising the Government's war policy – perhaps demonstrating his sanity rather than his insanity. It was that or be tried for treason, and the Government did not want that. The decision to send Sassoon to Craiglockhart was, unfortunately, political rather than medical. The best-known doctor at Craiglockhart was undoubtedly W.H.R. Rivers (1922), who treated both Owen and Sassoon, and who told his story in his autobiography after the war. The 'Regeneration' trilogy of Pat Barker, published in the 1990s, provided a vivid account of the experiences of the traumatised soldiers in Craiglockhart. Rivers was a strong advocate of the psychological cause of shellshock, believing that part of the problem was that civilian soldiers, who had been trained quickly, had been unable to build up effective defences against the intense emotions they were to experience as a result of trench warfare. Rivers believed, like Janet (1925) in Paris, in a cathartic approach, and in attempting to reintegrate the traumatic experience into consciousness.

Wilfred Owen illustrated both cognitive processing and avoidance through his poetry. In this instance, he shows how soldiers commonly used avoidance in relation to the deaths of their fellows:

Why speak not they of comrades that went under?

Hibberd (1992) claims that only soldiers would see the point of this question, because only soldiers have the memories of their experiences. Owen states that soldiers have problems with the emotions associated with memories of dead comrades and so they avoid thinking about them. Through literature we can gain an understanding of war experience, again in the words of Owen regarding battle:

> *I can find no word to qualify my experiences except the word SHEER . . .*
> *it passed the limits of my abhorrence. I lost all my earthly faculties, and*
> *fought like an angel.*

Owen recognises the traumatic nature of the war, that to experience war is to experience something entirely alien to normal behaviour, and something that is not possible to describe.

Not all medical practitioners were as enlightened as Rivers. Lewis Yealland became renowned for his physical treatments. He used Faradism, basically electric shock treatment, to 'cure' paralysis. Yealland, not unlike many senior military officers, believed that soldiers with functional symptoms had weak wills and that they needed strict discipline and harsh methods to be cured. While he claimed a high success rate, this was likely to be due to fear on the part of his patients. Patients experienced what we might now view as torture. One man was 'strapped in a chair for 20 minutes at a time while strong electricity was applied to his neck and throat; lit cigarettes had been applied to the tip of his tongue and 'hot plates' placed at the back of his mouth' (Jones, 2004). The patient had been told he could not leave the room until he was cured – 4 hours of electric shocks did the trick, according to Yealland (Binneveld, 1997).

The change in the idea from trauma being viewed as a psychological disorder with environmental causes rather than a physiological one was *the* fundamental change in thinking that enabled future psychologists to make progress in understanding and treating war trauma. Prior to World War One, the physiological argument reigned supreme. After the war, many accepted that an environmental event could be the cause. This was a Kuhnian paradigm shift that had been building up since Charcot's work in Paris in the 1880s, and was forced through by the unbearable horror of the trenches. Of course, even by the end of the war there was still strong disagreement about the existence of shellshock, with many claiming it did not exist as a disorder at all.

During the war, psychiatric battle casualties had been initially returned to the UK along with the wounded, but by the end of 1915 it was clear that the chances of a soldier being cured decreased the further they were sent from the front line. It was Myers who first suggested that the troops should be treated relatively near the front line, but far enough away so that they were safe. Sir Arthur Sloggett, who had the rather long title of the Director-General of Medical Services of the British Armies in the Field, agreed that Myers could open specialist psychiatric units in casualty clearing stations about 10 miles from the front. Sloggett himself was against psychological treatment, believing that shellshock could be treated with military discipline. Nevertheless, four treatment centres, termed 'NYDNs' (not yet diagnosed nervous) were established (Jones, 2004). The soldiers were rested and given encouragement to recover. This strategy was later described as 'PIE' – proximity, immediacy, expectancy – the basic principles of treatment for battle stress:

> *Proximity* The soldier must be treated as close to the front line as practicable.
>
> *Immediacy* He must be treated as soon as the symptoms appear. This relies on his officers being aware of the symptoms, and recognising them as traumatic stress rather than as signs of cowardice.
>
> *Expectancy* At all times the soldier must expect to return to his frontline unit. If the soldier was allowed to think that he was a casualty just like any physically wounded comrade, then the symptoms would be less likely to dissipate.

This few hours' or days' bed rest meant the difference for many men between breaking down completely and being able to cope. The dividing line between clinical PTSD and sub-clinical PTSD is not that clear. PIE probably helped many with sub-clinical disorders. The same issue arises now: we make little effort to deal with those who have sub-clinical problems, apparently not realising that by treating people before they have full-blown PTSD we might save a lot of heartache and pain.

These principles, though sound, were not widely applied during the First World War. After the war, when there were thousands of veterans suffering from chronic psychological trauma, there was very little in the way of effective treatment – whether psychological or physiological – available. Most of the sufferers were left in mental institutions, and many remained there for decades, never regaining their sanity, despite the good work of many psychiatrists and psychologists[2]. The conditions persisted, though many psychiatrists and others had believed that once a neurotic soldier had been discharged from the armed forces he would stop his 'subconscious malingering' and recover.

---

[2] These people were the unsung heroes of the interwar years, caring for many thousands of forgotten 'heroes', often with little success, but with much perseverance and care.

Charles Myers ended up serving in France through most of the war. When he was demobilised in 1919 he described how he was weary after his service. He was invited to contribute to the Report of the War Office Committee of Enquiry Into Shell-shock, but found that the revival of his memories was too painful for him. When he finally wrote up his wartime diaries in an account published in 1940, he found the experience of preparing the book exceptionally unpleasant. Clearly, Myers had been significantly affected by what he had seen.

In Austria, Sigmund Freud was applying his principles of psycho-analysis to the treatment of traumatised soldiers. Freud (1921) was aware that combat could lead to war neuroses. He suggested that there is a conflict between the superego and the id, and that war neurosis is a response to the horrors of combat, that there is a change in ego-state from peacetime to wartime, with the wartime ego being threatened with anni-hilation. Freud also recognised from the outset that war neuroses were functional rather than organic, psychological rather than physiological, which is in contrast to the allied First War World position which had encouraged the notion of shellshock as a physiological response to combat experience throughout much of the war. Here Freud was building on the seminal work described earlier with Charcot, Janet and others in Paris.

After the First World War, the 1922 Report of the War Office Committee of Enquiry Into Shell-shock recommended training medical officers in psychological problems relating to war, but this was not taken up with any seriousness. According to Jones (2004), the Journal of the Royal Army Medical Corps only published five papers on shellshock between 1920 and 1936. By the start of World War Two the treatment principles discovered in the First World War had been largely forgotten, because they had not been needed in the years of peace (Strecker and Appel, 1964). By 1939 there were psychiatrists attached to the British Army at the outset of the war but they were very few, and were in place mainly to help select personnel for appropriate soldierly tasks. Before the outbreak of war, the experts appeared to decide that war neuroses could be abolished by pretending they did not exist. More specifically, any problems that did arise were caused by an individual's inherited disposi-tion, not the fault of war experience at all. This would be a good means of reducing the burden of war pensions, and is still a tactic used today, where soldiers who are clearly traumatised by their soldierly experiences are considered to have a problem because of their genes or because of some childhood trauma. Some preparations were made for psychiatric casualties in the UK, particularly for civilians around the time of the Blitz, but these failed to materialise when London was actually bombed (O'Brien, 1994).

Drug treatments had become available to treat war trauma; barbiturates were used to sedate affected troops, to reduce the active symptomatology. According to Sargant (1967) there is evidence for the effectiveness of these treatments. It is certainly the case that after the Second World War there were far fewer chronic war neurotics than after the First World War, though barbiturates may not have been the only answer. The nature of World War Two was different. Society itself had changed fundamentally. The country as a whole was traumatised by World War One. All the soldiers in World War Two grew up with their fathers' stories of World War One. That just could not happen again. People would never respond in the same way.

William Sargant (1967) was one of the best known of the British wartime psychiatrists. He described his experiences of British psychiatry during the Second World War in his book *The Unquiet Mind* (Sargant, 1967). He worked at Belmont hospital near Epsom, and after Dunkirk British soldiers began to arrive: 'I shall never forget the arrival of these Dunkirk soldiers in their tin hats and filthy uniforms, some of them wounded, many in states of total and abject neurotic collapse, slouching along ... Men swarmed into the hospital, some raging mutinously against their officers for having deserted them in a panic and others swearing that they would never care to fight again ... Many were suffering from acute hysteria, reactive depression, functional loss of memory or the use of their limbs, and a variety of other psychiatric symptoms, which one would never see in such abundance except during a war' (pp. 114–15). Sargant then describes a case where a soldier had hysterical dumbness, with hands shaking as though he had Parkinson's disease, and paralysis of the bladder, which was enlarged up to his navel. Sargant administered an intravenous injection of sodium amytal – a sedative he kept for experimental use on air-raid casualties. He described the effect as 'startling. His bladder suddenly emptied, his speech returned, his hands stopped trembling, and he became intelligent, articulate and comparatively normal at least until the effects of the injection wore off' (p. 115). Sargant carried on using this treatment throughout the war. The drug had an important side-effect. Soldiers would suddenly remember details of their traumatic experiences. After reliving these experiences, they often improved. Perhaps this would have helped Hitler, who, in the First World War, was given a label of 'amauro-blepharitis' (hysterical blindness) but who had no sympathy with traumatised German soldiers in the Second World War.

Another case Sargant describes was one where a soldier's brother had been severely wounded. He had begged his brother to put him out of his misery, which he did. The soldier then experienced a paralysis of the hand which pulled the trigger. A sodium amytal injection resolved the problem.

Sedation was used to keep patients asleep for days or weeks. At the end of this period many soldiers would be much improved. (This was also a technique which had been applied in the Spanish Civil War.)

Modified insulin treatment was also widely used, by both the British and American forces (the latter used it with over 15,000 patients). This treatment, which was effective with emotionally disturbed patients, but not depressives, consisted of giving an insulin injection which made the patient very drowsy, and just before they slipped into a (potentially life-threatening) coma they were given plates of potatoes, which helped restore glycogen levels to normality.

It has been estimated that around 10–15% of the casualties sustained by the British Expeditionary Force (BEF) during 1940 were psychiatric cases (Keegan, 1976). Keegan also estimates that throughout the war the psychiatric casualty rate varied from 2% to 30%, depending on the conditions of the fighting, demonstrating the importance of the particular event, as well as the personality and resilience of the individual.

When the USA entered the war and became involved with major fighting in North Africa, their authorities noticed that frontline units were being rapidly depleted. Around 30% of all casualties were psychiatric ones. Psychiatric cases were being sent down the line and back to the USA with the physically wounded. They quickly realised that they needed fast and effective forms of treatment. They stopped sending most psychiatric cases down the line and reintroduced the PIE principles from the First World War. They also used the sodium amytal treatment being used by the British. These treatments ensured that around 60% of the psychiatric casualties could be returned to their units within a few days. The USA failed to acknowledge the help the British had given them regarding these treatments, claiming that their new treatment – narcosynthesis – relied not only on sodium amytal or Sodium Pentothal, but also on Freudian principles of psychoanalysis. In 1943, General George Marshall, the US Chief of Staff, was still complaining that more soldiers were being discharged on psychiatric grounds than were being inducted into the army. During the whole war 409,887 members of the US armed forces were admitted as psychiatric patients to overseas hospitals. Of these, 127,000 were returned to the USA (Babington, 1983).

It was medical personnel from the USA who introduced the diagnostic terms 'battle fatigue' and 'combat exhaustion' to try and remove the stigma associated with war neurosis. There was a recognition that most soldiers did not get used to combat; they put up with it for as long as they could. Soldiers would become ineffective after around 140 or 180 days, with the peak of effectiveness around 90 days.

The RAF used the term 'lack of moral fibre' to describe war neurosis in aircrews. Many airmen were labelled 'LMFs', due to the very high casualty rates in Bomber Command. There was little support for aircrew who experienced psychological problems. Some were grounded, around one-third managed to fly again, and a very few were invalided out. The social pressure is important here. Bomber Command experienced very high casualties – around 50% during the course of the war – and the men knew there was a limited chance of them surviving the war, so one way out could be traumatic stress. Because of the need for large numbers of trained aircrew, and a shortage of highly trained men, it would be difficult to *allow* people to become traumatised in this group. It was almost a throwback to World War One, with any signs of fear being seen as cowardice. The stiff upper lip was at its stiffest under the moustaches of the men of Bomber Command.

Later in the war, the large numbers of patients arriving after the Normandy invasion ensured that Sargant and his team, now based at Graylingwell Hospital, Chichester, would have to use emergency treatments at a level that would be difficult in peacetime. Typically there would be around thirty patients all being given the combination of deep sleep and modified insulin therapy simultaneously. It was around this time that Pavlov's work on classical conditioning became known in Britain and new forms of treatment were tried. Sargant started encouraging abreaction by forcing patients not to relive their own traumatic experiences, but an invented – related – experience, e.g. asking a tank-man to imagine being in a burning tank trying to save a comrade. In theory this led to an emotional release, after which the patient would improve. This is similar to the imaginal processing now widely applied as part of cognitive behaviour therapy.

Anderson *et al.* (1944) also described the condition of the men who had broken down after the Normandy invasion. The soldiers were labelled as having combat exhaustion, a controversial term which many psychiatrists would not accept as the soldiers were not exhausted on admission to hospital. Unfortunately some soldiers, learning the label of their condition, convinced themselves that they were too exhausted to leave their stretchers and that this would be a permanent condition. Anderson *et al.* state that 12% were unable to speak, 8% were temporarily blind, 7% had lost their hearing, and 15% developed a stammer. None was affected by paralysis. Around 70% had nightmares about their experiences. One difference between these men and those of the BEF 4 years before was that these had not lost their morale – no doubt a function of the defeat of the earlier BEF and the expected victory of the Normandy invaders.

Sargant's wartime experiences led him, along with his colleague Slater, to produce the classic book on psychiatric treatment, *An Introduction to Physical Methods of Treatment in Psychiatry*. The Second World War had seen an improvement in the methods used for treating traumatised individuals. The treatment was designed to remove the unpleasant memories and emotions of the traumatic event (Wilson, 1994). Dollard and Miller (1950) used combat as an example of learned repression. They proposed that there are several stages of learning to repress memories: (1) during combat there are many external and internal cues; (2) the traumatic conditions attach strong fears to *all* these cues; (3) afterwards when the soldier thinks about combat these thoughts are the cues that evoke fear; (4) when he stops thinking, the fear diminishes; (5) the decrease in fear reinforces stopping thinking, so the veteran does not think about the war. These methods are again not dissimilar to those used in modern treatments.

This chapter has provided an outline of some of the historical moments in the understanding of war trauma up to the Second World War. It is clear that the language of trauma has changed – only recently is it intelligible in modern terms – and it is with difficulty that we interpret the feelings of people who wrote letters home from battle before the mid-nineteenth century. This has been a flavour of war trauma, a background and context for developing our understanding throughout the twentieth and into the twenty-first century. The next chapter takes up where this one left off, with the research conducted during the Vietnam War which led directly to the introduction of PTSD into the modern vocabulary of mental illness.

3   Methods and ethics

Trying to understand and treat war trauma requires a good practical and theoretical understanding of the subject. In order to obtain such an understanding, effective methods must be used. Within psychology we have developed a whole range of methods, from experimental through to qualitative approaches; all can provide us with good theory, but in order to do so they must be used appropriately. As in all science, there is good and less good practice. It is not just that some methods are applied inappropriately, with our ever-advancing technological and methodological understanding; researchers are constantly at the forefront of new techniques and approaches, so it is inevitable that there will be problems along the way. Another difficulty faced by trauma researchers is that the work is often carried out in difficult circumstances, so compromises with regard to method are often made. It is difficult to design the ideal experiment in a battlefield situation.

Another area of importance is that of ethics. While psychologists have broadly conformed to ever more sophisticated ethical codes and procedures over the last few decades, particularly in the West, there is an ongoing debate about ethics, both in the protection of participants and in ensuring the safety of researchers themselves. Ethical issues play an important part in war trauma research. Inevitably, this research involves some danger to both participants and researchers, and there are no clear boundaries between what is acceptable and what is not acceptable. Traumatised participants are often personally vulnerable, and there is a possibility of further psychological damage occurring as a result of taking part in a psychological study. We also must take care as researchers, particularly when conducting research in war zones, though sometimes participants can themselves present a danger to researchers – traumatised people can be aggressive and dangerous. These issues are contentious, and it is important that we discuss them and act appropriately when designing studies. It is equally important that we do not become so rigid that a lot of good research cannot be conducted for ethical reasons.

A range of methods

Researchers have used virtually every methodological technique available to the discipline of psychology, which is one thing that makes the area exciting – it is an area where we can genuinely triangulate research from different methodological sources, and thus attempt to strengthen our theories.

There are studies involving the so-called 'gold standard' technique of medical science – the randomised controlled trial – where the researcher wishes to determine the effectiveness of a particular treatment, e.g. cognitive behaviour therapy, and compare it with either another form of treatment, or with a no-treatment control group. Traumatised participants are randomly allocated to one of the groups, and after the treatment is completed the groups are compared to find out whether the treatment group has improved to a significantly greater extent than the control group. If so, it is argued that, assuming all key variables have been controlled for, the treatment is effective with this group.

Researchers have used brain scanning technology such as magnetic resonance imaging (MRI) to explore those areas of the brain that are thought to be important for war trauma, such as the amygdala (which is involved with emotion and conditioning), the hippocampus (which is important for memory input) and prefrontal cortex (involved with attention, decision making and working memory, all important in trauma theory). By comparing traumatised and non-traumatised people, and looking at the differences in brain structure or function, we can draw conclusions about which areas of the brain are affected by trauma.

Other researchers use self-report questionnaires, which measure a range of psychological variables, so we can see which variables play an important part in how and why one person becomes traumatised and another does not. For instance, we can measure extent of trauma, along with age, sex, coping styles, social support and personality, and see which of these predict a poor outcome after war experience.

Clinicians carry out detailed assessments of their clients throughout a treatment programme. These can be used as the basis for case studies, a method which allows the researcher or clinician to take a very detailed look at the factors associated with trauma. These are illuminating to the theoretician.

Interviews have been widely used as a method for the study of traumatised individuals because they enable the participant to discuss their memories and feelings in detail, in the way they want to discuss it, providing the information the participant wants to provide, i.e. focusing on the issues that are important to them as individuals rather than the issues the researcher thinks are important – they may not be the same thing. It is possible, through interviews, to develop a detailed understanding of the problems and issues faced by the person with war trauma.

The narrative interview is a specific method linked to theory that is important in this book. Narrative refers to a broad approach to a general understanding of war trauma, and relates not only to the trauma itself but also to the participant's life in general, so providing a fuller and more coherent picture of the role of the traumatic event in the person's remembered experience. Narratives can be derived from a number of sources, clinical interviews, narrative therapy, research interviews, unpublished or published writings, etc., but if we are going to deal with these we have to know how to carry out narrative analyses; we need to apply a narrative method.

As in all science, understanding method is a critical pre-requisite for understanding theory. Only by knowing *how* we studied an area can we understand the potential strengths and weaknesses of a particular theory. What follows is not a detailed consideration of each method – this is not a book on methods – but an outline of some of the key issues.

Randomised controlled trials

While the randomised controlled trial (RCT) is the gold standard for medical research, there have been relatively few of these trials carried out within the field of war trauma. This is for a number of reasons, but there is a need for further research in this area, as this will help us determine the kinds of treatments that are effective for traumatised people. But there is a problem. RCTs were devised for use in medical science, where a specific drug is tested for efficacy in treating a specific disorder. The science is clean, and largely free from confounding variables. A person is randomly assigned to either the treatment (drug) or control (placebo or no drug) condition, administered the treatment and then tested to see whether there is any effect. Most (though not all) physical illnesses are definable and discrete. They consist of a given set of symptoms defining a specific syndrome. Unfortunately, war trauma is not like that. Each person has a unique set of symptoms, some of which need to be treated using different methods. There is not, and probably will not be, one drug that will treat all of these various symptoms. The diversity of experience, symptoms, personality and social settings makes it difficult to state that a particular form of treatment is most effective. Treatment A may be very useful for Person X, but not for Person Y, whereas Treatment B may work with Person Y but not with Person A. Treatment C may be better for dealing with startle reactions, and Treatment D for faulty beliefs. It is complicated. Cognitive behaviour therapy (CBT) is recommended by the NICE guidelines in the UK as the most effective treatment for PTSD (NICE, 2005), along with eye movement desensitisation and reprocessing. But CBT is only useful and effective for certain kinds of people. Generally, they have to be people with some insight into their condition, they have to be relatively intelligent in order to understand how the treatment is meant to work, they have to be motivated to help it work, and they have to be able to cope with the severe emotional distress that will often result from the treatment. CBT will not work for everyone.

Another problem with RCTs in this area is that they assume that a patient can be randomly allocated to either a treatment or a control condition. This is often just not possible. A lot of treatment for war-traumatised people such as refugees takes place in the field, in the country where the war is taking place, or in a refugee camp nearby. This may not be the situation where an RCT can be used. People need treating, and a war zone or a refugee camp is not always the best place for exact science. Therapists have to be practical. One of the problems psychologists working in this area face is criticism from the medical community regarding the inadequacy of our methods. The situation when treating traumatised people, especially in the field, is very different from a hospital in a safe country where participants can be easily accessed for the study.

This is also an ethical issue. If the clinician believes that a particular treatment alleviates war trauma, and there is already some evidence that this treatment works, then they may consider it their duty to use that treatment. Refusing such treatment to psychologically damaged people goes against the ethical principles of the professional psychologist. This can sometimes be resolved if a waiting list control is used, i.e. where one group receives immediate treatment, and the other group receives treatment after a specific period of time. The key measurement is carried out before the second group starts treatment. Again, while this is a good experimental design, it may not be practical if the clinician is working in the war zone.

Health service ethical procedures are – at least in the UK – very strict, and there can be more emphasis on design matters than on ethics. That may be appropriate in the hospital setting, but the problems faced by psychologists should be recognised. As we can see from the above, sometimes the most ethical solution for a study is to design it 'badly', in terms of medical ethics. If this makes sense, the well-designed study may be unethical while the 'poorly' designed study may be ethical.

Any findings may be limited in scope because of the compromise, but they will be helpful, and the study will still be scientific, if not quite as methodologically rigorous as might be desired. The ethical procedures for psychologists who are studying the complexities of human behaviour should be separated from the procedures used for medical practitioners testing drugs. The fundamental rules are so different that sharing the same ethical procedure when studying patients is extremely problematic, as we have seen in the UK over the last few years.

As an example of the problems faced by designing good RCTs, we carried out a systematic review of the literature regarding the treatment of traumatised refugees. We initially found around 800 studies looking at the treatment of refugees, but once we had applied strict criteria relating to the use of RCT – the gold standard, remember – we found that only 6 studies fulfilled the criteria. The reason that many studies had to be excluded was that they were carried out in war zones or refugee camps, or with groups of extremely distressed people. There is no time for sophisticated techniques when there are damaged people. We found that the most effective techniques were CBT and narrative exposure therapy (Schauer *et al.*, 2005). Both were significantly more effective than controls. The problem with drawing a conclusion from this review is that it is based on 6 studies rather than 800. An analysis of all 800 studies (but recognising their limitations) might lead to a very different conclusion regarding efficacy of treatment.

Other experimental techniques

A true experiment involves the manipulation of an independent variable (the psychological factor that we are interested in, e.g. whether or not the person has PTSD, or whether or not a rat has had its amygdala lesioned) and the measurement of a dependent variable (e.g. the reaction time to trauma-related visual stimuli, or the number of trials it takes a rat to learn to avoid an electric shock). Participants should be randomly and independently allocated to groups, so that potential confounding individual variation (e.g. cognitive processing speed) is spread equally across conditions. While true experimentation is difficult with much research into war trauma, useful research has been carried out both on the cognitive factors involved in trauma, and on work with animals, particularly relating to conditioning paradigms and lesion studies.

Experimental work has played an important role in many ways, from identifying particular brain regions that are important for emotional processing and memory, to developing an understanding of the cognitive problems experienced by traumatised people.

Again, there are ethical difficulties when carrying out certain types of experimentation in this area. Obviously, it is not ethical to traumatise people and randomly allocate them to groups. That means that our experiments on humans are generally quasi-experiments, where we compare already traumatised people with those who are not traumatised, attempting to match them according to traumatic experience and other variables we consider to be relevant. We then test to see whether they perform differently on, for example, a cognitive task (e.g. memory, attention or perception). If there is a difference, we may claim that this is because of the presence of PTSD. The problem is that the participants effectively self-allocated themselves to the groups (due to their traumatic stress). It may have been that the difference was already there before the traumatic experience. We have no way of telling when we are working retrospectively in this way.

There are further problems with experimentation in psychology that are general ones, not associated specifically with war trauma. Experimentation, by its nature, manipulates only one or two variables. Humans vary on many thousands of factors, and so it can be difficult to tease out an effect that is specific to the experimental design. When this effect is small, as is the case with many cognitive tasks, then this can become even more difficult.

Problems notwithstanding, experimental procedures have produced some of the critical findings for our understanding of traumatic stress, and these should not be overlooked. These will be examined in more detail in the next two chapters.

Brain-imaging techniques

Brain imaging has become very popular in the last 20 years or so. A plethora of technology is now available to look at what is happening inside the brain, where it is happening and how activation in a specific area of the brain is related to specific behaviours. This is a major advance in psychology which is fruitful for theory and understanding. There is a wide range of technology available, including magnetic resonance imaging or functional magnetic resonance imaging, positron emission tomography and computed axial tomography scans, and the newest approach – transcranial magnetic stimulation (TMS). All are invasive techniques, particularly TMS, which involves deliberate stimulation of specific brain areas and the analysis of the responses to that stimulation. These techniques are used to help identify which regions of the brain are active while people are displaying certain behaviours, or how the brains of different groups of people (e.g. traumatised vs non-traumatised) differ. They have transformed our understanding of the brain in the last couple of decades. They have changed the whole nature of neuroscience. This is a Kuhnian revolution in our understanding of the brain.

One of the problems with many imaging studies is that they only show that activity is occurring in a certain area in the brain. This in itself is not demonstrating a great deal. At one level these studies have little more explanatory value than Gall's phrenology, the measurement of bumps on the head. The correlation between brain activity or size and behaviour may be closer than Gall's approach, but it does not go much further than correlations. Fortunately, as we shall see in later chapters, brain-imaging techniques, though they are still in their relative infancy, have helped our theoretical understanding of trauma enormously. We now have a far more detailed understanding of the neuropsychological mechanisms underlying trauma than we did even 10–15 years ago.

A good example of the kind of work that has been carried out in the field of traumatic stress is that of Doug Bremner *et al.* (1995, 2005). Since the 1990s this team has been trying to establish the important sites relating to traumatic stress. Using PET, they have assessed a number of different traumatised populations and consistently found that traumatised people compared with non-traumatised people have a smaller volume in the right hippocampus, an area of the limbic system that is critical to the storage of explicit, verbal, conscious memories. This finding is contentious, and other research has shown the relationship to be more complex. Yehuda *et al.* (2006) found that veterans with PTSD did not differ in hippocampal volume from matched veterans without PTSD (though they did show lower urinary cortisol and poorer memory performance on the Wechsler logical memory test and digit span). Smaller left hippocampal volume was found in veterans who developed PTSD in response to their first reported traumatic exposure, compared with veterans who experienced PTSD after a second or subsequent exposure. These researchers concluded that smaller hippocampal volumes may be associated with specific risk and resilience factors. This is a demonstration of the difficulty of carrying out good experimental research in this area. It is not clear from this quasi-experimental study whether or not the veterans with a smaller hippocampal volume had this before they were exposed to the trauma or whether it was caused by the traumatic event. Teasing this apart is essential to establishing causality. This demonstrates the need for longitudinal studies (see Jelicic and Bonke, 2001) to establish hippocampal volume before exposure to traumatic events, e.g. using samples of members of the armed forces or the emergency services – people who can be assessed at an early stage in their training, but who can be predicted to be exposed to traumatic events during their career.

These relatively new methods are at an exciting stage, and both methodological and subsequent theoretical developments are taking place at a rapid rate. As yet there are still significant gaps in our understanding, particularly with regard to more complex processes, such as narrative. These methods have not yet been effective at describing the neuropsychological processes underlying narrative, as this involves complex integration of comprehension and production. From the limited evidence available, story comprehension involves a network of frontal, temporal and cingulated areas that supports both theory of mind and working memory processes (Marr, 2004). It is at the level of the integration of processes that researchers have not yet succeeded in analysing the neuropsychology of narrative.

Self-report measures

The self-report questionnaire is probably the most common method used in war trauma research, and the one that has the most problems – in practice if not in theory. There are a number of reasons why it is the most ubiquitous method, and they are not always good ones. The questionnaire, used well, can provide very useful information about a person. Questionnaires are used to measure the type and extent of the trauma, coping styles, social support, dissociation, anxiety, depression, substance abuse, general demographic details (age, sex, socio-economic status) and a host of other variables. Many of the measures used are based on good psychometric principles. They have been standardised using appropriate populations, and are reliable across time (assuming the construct is stable across time) and measure (if there are two measures of the same construct). It is usual for a good standardised psychometric instrument to have norms established so that a person can be assessed against those norms. For instance, if we have a measure of coping, we may be interested in knowing whether a person uses a particular coping strategy more, less or about the same as the average person. Similarly, we need to establish cut-offs for many measures. If we want to find out what proportion of people have PTSD after a particular incident, then we need to establish an accurate cut-off so that we can conclude with some confidence that people who score X or above are likely to have PTSD, while those who score below X are unlikely to have PTSD. We do not draw a firm conclusion from any self-report measure. An assessment of PTSD or any other mental disorder requires an in-depth assessment by a qualified clinician.

If a questionnaire is going to be useful, it must be based on sound theory. For instance, if a researcher is going to accept PTSD as a suitable description of the psychological response to war, that the medical model is appropriate for the measurement of this, and that the diagnostic criteria supplied in DSM and ICD are appropriate and accurately reflect the symptoms experienced by a traumatised person, then the measure used must be equivalent to a measure of PTSD; that is, it should assess the event itself and the person's emotional reaction to it, intrusive thoughts, avoidance and emotional numbing, hyperarousal, a temporal component (how long the person has had the symptoms), and the impact on work, family and/or social life. The items in the measure should cover all of these. And many measures do. They have been constructed according to these principles and work effectively. Both researchers and clinicians use questionnaires extensively and effectively.

Problems with self-report measures

Unfortunately, there are a number of problems with self-report questionnaires and hence with many of the studies that have used this technique. When reading the literature it is important to be aware of these limitations and the impact they will have on the findings and conclusions of a study. Here are some of the key problems.

There are too many measures

Many researchers appear to think that it is good practice when designing a piece of research to make up their own measure, and call it after themselves or the university or city in which they work. Many measures that are presented in the literature do not appear anywhere else; they are not used in further research. There may be little or no validation, nor any clear justification for the development of the new measure. Psychology as a discipline is in rather a mess regarding questionnaires; it is not simply a problem for researchers in the field of war trauma.

It is difficult to estimate the number of measures available only in the English language. And there are, of course, many available in other languages, and translations of English measures in other languages. These purport to measure a whole range of psychological constructs. Some are well validated and have a lot of evidence to support their use; others have little or no such support. Researchers should always try to find good well-validated measures of the construct they are interested in rather than try to make up a new scale just to add to the plethora. On many occasions, researchers do not use measures that are available, reliable and valid for other reasons. A measure might only be commercially available, and be very expensive, or the researcher may simply not know about it because of the sheer number of questionnaires that have been published in the literature, and there are not always good reviews of measures available.

Measures are not always based on good theory, or they do not cover the full range of the theoretical construct

If there is no good measure available for a specific construct, then this is when it is appropriate to develop one. Trauma theory is in flux. Though we have a clear idea of the key concepts, new and revised theories are being developed all the time, and a good self-report questionnaire must accurately represent the theory it is attempting to measure, i.e. it must have construct validity. If a researcher is interested in studying coping, then there are several theories that propose anything from two to twenty, or more, coping strategies. How should a researcher first of all decide which coping theory is appropriate, and then which measure is the best test of that theory? It is a daunting task, and one which the best researchers have not resolved. If we cannot agree a theory, then we cannot (by definition) agree a theoretically sound measure.

Associated with the previous point is that a self-report questionnaire may not cover the full range of material required

Assuming that we agree that PTSD is an appropriate theoretical approach, then a measure of PTSD is appropriate for people we assume have PTSD, but difficulties arise with war trauma for the reasons described below.

First, the people in whom we are interested may belong to a non-western culture, and if the measure is validated on a western population it may not contain the necessary items for people from other cultures. This is a common problem in war trauma research that has not been resolved. PTSD is a western construct but wars usually take place in non-western countries (even though most are backed by countries in the West). We do not know the extent to which PTSD is applicable in many countries. For instance, de Silva (2006) argues that the responses of Buddhists in Sri Lanka to the tsunami of 2004 were very different to classic PTSD, at least partly because Buddhists accept a version of fatalism which is more accepting of events; hence there may be no post-traumatic reaction because the event is not perceived as traumatic in the first place. If there is no traumatic event, there can be no PTSD. There may be similar psychological symptoms, intrusive thoughts, avoidance, etc., but the overall pattern will not be the same, so a PTSD questionnaire would not be appropriate.

Second, war trauma is more complex than simple PTSD. Not only do war-traumatised people experience PTSD, they also have problems with depression, anxiety, substance abuse, coping and social support – a whole range of problems – so a measure of PTSD alone will not suffice. Added to this there are specific issues relating to particular wars. For instance, in the civil war in Sierra Leone, many males had their arms chopped off, a traumatic incident not usual in war. In Bosnia, women were systematically, politically even, mass raped. These kinds of incidents must be accounted for in any self-report questionnaire that is being used to assess war trauma, because one key part of war trauma is the type of incidents that occur. This does not obviate the need for the basic PTSD measure, but it does mean that there will often be adaptations to existing measures in order to obtain full coverage of the material required.

Measures may lack face validity, or be ambiguous to the user

There is little point in presenting a questionnaire for a person to complete if they think that it bears no relevance to their situation, no relevance to their experiences or their life. Psychology students in the UK may be very used to completing questionnaires, but that is not the case for most people in the world. A measure has to have face validity: the person completing it has to believe that it is measuring something worthwhile. If they do not believe this, then there is no reason for them to complete it accurately, or at all. There are many reasons why a measure may not have face validity. Many participants will not be familiar with questionnaires, and why questionnaires are used. To resolve this problem the person administering the questionnaire must show the participant that the information being obtained is valuable and will contribute significantly to the research project, and that the project itself is of value, particularly to the people completing the questionnaire. Regarding content, the participant may not understand why certain items have been included in a questionnaire. People who produce questionnaires consisting of scales may deliberately include unusual items, perhaps because they have useful psychometric properties, such as detecting lies or a high item–scale correlation. While such niceties are acceptable to psychometricians, someone in a refugee camp may not appreciate their usefulness. We have to trust the creator of the questionnaire to know what they are doing and to have done a good job, which is not always easy in the war trauma situation, where the participant may well see a questionnaire as trivialising the issues.

*The items do not have theoretical equivalence but
they are given mathematical equivalence*

This is a problem common to most, if not all, psychometric questionnaires. A measure might have, say, twenty items. These items may cover
twenty different aspects of PTSD. The scale is scored on a 1–5 scale,
with 5 being high and 1 being low. The participant's overall score is
obtained by adding up the number they record for each of the twenty
items, leading to an overall score of between 20 (very low) and 100 (very
high). The fundamental problem is that not all of the items have a
theoretical equivalence. An item on 'intrusive thoughts' might be the
key item, which determines whether the person has PTSD, but it may be
scored in exactly the same way as an item on, for instance, 'having sleep
difficulties', which might be inconvenient but not a serious problem.
Items are not generally weighted according to the emotional significance
of the particular symptom that is being measured. This can lead to a
distortion of the final scores. This is linked to the next problem.

*Each person's interpretation of what is meant by
an item may differ*

One person's war trauma may be mainly about nightmares (and hence
sleep problems) whereas another person's trauma might be about intrusive thoughts during the day, whilst at work or with the family. Items
mean different things to different people. This, again, may distort the
overall figures obtained, and the questionnaire will not reflect the severity of particular symptoms for individuals. One solution to this is to
include a 'severity' score for each item, so the participant can indicate
not only whether they have a symptom, but also how severe it is to them.

A related issue is how a participant scores a questionnaire

For instance, if there is a 5-point scale stating 'I am having nightmares'
(the sort of item that does appear), then one person might put '5' when
they are having one nightmare a month. Another person will put '1' in
the same circumstances. Another person will put '5' because they are
having nightmares every night. Without actual behavioural markers –
indicators to the participant about how to relate actual behaviour
to scores – e.g. 'a nightmare every night' = 5, 'a nightmare once a
month' = 2, it is very difficult to ensure that self-report questionnaires
are filled in in the same way by everyone. A further complication, even
with behavioural markers, is that one nightmare a month may be a very
emotional event for one person, and a nightmare every night may have
fewer psychological consequences for another.

Specific items within the questionnaire may be interpreted
in different ways by the user and by the researcher

This is linked to the previous point. A researcher – naïve but normal – may assume that having a nightmare every night must be worse than having an occasional nightmare. This will again lead to problems with interpreting the questionnaire, if there is not more information available.

Questionnaires are useful for group data but of little
use relating to an individual

There are circumstances where looking at group data shows something of importance: the value of a therapy for a group, the role of PTSD in war trauma, the extent of war trauma in a given population, or the relationship between war trauma and particular individual variables (coping styles, intelligence, etc.). What we must not do with questionnaires is, when they are self-report, extrapolate from the group to the individual. Just because there is a group link which shows that people with a processing coping style are less likely to have war trauma, this does not mean that Person X, who uses a processing coping style, will not have PTSD.

This has been a relatively long discussion because so much research is based on self-report measures. It shows that there are a number of serious deficiencies with self-report questionnaire measures that the researcher must consider when devising their study. I hope that the above discussion will not stop people from using questionnaires, nor from devising their own, but it should show that care should be taken when choosing this method. There are many pitfalls, some of which can be easily avoided, some of which are difficult to avoid. Never take anything for granted, even with a well-validated questionnaire. For instance, in one of our studies (Hunt and Robbins, 2001a), Second World War veterans completed the Impact of Event Scale (Horowitz *et al.*, 1979) – a well-validated scale – as one of the measures. Many veterans scored very highly on the 'Intrusion' scale, even 50 years after the war was over. This showed that veterans experienced intrusive thoughts decades after the war. However, another analysis of the individual items compared the IES with other measures. It turned out that many of the veterans, rather than demonstrating intrusion, were actually showing an interest in the war. They liked talking about it, they liked reading about it and they liked watching films. This interest was showing up in some of the items, such as 'I thought about the war a lot.' So even when there is a well-validated measure, things can go wrong!

Clinical assessment and case studies

This is one of the most effective means of developing trauma-related theory. Case studies provide very detailed accounts of particular individuals with war trauma. They may be cases that have been written up by a clinician, or they may be individuals who have been extensively studied by an individual researcher. They are usually presented in the literature because they have something of particular interest. An individual may have been through very difficult war-related circumstances and managed to survive without serious psychological injury, or they may have responded well to a new treatment, or they may have severe problems which are of a different pattern to the norm. With regard to method, data may have been collected using any of the methods already discussed, but it will include a detailed assessment, using appropriate measures and interviews.

Clinical assessment is one area where there is a tremendous amount of data that have not been written up, because the clinician may not have time. There is a wealth of unpublished material based on evaluating and treating patients.

Interviews

The interview is a very useful technique used widely by researchers. The interview avoids many of the disadvantages of the questionnaire, though it is, in its own ways, a potentially very imperfect instrument. Interviewing comprises a number of techniques, from highly structured (where there is a questionnaire to which the respondent provides specific answers), to semi-structured (where there are open-ended questions, but the questions are still specific and there is a set order), to unstructured – rather a misnomer, but where there are a number of topics the researcher wishes to address, and where the interview can flow in different directions, depending on the way the respondent talks. The researcher's role is to ensure that the topics are adequately covered.

There are many different ways to analyse interviews. Analytic technique is the subject of many books, and it is not necessary to go into detail here. There are many disagreements among psychologists not only about how to conduct interviews, but also about how to transcribe them and analyse the data. Some interviewers use content analysis – a quantitative approach – where the analysis involves adding up the number of times something is said and analysing these frequencies. More commonly, interviews are analysed using qualitative techniques, of which there are many, for instance grounded theory (Strauss and Corbin, 1998), interpretative phenomenological analysis (Smith *et al.*, 2009), various forms of discourse analysis (e.g. Potter and Wetherall, 1988), or narrative analysis (Crossley, 2000; Burnell *et al.*, 2006). All have their uses. Though there are different analytic approaches, there are a number of general rules underlying most techniques:

(1) *Transcribe the interview carefully.* According to the analytic technique used, one may have to just transcribe relevant passages, or it may be important to transcribe not only every word but also the pauses, exclamations, etc., i.e. the non-verbal components. It is best if the interviewer does the transcription, as he/she is more knowledgeable about what happened during the interview.

(2) *Pick out the phrases, sentences or paragraphs (units) that are meaningful,* i.e. the statements made by the participant that may be helpful during the analysis.

(3) *Group these units together in categories or themes.* These categories or themes should emerge as the units are grouped. They often emerge as the researcher is extracting the materials from the original transcript. The units should be grouped and regrouped until a meaningful structure emerges. This may involve over-arching themes and sub-themes.

(4) *Validate these themes.* At this stage one should be able to write a few sentences explaining what each theme represents. Do the themes accurately represent the units?

(5) You should now conduct further interviews to validate the theme structure, altering this structure as necessary as you carry out further analysis. This continues until the categories are saturated, when no more changes are apparent, and you have the most economical framework of explanation.

(6) *Write up using the themes as key discussion points.* A straightforward way to do this is to use the themes as subheadings, describe each, and use appropriate (not too many) unit examples.

These are the fundamental principles, though researchers argue about the relative importance of the style and depth of transcription, about how to extract and group phrases, about how to validate the themes and about writing up.

The interview, particularly the semi-structured or unstructured interview, is a valuable tool for researchers interested in war trauma. Many participants are upset by the use of questionnaires because they are very restrictive and do not reflect their experience. War-traumatised individuals are very sensitive to the *meanings* of their problems. They want to put across the issues that are important to them in their own ways – to explore particular ideas, to look at how they have coped (or failed to cope), their memories and their experiences. They want to discuss the story of their war. A questionnaire is often seen as trivial, asking the wrong questions. By devising an interview that has a number of themes (e.g. the war experience, memories, coping styles), the researcher can enable the participant to discuss what is important about these themes.

The researcher must be a good interviewer. They must be able to draw out relevant information, even if the participant is reluctant to discuss an issue. They must also be prepared to deal with the often raw emotions that such interviews bring out in participants – not just upset, crying and bewilderment, but anger and sometimes aggression. The full gamut of human emotion can be present in an interview with a victim of war trauma.

Narrative approaches

As narrative is central to this book, it is important that we examine narrative methods. Narrative methods are used with a number of sources of data, mainly the one-to-one interview, but written accounts (e.g. diaries, journals, books) can also be analysed using narrative methods. Narrative methods arose in part from the style of answer that many participants made to interviewers' questions. They typically tended to be long-winded, and represented a fuller story than the interviewer had actually asked for. There is a tendency for people to tell stories when they are being interviewed, and it is every interviewer's painful experience to hear such stories when they wanted just a short answer to a simple question. Narrative methods had to be developed to take into account people's normal behaviour, which was to refuse to allow the interviewer to fragment the coherency of their lived experience. Of course, it was not that simple, but it is good to think that the ordinary non-specialist has some power over the academic researcher.

According to Bamberg and McCabe (1998), human agency is critical to narrative: 'people strive to configure space and time, deploy cohesive devices, reveal identity of actors and relatedness of actions across scenes. They create themes, plots and dramas. In so doing, narrators make sense of themselves, social situations, and history' (p. iii).

Mishler (1986) was one of the earlier proponents of a narrative approach, though much work had been carried out prior to this. The so-called 'narrative turn' has affected many disciplines in one way or another, for instance sociology, history, anthropology, law, social work and, of course, psychology. Academics in each discipline have used different narrative methods in their research, but this is not a full review of narrative methods, so we will focus on methods used in psychology.

The difficulty with narrative methods lies in the complexity of the subject matter. At the heart is the story, but what forms should the story take? It can be anything from a clearly written account, to the jumbled words of a traumatised person who is having difficulty in telling their story because it is so painful. Often an interviewer will have a structured set of questions that relate to the notion of 'story' in general. Is this appropriate or should not the person telling the story tell it in the way they want? There is also the issue of the extent of the story. If we are interested in trauma, then do we just want to hear the story of the event and its direct consequences, or do we want the person's full life story so we can understand something of the causal chain of events that led to them being traumatised by their experiences? Stories are also interconnected. A person's trauma story may be linked to their narrative about their subsequent career, or their family relationships. The network of narratives can extend out endlessly, so it is important that the researcher has a clear idea from the outset about what kind of story they are looking for. This, in turn, leads to another critical issue – that storytelling is an interpersonal exercise. The storyteller needs an audience, and the audience needs to make some sort of response. As psychologists, we are very aware of the impact of someone in authority on the behaviour of others. The researcher can be that person of authority to the narrator, and this will affect the story that is told. Other aspects of the status of the interviewer can affect the story told. When I was interviewing WWII veterans (see Chapter 10), I was sometimes not made particularly welcome by veterans, who were only happy telling their story to people of 'their own ilk', which generally meant other soldiers. However, when they found out that I used to be a bricklayer, i.e. a 'proper man's job' (rather than an academic, which clearly is not a proper man's job), these people were much more willing to talk.

Narratives about traumatic stress are much more than personal narratives. As discussed in Chapter 1, trauma itself is not only psychological – it is interpersonal, social and political – so it is inevitable that people's trauma narratives are going to contain social and political elements. Narratives may be just as much about history and about politics, as about the psychological state of the narrator. This brings in another issue about the trauma researcher who is interested in narrative. It is important that they understand the politics and the history that the narrator is discussing. If they do not, then the narrator will be less willing to put across their story. If the narrative is about World War Two, then the researcher should know about World War Two – both the historical and political situation – and also the social constructions that the narrator is likely to hold because they are of that particular generation. This will be discussed in more detail in Chapter 10. The social constructions held by any narrator must be understood by the researcher. Narrators can position themselves as victims of their story, or as agents who assume a level of control over events. The positionings of the self in personal narratives indicate the performance of identity (Riessman, 2000).

The difficulty with narrative is the analysis itself, deciding exactly what to analyse and interpret. The rules are not as strict as they are for statistical analysis; they cannot be. Narrative analysis does not assume objectivity but is concerned with position and subjectivity (Riessman, 2000), though some argue that large parts of any story can be factually verified (Bertaux, 1995), though there is often little point to this. Verification is usually more about matters of law than psychology. It is down to the researcher to determine which elements, which segments of text, are important and why. The researcher must interpret the text, and place appropriate boundaries regarding the beginning and end of the story, and determine the structure. This can be a complex task. In narrative analysis this is sometimes carried out with the narrator, with the researcher analysing and drafting the writing up of the research, and then asking the narrator to comment on it. In the end, the narrative is that of both the narrator and the researcher; and in this way is sometimes criticised. Nevertheless, without the researcher imposing analysis and boundaries the narrated story is less useful to psychological science.

Narrative methods have been criticised by many people, and it is true that such methods are not appropriate for many types of research (Atkinson, 1997; Atkinson and Silverman, 1997). If we need representativeness of the population, then narrative methods are not appropriate, nor are they when it comes to understanding the neurophysiology of the brain or cognitive mechanisms of memory. Nevertheless, narrative methods are essential if we are to fully understand the response to trauma, as narrative is itself a central part of that response.

Ethics

The researcher who is interested in war trauma will always come up against ethical issues. All professional psychologists are bound by their code of ethics, which means that they must ensure that the work they do is within the bounds of their professional competence, that they do not cause harm to others, and that they do not place themselves under significant risk. The British Psychological Society's (2006) *Code of Conduct and Ethical Guidelines* provides full details.

Any code of ethics presents problems to the researcher interested in war trauma. By the very nature of the research we are asking people to discuss those things that have caused them the most distress. By asking them about their war experience we are deliberately causing them further distress – without even the promise of effective therapy. At the same time the researcher is exposing him or herself to stories which might be personally damaging. Furthermore, researchers who travel to war zones can run significant personal risks. How do we deal with these issues?

Much of what follows is about interviewing traumatised individuals, though the material is relevant for other methods.

Causing distress to the traumatised participant

It is almost inevitable that, during the course of the research, particularly when the participant is being asked to describe traumatic events in detail, a traumatised participant will become distressed. In a way, the researcher is deliberately setting out to distress the participant, because understanding the emotive nature of trauma requires an account of what happened and how it made the person feel, think and behave. At first sight, this may appear to contradict professional ethical guidelines, but it is an inevitable consequence of discussing extremely distressing events.

There are several levels to resolving this problem. First of all, each participant must provide full informed consent. The initial request for participants to take part in the study must inform people at the outset that they will be asked to disclose distressful memories. It is not enough to provide them with the information after they have volunteered, because many people, once committed, will feel they have to continue with the study once they have volunteered, even though they might prefer to drop out. They do not want to let down the researcher.

The second stage is about volunteering. If a person comes forward after receiving information about the nature of the study, the researcher must then tell them in detail what is required, and make it absolutely clear that they do not have to take part. Sometimes this will mean sending out the detailed protocol to the participant in the post, and then hearing nothing back, not even a tick in the 'do not want to take part' box. The researcher should not pursue people. It is acceptable to send one follow-up request, but the person must not feel hassled or forced into agreeing to take part in the study. These are vulnerable people. They change their minds about participation for their own good reasons.

The next stage, when the researcher meets the participant (who has now signed consent forms), is to deal thoroughly with any questions, before starting data collection, and to again make it clear that their participation is voluntary and that they can withdraw at any time. If they are still agreeable, the data collection takes place, with the participant able to stop at any point. After the data are collected, the researcher should still ask whether the participant is happy for their information to be included. The participant should then be provided with a list of possible help points in case they have issues they wish to discuss further (e.g. with a doctor or counsellor). The researcher should follow up the meeting a few days later, just with a telephone call to make sure the person is all right, to guide them to help if necessary, and – importantly for interviews – to ask if there is anything they wish to add to what they said. It is very common for people, after being interviewed, to think about the issues over the next few days and either regret something they said or want to add further details.

In the end, data collection with traumatised people is difficult for the participants. They are likely to get upset; they are likely to cry. While they should be free to stop the interview at any point, it is likely to be more damaging to stop when the person is distressed than to continue through the distress until they emerge at the other side.

There are added complications if the data collection is taking place in a war zone or a refugee camp, perhaps with people who are not literate. The rules stay the same; it is just that the method of dealing with the rules changes. The researcher still has to obtain full informed consent, and there should be no pressure on the person to take part in the study.

The participant must always be a volunteer. It is ethically questionable to try to force people to take part in any research; it is particularly unreasonable to ask traumatised people to discuss issues that many of them do not wish to discuss. This does mean that samples are not representative; it also means that any figures you obtain cannot be generalised to the traumatised population. Owing to the nature of trauma, there are some types of people who want to talk about their experiences in details, and others who do not want to talk in any circumstances. These differences must be respected, even though it means there will be a methodologically and theoretically significant proportion of the population who are not in your study, hence your findings may be biased. These factors are a function of this type of research – design compromise before ethical compromise. As long as the issues are addressed fully, including in the written report, this is still good science.

Self-exposure

The researcher who interviews traumatised people may experience some symptoms themselves. When one constantly hears terrible stories about death and cruelty, and about unbearable emotions, the stories themselves can affect you. There is a whole literature on this. It is known as 'vicarious traumatisation', and relates to both the effects on researchers and on clinicians who treat traumatised people (Figley, 2005).

While the symptoms the researcher experiences are not symptoms of trauma (they have not experienced an event, just a reporting of an event), they can be distressing; and so it is important to be prepared. First of all the researcher should be aware of the kinds of material to which they are likely to be exposed. Second, while it is important to demonstrate empathy with a traumatised person, the researcher should not get 'too involved'. It is important to stay emotionally detached from one's participants. While this can be difficult, it must be achieved. It is important not only for the research, but also for the researcher–researched relationship. The traumatised person would not expect you to become emotionally involved; you are the one who exerts the control within the relationship. The participant often appreciates the opportunity to be open to someone with whom they have no emotional relationship. In these circumstances they can talk openly and emotionally without fear of hurting someone they know and care for.

Of course, some people will disagree, and argue that the interview is between equals and that emotions should be shared and understood if the interview is to be a success. While this viewpoint is relevant to many interview situations, it is arguably less so when it comes to trauma. The person who is traumatised needs help and guidance to be able to discuss their problems – not someone to share their misery. They want to feel better after an interview, to have helped, to be useful. They do not want the responsibility of upsetting the interviewer, and so, for this reason, it is beneficial not to treat the interview situation as one of equals or co-researchers, but of interviewer and interviewed.

Another issue for the interviewer is that of appropriate training in interview techniques. An interview – especially in this field – is not a conversation. It needs structure and guidance. The interviewer needs to know how to make progress in the interview, to cover the points required, to know when a discussion is a 'blind alley' or is likely to lead somewhere useful.

Finally, and perhaps most importantly, the researcher who is studying trauma needs to have someone to talk to about their own feelings. Being upset after an interview is perfectly human and normal, and it helps to have someone to chat to about it, someone who understands, for instance a co-researcher or supervisor.

Visiting war zones or dangerous places

Most researchers work for an organisation such as a university, and such organisations have a duty of care towards their staff. This duty of care means ensuring that staff are not put in any situation that increases their risk. Obviously, if a researcher visits a war zone, then they are putting themselves at risk, so who is responsible for this? Any risk assessment carried out in such a place would show *very high risk* on all categories, and that would normally mean the member of staff should not visit the war zone. If these findings were actually applied, then a lot of good research would not get carried out. It perhaps illustrates one way in which the health and safety culture has gone too far. While we want to be reasonably healthy and reasonably safe, we also need some autonomy in deciding what we consider appropriate. A university should never force someone to work in a dangerous situation but, in the end, the responsibility has to lie with the researcher. If they need to visit a war zone for their research, then so be it. The employer should take reasonable steps to protect the safety of the employee, but not to the extent of banning travel for bona fide research.

Ethical issues – a conclusion

In the context of ethical procedures for most psychological research, there appear to be some serious problems for conducting research into war trauma but, as we have seen, these do not present insurmountable difficulties. A researcher should always design their studies with ethical considerations to the forefront of their minds. This will, in areas such as this, lead to design compromises. As stated earlier, this is better than ethical compromises, and is still good science.

4   Current theory: post-traumatic stress disorder

Introduction

This chapter focuses on our current understanding of war trauma. This is a rapidly changing area, and space does not permit a thorough coverage of all theories. Instead, the focus will be on the key constructs and the relationship between them. The area of war trauma is fascinating because it is an area within psychology that allows us to draw together the often disparate and contradictory perspectives, particularly psychoneurology, cognition, psychodynamics, behaviourism and social theory. The purpose of the chapter, then, is not to provide a full theoretical account of our understanding of war trauma, but to provide the scaffolding from which we can build that understanding. Chapter 7 focuses on memory, particularly traumatic memory. This chapter discusses the construct of post-traumatic stress disorder (PTSD), and associated comorbid disorders. PTSD is the main classification that is used in the diagnosis of war trauma, and it has been an effective heuristic, helping bring about many thousands of publications on the subject. While it is a popular diagnosis, and very useful for clinicians, there are some problems with it, and there is debate about the structure of the syndrome (its symptoms have been revised with each revision of the diagnostic classification system) and some question as to whether it should even be retained.

PTSD

As described in Chapter 2, the construct now known as PTSD has existed for many years under a variety of formulations and names, mainly relating to battle experience (battle fatigue, combat neurosis, etc.). These terms all refer to a specific set of symptoms that are the result of a traumatic experience. In the twentieth century, interest in the subject understandably tended to increase around wartime and decrease during peacetime, though since 1980, when PTSD was itself introduced, there has been a plethora of papers and books published. The PILOTS database (Published International Literature on Traumatic Stress), which is designed for bringing together research on PTSD, lists over 22,000 papers for the term 'PTSD' (September 2009). It also has 295 publications for war trauma. The construct of PTSD has been a useful heuristic for the generation of trauma-related research.

There are two key classification systems: the International Classification of Diseases (ICD) and the Diagnostic and Statistical Manual of Mental Disorders (DSM). Both have listed PTSD from roughly the same time – around 30 years ago – and both have adjusted the classification several times since then. They are largely consistent with each other, and here we will examine the DSM, as it focuses specifically on mental disorders. Both classification systems use the same coding system.

The original DSM-I was published in 1952 by the American Psychiatric Association, and has been revised several times. DSM was introduced partly on the basis of work carried out during World War Two, to provide diagnostic criteria for mental disorders, and is based on the key research for each mental disorder. Over the decades, new disorders (such as PTSD) have been introduced, and old ones have disappeared.

DSM-I recognised traumatic neurosis (American Psychiatric Association (APA), 1952), which was classified as an anxiety disorder. DSM-II was published in 1968, before the USA really recognised the psychological problems emerging from the soldiers returning from Vietnam. The term 'trauma' generally referred to physical trauma resulting in psychological problems, e.g. problems arising due to a difficult birth or to brain damage. People with psychological problems associated with a traumatic event might be diagnosed with transient situational disturbance, which was an acute reaction to overwhelming environmental stress. Here, if the symptoms did not diminish as the environmental stressor diminished, then 'the diagnosis of another mental disorder is indicated'. Specifically, if someone reacted due to combat stress, then they would be classified as having an 'adjustment reaction of adult life', which was 'fear associated with military combat and manifested by trembling, running and hiding' (APA 1968) – a rather simpler definition than we now use.

The term 'post-traumatic stress disorder' was introduced into DSM-III (APA, 1980). This was largely due to the work of a number of authors, particularly Mardi Horowitz, working with US Vietnam War veterans. Since then, research has demonstrated that people have similar symptoms irrespective of the nature of the traumatic event. DSM-III recognised some fundamental changes in the way we classify mental disorders. Instead of the broadly defined entities of earlier versions, which looked at mental disorder in terms of a continuum from normality to abnormality, DSM-III recognised that diseases should be symptom-based and categorical (Mayes and Horowitz, 2005). PTSD was initially a controversial diagnosis, argued over and debated for years. This was partly because it related to a specific environmental event, unusual in DSM (and necessary for a diagnosis of PTSD to be made), partly because there was debate over whether it should be classified as an anxiety disorder, and partly because the research findings relating to the disorder were inconsistent. The stressor was classified in DSM-III as an event outside the range of normal human experience; this referred to war experience, natural and man-made disasters, rape and sexual abuse, and other significantly stressful events. It was an attempt to differentiate traumatic events from the more normal stressful events of life such as divorce, losing one's job, or being in a fight. There was an assumption that people should normally be able to cope with everyday stressors, but not necessarily with traumatic events.

PTSD was revised for DSM-III-R (APA, 1987) and again for DSM-IV (APA, 1994). A text revision of DSM – DSM-IV-TR – was later published in 2000 (APA, 2000), with some changes to diagnostic categories.

PTSD lists the characteristic symptoms following exposure to an extreme traumatic stressor – not just war, but also rape, sexual abuse, exposure to natural or man-made disasters, and other forms of extreme stress. The diagnostic criteria are as follows:

Criterion A: The person has been exposed to a traumatic event in which both of the following were present:

(1) The person experienced, witnessed or was confronted with an event or events that involved actual or threatened death or serious injury, or a threat to the physical integrity of oneself or others.
(2) The person's response involved intense fear, helplessness or horror. *Note:* in children it may be expressed instead by disorganised or agitated behaviour.

Criterion B: The traumatic event is persistently re-experienced in at least one of the following ways:

(1) Recurrent and intrusive distressing recollections of the event, including images, thoughts or perceptions. *Note:* in young children, repetitive play may occur in which themes or aspects of the trauma are expressed.
(2) Recurrent distressing dreams of the event. *Note:* In children, there may be frightening dreams without recognisable content.

(3) Acting or feeling as if the traumatic event were recurring (includes a sense of reliving the experience, illusions, hallucinations and dissociative flashback episodes, including those that occur upon waking or when intoxicated). *Note:* in children, trauma-specific re-enactment may occur.

(4) Intense psychological distress at exposure to internal or external cues that symbolise or resemble an aspect of the traumatic event.

(5) Physiological reactivity on exposure to internal or external cues that symbolise or resemble an aspect of the traumatic event.

Criterion C: There is persistent avoidance of stimuli associated with the trauma and numbing of general responsiveness (not present before the trauma), as indicated by at least three of the following:

(1) Efforts to avoid thoughts, feelings, or conversations associated with the trauma

(2) Efforts to avoid activities, places or people that arouse recollections of the trauma

(3) Inability to recall an important aspect of the trauma

(4) Markedly decreased interest or participation in significant activities

(5) Feeling of detachment or estrangement from others

(6) Restricted range of affect (e.g. unable to have loving feelings)

(7) Sense of a foreshortened future (e.g. does not expect to have a career, marriage, children or a normal life span)

Criterion D: There are persistent symptoms of increased arousal (not present before the trauma), indicated by at least two of the following:

(1) Difficulty in falling or staying asleep

(2) Irritability or outbursts of anger

(3) Difficulty in concentrating

(4) Hypervigilance

(5) Exaggerated startle response

Criterion E: Duration of the disturbance (symptoms in Criteria B, C, D and E) is more than 1 month.

Criterion F: The disturbance causes clinically significant distress or impairment in social, occupational or other important areas of functioning.

It must also be specified whether the duration is of less than 3 months, in which case it is classified as 'acute', or 3 months or more, in which case it is 'chronic'. It is classified as 'delayed onset' if the onset of symptoms occurs at least 6 months after the event.

There is a good range of evidence in support of PTSD. A review by Nemeroff *et al.* (2006) provide a good account of the literature. There are individual factors that help predict PTSD (at least in groups). Women are usually more likely to get PTSD than men. Kessler *et al.* (1995), in a US study, found twice as many women with PTSD than men. Frans *et al.* (2005) found similar results in a Swedish cohort. It is not clear why women are more likely to be diagnosed with PTSD, though there are a number of possible reasons. First, women are exposed to different types of trauma, e.g. rape and sexual abuse, which may be more personally violating, and hence more traumatic. Second, there is the 'depression effect', whereby women are more likely to be open and honest about their symptoms; they are more likely to go to the doctor and report that they are experiencing problems than men. However, the results are not clear, as some studies seem to show that PTSD rates can be similar for men and women when they are exposed to similar events. For instance, Kang *et al.* (2005) found that male and female US veterans of the Iraq and Afghanistan wars have similar rates of PTSD. As Nemeroff *et al.* (2006) discuss, female gender is usually a strong risk factor for the development of PTSD, though the mechanisms for the disparity are uncertain. There are other risk and resilience factors that help to predict PTSD. The presence of effective coping strategies is a good predictor, as is the presence of perceived social support, and previous mental health conditions – including PTSD (e.g. McCauley *et al.*, 1997).

PTSD is recognised in British law, so people who have been traumatised should expect to be treated justly according to the law because they can get a diagnosis of PTSD. The 'Belmarsh 12' were a group of individuals who were locked up without trial in 2002 because the British government perceived that they were a 'terrorist threat'. Usually recent British governments have respected habeas corpus, and have not tended to lock people up without just cause. A person is charged, and then they are sent to trial, where it will be determined whether they committed a crime and, if so, what the punishment should be. The Belmarsh 12 were not charged, and were imprisoned without any knowledge of whether they would be charged or when they might be released. A group of psychologists and psychiatrists assessed them, and concluded that they were experiencing PTSD as a result of the trauma of being locked up without charge. In the end the courts recognised this and controversially freed the men (Robbins, 2007).

PTSD has proved to be a useful diagnostic category for people who are in need of treatment for traumatic stress. While the response to traumatic events can be complicated, there are therapeutic procedures that work with the symptoms of PTSD, at least for some traumatised people. Providing therapy can benefit people's lives by reducing their symptoms. There are a range of therapies available. The NICE (2005)

Guidelines recognise cognitive behaviour therapy and eye movement desensitisation and reprocessing as the most effective forms of treatment, though they do not work for everyone. If someone is to receive psychological treatment, they need to be prepared for the possible consequences of that treatment, and they need to be aware of their own symptoms and be highly motivated to reduce them.

PTSD has also worked as an effective heuristic, helping to develop research and theory about trauma. Without PTSD it is unlikely that such a tremendous amount of research would have been carried out. Research funding often relies on a clear description of a disorder, and PTSD provided that label. As noted above, there are now many thousands of scientific publications relating to PTSD, which have helped to improve our understanding of traumatic stress.

Critique of PTSD

While PTSD has some very positive features, there are problems with the construct. There is the complexity of the psychosocial response to traumatic events. While people do consistently display the symptoms described in DSM, the construct of PTSD is not entirely coherent or consistent. Many, if not most, people with PTSD also experience other diagnostic constructs, or symptoms from other such constructs. This means that if we were to apply a medical diagnosis strictly, we would have problems in recognising PTSD as a construct.

Many researchers and clinicians are critical of PTSD. At some levels this does not matter. If treatments arising from a diagnosis of PTSD work, then why should we worry too much? The problem is that PTSD is, as stated earlier, recognised in law.

If a person can prove that they contracted PTSD as a result of their working conditions they can sue their employer. If a diagnostic category is going to be used in law, it must be as good at assessing disease as possible. Rosen and Lilienfeld (2008), in a recent review, carried out an empirical evaluation of the core assumptions of PTSD, and the results were very critical of the construct. There were a number of key issues that they addressed, starting from the position that PTSD rests on a number of core assumptions, particularly that a class of traumatic events is linked to a distinct clinical syndrome. This should, theoretically, distinguish PTSD from other mental disorders. Rosen and Lilienfeld argue that, though research has attempted to distinguish markers for PTSD, for example biological or cognitive, it has largely failed to do so. In the end, the authors conclude that virtually all of the core assumptions and mechanisms relating to PTSD lack compelling or consistent empirical evidence.

Criterion A (p. 52) has always been difficult for PTSD. There is, unlike most diagnostic categories, an assumption that there is a specific environmental cause for the resultant disorder. There must be a link between the traumatic event and subsequent symptoms. The key problems are that: (a) there is no clear definition of what a traumatic event is; (b) it is not always possible to determine whether a traumatic event has taken place; (c) it is not always possible to determine whether the event actually produced the symptoms; and (d) the causal event is not necessarily sufficient to lead to PTSD. Many – usually most – people, after a traumatic event, are not traumatised. Criterion A has developed and changed throughout the various editions of DSM in order to try to clarify the first of these problems. Initially, in DSM-III, the event was considered as 'something outside the range of normal human experience' (American Psychiatric Association, 1980). This would immediately exclude war experience, the death of loved ones, and many other traumatic stressors, and was clearly designed with the safe western person in mind. In DSM-IV (American Psychiatric Association, 1994) there is confusion between the event, which is something that leads to, or threatens to lead to, death or injury, and the person's responses to the event, feelings of fear, helplessness or horror. This confusion between the event and the psychological response to the event is no improvement on earlier versions of DSM. By confusing what happened with how someone feels about it, the authors open the possibility of excluding those people who experience the event, but who do not experience any symptoms at the time or in the immediate aftermath, and who develop symptoms at some future point. Perhaps this is why some people argue that PTSD should not be linked specifically to a traumatic stressor.

Of course, there is the further problem with the stressor criterion – that some people develop a more positive and understanding outlook on life after going through a traumatic event. This will be covered in more depth in Chapter 6, but it is another reason why there is a problem with the stressor criterion; such an event does not predictably lead to the particular pattern of symptoms we call PTSD.

PTSD is defined within the traditional medical model of a number of symptoms regularly clustering together and forming a coherent syndrome. Unfortunately, there is no clearly definable group of symptoms that leads to a definite syndrome of PTSD. This may be a criticism of the use of the medical model in these circumstances. The model may be relevant to most physical disorders, and many mental disorders, but it becomes problematic when considering complex psychological disorders. Most research into PTSD has shown that there is nearly always a comorbid disorder – often depression, sometimes generalised anxiety, substance abuse, or aggression and violence-related problems. We should question whether the medical model is appropriate when perhaps 90% or more of the people with a disorder have comorbid problems. If PTSD is to represent a coherent clinical syndrome, any diagnosis must show that it is not just an amalgam of symptoms that can be assigned to other extant disorders (March, 1990). We should always seek out the most parsimonious explanation for symptom patterns, and perhaps PTSD is not the most parsimonious explanation.

The overall factor structure of PTSD has been critiqued, though many studies support the three-factor structure represented in the diagnostic criteria (intrusive re-experiencing, avoidance and hyperarousal) (e.g. Foa *et al.*, 1995; Anthony *et al.*, 1999), with others supporting a two-factor structure (e.g. Buckley *et al.*, 1998), The majority of people have, according to Rosen *et al.* (2008), fitted a four-factor structure, which is often labelled as re-experiencing, effortful avoidance, emotional numbing and hyperarousal (e.g. Amdur and Liberzon, 2001; Simms *et al.*, 2002; McWilliams *et al.*, 2005). If PTSD is to be an accurate diagnostic category, then the number and names of these factors should correspond very closely with the actual diagnostic criteria. This is not clear, though the four-factor solution, separating avoidance and emotional numbing, has been argued for on a number of occasions.

A further problem results from the variability of symptom patterns observed in patients with PTSD. As Foa *et al.* (1995) noted, two people may receive the same diagnosis of PTSD yet share no symptoms. This occurs because there are seventeen symptom criteria, but only six are needed for a diagnosis. While one person can report that they are experiencing intrusive thoughts, avoidance of reminders, an inability to recall aspects of the event, irritability and hypervigilance, another might report nightmares, a loss of interest in normal activities, emotional numbing, sleep disturbance and problems with concentration (Rosen *et al.*, 2008).

In the end, when critiquing PTSD, we always return to comorbidity. Not only do the diagnostic criteria fail to combine particularly effectively, except at the more holistic level, and not only do people present with a range of different symptoms within the diagnostic category of PTSD, but most people also receive a diagnosis of other disorders, such as depression, generalised anxiety, or substance abuse. This problem of comorbidity questions whether PTSD can be differentiated from other disorders (Yehuda and McFarlane, 1995). If there are high levels of comorbidity, then we can question the validity of the diagnostic category; it simply is not functioning as an independent disorder. Rosen *et al.* (2008), reviewing the literature on comorbidity, note that some of the Criteria for PTSD are markedly similar to those for other disorders.

For instance, while criterion B-4 for PTSD is 'intense psychological distress at exposure to internal or external cues that symbolise or resemble an aspect of the traumatic event', Criterion A for Specific Phobia is 'marked and persistent fear that is excessive or unreasonable, as marked by the presence or anticipation of a specific object or situation'. Similarly, Criterion C-4 for PTSD is 'markedly diminished interest or participation in significant activities', while Criterion 2-A for Major Depression is 'markedly diminished interest or pleasure in all, or almost all, activities most of the day, nearly every day'. Again, intrusive thoughts are considered to be critical to PTSD, but studies have found that there is virtually no difference in intrusive thoughts between the intrusive memories of depressed patients and PTSD patients (Rosen et al., 2008, p. 845). While these similarities do not preclude PTSD from being a viable diagnostic category, it can only be viable if the diagnostic criteria themselves are stable, and as we have seen, they are not stable.

There are further criticisms of PTSD – the lack of distinctive biological markers (though there are such markers, as we shall see in the next chapter) and the complications of traumatic memory – but it is not the purpose of this book to determine the ontological status of PTSD. It is enough to say that there are problems with the diagnosis, and for the purposes of the following discussion, the focus will be on war trauma as a disorder, one that is not recognised in either DSM or ICD, but which subsumes PTSD, depression, anxiety, phobias, substance abuse and other problems that emerge as a result of the experience of war. The complicated nature of war trauma has been recognised. Herman (1992) draws a distinction between the disorder that arises as a result of a single discrete event (simple PTSD) and that which arises as a result of long and complicated events (complex PTSD). PTSD, as it is currently represented in DSM, does not tease out the differences between these disorders, though clinicians who treat PTSD have to in order to effectively reduce the symptoms.

Whatever the arguments regarding the transition from DSM-II to DSM-III, there is a continuum of response to a difficult event, ranging from few or no symptoms, through some distress, to traumatisation. While it can be argued that the continuum is broken at the point where the response to the event is traumatic, the position is not clear. The idea of a traumatic event involving some kind of rift is a good one, but it is also problematic because many people after the event have such a wide range of symptoms that it is difficult to determine which ones should be classified as disordered. In effect, many people have subclinical problems, but PTSD does not effectively separate the groups.

What are the symptoms of war trauma?

War trauma is not a recognised psychiatric entity, though there are arguments for making it so. It is a complicated disorder, dependent to some extent on the kinds of experiences people have during war. Unfortunately, these experiences cut across the full range of traumatic experiences, from seeing people die to killing them, along with apparent man-made disasters such as the physical destruction of buildings, and the maltreatment of people from rape through to starvation. People who are traumatised by war are generally labelled as having PTSD, often with some comorbid disorder such as depression or problems with aggression. The patterns of symptoms for someone with war trauma vary, but they seem to depend at least to some extent on the particular war in which the individual was involved, and the role they played (e.g. as soldier or as civilian, perpetrator or victim, and the kinds of events that happened). The pattern is not clear. People who are traumatised by war display a wide range of symptoms that have some overlap, partly through the PTSD classification, partly through comorbid classifications. The symptoms can be more or less serious and last for shorter or longer times. They may have a greater or lesser impact on the person's life, depending on other factors, often beyond the person's control. The symptoms themselves may be present for life. If a person becomes a refugee, then there will be a significant environmental and psychosocial impact. People who become refugees are often damaged more by their arrival and reception in the new country than they are by the events they witnessed or experienced in their homeland (Hunt and Gekenyi, 2003).

If we accept the medical model for mental disorders, then there is a case for arguing that we need to have a diagnostic category of war trauma distinct from PTSD, as PTSD covers only a proportion of the symptoms experienced by people suffering from war trauma. Rather than take that approach, we may help victims of war more effectively by using a narrative approach that takes into account the breadth of their experience, the full range of symptoms they are experiencing, and by exploring different ways to improve their mental and physical health through the development of a narrative about their experiences – which can involve both traditional treatment and a wider range of activities. This can also account for the more positive outcomes that indubitably occur among many people as a result of experiencing war. This will be discussed in detail in Chapter 6. Many people who have experienced war talk about the excitement, the buzz, and about learning about themselves, and the development of new skills that are useful in later life, and these experiences are just as valid as the negative symptoms experienced by others.

An understanding of war trauma must take into account this range of experience.

People with war trauma usually experience the symptoms of PTSD: intrusive thoughts, avoidance, emotional numbing and hyperarousal. They have difficulty in sleeping and in communicating with friends and family, and they may also experience broader symptoms which do not fit with PTSD, such as depression, displays of anger, substance abuse or problems with relationships. The complexity of war trauma is such that these symptoms may not always be present; the pattern changes over time, partly as a result of the person dealing with their memories, partly as a result of environmental and social changes.

There are added problems. Wars are not mainly about traumatic and stressful experiences; they are about people living normal lives – eating, drinking, getting bored, having sex, being sent to school or college. Life goes on, but it goes on differently. The person who has been through war has experienced all these things so it is not surprising that when they look back at their war they experience the full range of memories regarding the war, not just traumatic ones. The problem for the more seriously affected is that the traumatic memories are the ones that dominate, often to the exclusion of everything else. What the person needs to do is to put these traumatic memories in context.

Concluding comments

While there is much to say in criticism of the construct of PTSD, it has proved to be very useful in guiding clinicians regarding the treatment of traumatised individuals. It has also been an effective heuristic, generating a great deal of research around the world. Without PTSD, it is difficult to imagine that our understanding of the response to traumatic incidents would be anything like as good as it is now. Nevertheless, while some people have argued the case for introducing a construct of complex PTSD, the case of war trauma does show that there is a need to have a broader explanation of people's responses to such complex events as war. The next chapter focuses on the role of traumatic memory in enabling a deeper understanding of war trauma.

5 Approaches to understanding trauma

Theories of traumatic memory are in large part consistent regarding the structure and processes involved in traumatic memory; though they tell different parts of the story, they converge fairly well, even if there is disagreement over the terms used. Traumatic memory is an area where we can integrate work across different approaches in psychology, including biological, cognitive, social and psychodynamic perspectives. This chapter provides an outline of the different approaches, and how they cohere.

Cognition and emotion

A great deal of research has been carried out to determine the impact of trauma on basic cognitive processes such as attention and perception. The findings indicate that people who are traumatised are more likely to pay more attention to, and be more perceptually aware of, environmental stimuli that remind them of the traumatic event than people who are not traumatised. This is understandable from an evolutionary point of view. If a person has experienced a traumatic event and survived, then they will be programmed to respond quickly to similar environmental stimuli and hence increase their chances of surviving again. The traumatised person is distinguished from the non-traumatised one in being unable to separate the traumatic situation from the normal environment.

Attentional bias has been demonstrated through the Stroop test. The original Stroop test consisted of the rapid presentation of colour words that were presented either in the same coloured ink or in different coloured ink. The participant has to say what colour the ink is, and their reaction time is measured. When the colour of the ink is discrepant to the colour word, the response time is slowed. Using a similar paradigm with traumatised people, except for using subliminally presented trauma-related words with the person naming the colour of the ink, there is evidence for slowed colour naming (Harvey *et al.*, 1996), and also speeded reaction time to trauma-related words when using a dot probe paradigm (Bryant and Harvey, 1997), i.e. a bias towards noticing trauma-related words. Less positive results were found in an auditory recognition test using traumatised Vietnam veterans (Trandel and McNally, 1987). One of the problems with this type of research is that traumatised people are not particularly conditioned to respond to words – it is particular sights, smells and sounds that they respond to – so it is not surprising that a task using words may generate conflicting results.

People experiencing a trauma experience a range of emotions, depending on their own characteristics and on the type of traumatic experience. As the first diagnostic criterion for PTSD includes fear, horror or helplessness as concomitant to the event itself, it is not surprising that there is a strong relationship between these reactions and the risk of PTSD some time later (Brewin et al., 2000). Other people report shame or anger at the time of the trauma. It depends on the person and the situation. Another useful emotional concept is that of 'mental defeat', which goes beyond the normal reactions and is concerned with a breakdown of identity. This was demonstrated in former political prisoners in East Germany (Ehlers et al., 2000). Those who experienced mental defeat were still more likely to have PTSD many years later. Mental defeat is a useful concept when discussing trauma and narrative, as it indicates a total breakdown in the narrative that is difficult to rebuild and restore.

The emotional response is also associated with people's beliefs. Emotions have to be at the core of any understanding of why we think as we do. Janoff-Bulman (1992) argued that traumatic events shatter people's basic beliefs and assumptions about the world. Her view is that we have fundamental beliefs that the world is meaningful, that it is benevolent and that the self is worthy. Trauma disrupts those beliefs, and recovery is about rebuilding them, or developing a narrative. A similar notion was put forward by Bolton and Hill (1996), who proposed a slightly different set of fundamental beliefs – that the self is sufficiently competent to act, that the world is sufficiently predictable, and that the world provides a sufficient satisfaction of our needs. Again, the traumatised person has these beliefs shattered.

Dissociation

Dissociation was discussed widely in the nineteenth and early twentieth centuries, and has been revived in trauma theory. It is not clearly defined, but relates to a breakdown of what is normally a relatively continuous set of interrelated processes that help us to deal with the world, whether that of the present, or the links between the past and the present. Dissociation may occur in traumatised people as a kind of automatic coping mechanism.

Janet (1925, p. 597) showed that traumatised individuals have an unclear verbal memory of the traumatic incident. He used the term 'psychological automatism' and suggested that the traumatic memory constituted 'images and movements' that were unconscious, but would, over time, begin to encroach into consciousness. This leads to psychological symptomatology. After a trauma, memories remain unconscious ideas until they have been translated into narrative form through conscious action, or processing.

Janet discussed repression as a defence against traumatic memories emerging into consciousness, in a similar way to how 'avoidance' is used. Memory that is persistently repressed becomes subconscious and lives apart from consciousness. Dissociation thus results from repression. Dissociation is experienced by a small proportion of the adult population at any one time (Mulder *et al.*, 1998).

Since the 1980s, research has moved quickly in the field of dissociation. Researchers have moved beyond the study of multiple personality disorder to recognise, as Janet did so many years earlier, that dissociation can help us to understand the mechanisms of the response to trauma. For some, this follows the psychoanalytic tradition. Gardner (1997) has argued that what he tortuously calls 'Embedment-in-the-Brain-Circuitry Phenomenon' is a contributory factor in the development and perpetuation of psychopathology. Gardner argues that seemingly purposeless mental material persists in brain circuitry for an indefinite period of time, long after it serves a useful function. Similarly, but with the apparent chaos outside, Sel (1997) argues that dissociation is a consequence of adaptation to a chaotic environment rich in contrasts, which is applicable to traumatic situations.

The impact of dissociation is that people will not be able to fully access their memories. In extreme cases, dissociative identity disorder may result, previously known as 'multiple personality disorder', but this is rare in trauma cases. The kinds of symptoms that are normally experienced include emotional numbing, depersonalisation and getting 'stuck in the past'. They relate to the severity of the perception of the traumatic experience (Holman and Silver, 1998). When dissociation occurs at the time of the traumatic event, it is known as 'peri-traumatic dissociation', and it is closely correlated with later PTSD (Murray *et al.*, 2002). The symptoms tend to relate to the 'freeze' that occurs in animals, rather than the typical fight or flight response to a stressful situation.

Bremner and Brett (1997) noted that PTSD patients (Vietnam veterans) reported higher levels of dissociative states at the time of combat-related traumatic events than non-PTSD patients. Other authors have found similar results (e.g. Shalev *et al.*, 1998). Michaels *et al.* (1998) found that dissociative states were more likely to persist in PTSD patients.

Cognitive processing

A cognitive processing model of trauma proposes that a person enters a traumatic situation with pre-existing schemata about the nature of the world, their belief systems, and expectations regarding the future. The experience of trauma confronts individuals with information that is inconsistent with these schemata, which contain information about safety and invulnerability. Horowitz (1986) argued that, for recovery to occur, the individual must process the traumatic experience such that the new inconsistent information is resolved and incorporated into the person's schemata via a process of adaptation. In order to do this, the pre-existing schemata must be adjusted to incorporate the new information. The individual's attempts to assimilate the trauma-related information will inevitably lead to increased arousal and hence a desire to escape from, or avoid, thoughts and reminders of the event. Horowitz argued that until the trauma-related information is assimilated, it is stored in active memory, and will continue to produce intrusive recollections. Psychological numbing of responsiveness is a psychological defence mechanism against such intrusive thoughts.

Creamer *et al.* (1992, 1995) argued that there is little empirical evidence to support Horowitz's work, and so presented a general model of cognitive processing in a way that would allow for longitudinal empirical testing (see also McFarlane, 1992). Their model is an attempt at a synthesis of previous models, but it has the limitation that it fails to include many elements that affect post-trauma adjustment, such as personality, social support and biological factors. It consists of five stages:

Objective exposure

The severity of exposure to the event has been found to be a critical factor in the development of subsequent pathology (e.g. Foy *et al.*, 1987; Speed *et al.*, 1989). But the severity of the stressor is not the only determinant. The model proposes that the effects of the stressor will be mediated by processing variables. These processing variables are intrusion and avoidance.

Network formation

This can only happen if the person subjectively appraises the event as being traumatic. The formation of the traumatic memory network in implicit memory will be determined by characteristics of the traumatic experience (stimulus, response and meaning propositions). It will also be affected by factors such as pre-trauma personality and prior experiences.

Intrusion

The memory network must be activated for processing to take place (Foa *et al.*, 1989). This occurs when the person is presented with information that matches stimulus, response or meaning information in the memory network (i.e. a reminder). Activation of the network results not only in intrusion but also the accompanying aversive responses. These intrusive memories, while causing distress, may also relate to cognitive processing. Exposure allows stimulus–response connections to be weakened and encourages modification of the meaning associated with the incident. Intrusion can be functional in this way, or it can be dysfunctional, perhaps because it can result in very high arousal and can prompt attempts to avoid the traumatic memories. Creamer *et al.* (1992) conceptualise avoidance as a coping mechanism that is activated when intrusive thoughts become too difficult for the person to deal with. Intrusion leads to the automatic fear response, which is too strong for the individual, who reverts to a strategy of avoidance; thus no processing of the traumatic information takes place. Creamer *et al.* propose that resolution occurs not only through intrusion, but also through more adaptive processing, e.g. discussion of the trauma with family and friends.

Avoidance

Avoidance is a coping strategy, a response to the discomfort caused by the intrusion stage. Network activation produces a state of high physiological arousal. People may attempt to escape this by avoiding reminders of the past. Our work (Hunt and Robbins, 2001a) suggests that avoidance can be a very successful long-term coping strategy for some individuals. Creamer *et al.* (1992) argue that it can be maladaptive if relied on to excess. They suggest that high levels of avoidance will be associated with the continued presence of psychological symptoms. While this is true, it is also the case that avoidance may be a very effective strategy for people for life. It is difficult to determine whether someone is using avoidance effectively or whether they really do have no potential symptoms. This presents another methodological difficulty.

Avoidance levels will also be determined by prior coping strategies. While avoidance may successfully alleviate symptoms, traumatic information cannot be processed. Creamer *et al.* predict that high levels of avoidance will be associated with continuing symptoms. This stage is critical for combat veterans. During combat, individuals use avoidance as an important coping strategy. After World War Two they were told to forget about what they had done, and wives were discouraged from talking about it. But evidence, even from the 1940s, suggests that those who avoid discussing a trauma may have more severe longer term consequences (Lindemann, 1944).

Outcome

Recovery is achieved through activation and modification of the fear network. This is evidenced by high levels of intrusion, which lead to high levels of symptomatology at the time, but reduced symptomatology later.

Creamer's theory has had some influence on the development of trauma theory, but there are difficulties. One of the biggest problems is that it is difficult to test because it requires detailed longitudinal work, and people's complex reactions mean that they may be in several of the above stages at any one time. Those who have apparently achieved outcome may revert to earlier stages when they are reminded of their traumatic event. It may not make sense to think of people being in particular 'stages' of recovery at all.

Another difficulty concerning processing is that it is assumed that, when the memory network is activated, it 'automatically' begins processing. There is no reason to suppose that this is the case. If an individual simply goes over and over the memory, it will not necessarily become less horrific or traumatic. This is simply depressive rumination. As Weine et al.'s (1995) victim of ethnic cleansing stated, the memories may be like films played over and over again. Another problem is that 'recovery' is oversimplified. In learning terms, the model suggests that a kind of behavioural flooding takes place, and that if the person has high symptom levels, then these will reduce over time through a process of extinction. There is no evidence that this is the case. In order for recovery to take place, the individual has to act on the memories. This is where the link with the work on explicit and implicit memories and developing a narrative is important. Creamer's notion of processing is equivalent to the development of the narrative (van der Kolk and Fisler, 1995): if traumatic recollections are 'avoided', then they remain in implicit memory, and are in a position to be activated should the right stimulus conditions be experienced, and as they are implicit memories, they are not being acted on or narrated.

A full model of the response to trauma has to take into account how the individual's schemata interact with traumatic recollections when developing the narrative, though even over the long term, the individual's response can be broadly defined within the two mechanisms of processing and avoidance. The individual either learns to adapt to the traumatic memories by avoiding them through 'keeping busy' with work, family, etc., or works on the memories through processing – changing the nature of the memories to stop them being traumatic – to integrate them into his/her belief systems.

Learning theory

Learning theory has been productive for theory, for empirical work and for treatment of trauma. The basic assumption is that a person develops fear through classical conditioning, usually taking the form of one-trial learning known as the 'Garcia effect',[1] which is a basic survival mechanism. If a person behaves in a particular way in a life-threatening situation and survives, then they automatically remember this for a similar situation in the future. While this may be adaptive in the traumatic situation, it may be less so in other situations. The problem, as we shall see, is that the memory is not just of the survival *behaviour* in the appropriate context, but also the emotional, cognitive and behavioural elements, which constitute traumatic stress. Any reminder of the traumatic event can automatically activate the fear memory. This works for the conditioning process as well. Orr *et al.* (2000) showed that people with PTSD develop conditioned responses to aversive stimuli much more readily than people without PTSD.

Lang (1979) suggested that emotional images are composed of three main classes of propositional unit; these are concerned with stimulus information (e.g. location and physical characteristics of the situation), response information (verbal, physiological and behavioural responses) and meaning information (interpretation of the stimulus and response elements and their significance for the individual; this is tied to narrative development, as will be discussed in Chapter 8). Lang proposed a prototype fear image stored in memory. New events are tested against this prototype. If there is a sufficiently close correspondence, the stored memory, complete with response elements, is activated and the individual experiences fear. This programmatic construction explains how the fear information is only sometimes available to consciousness, in effect when the individual is provided with a reminder.

The emotional processing of fear and the construction of memories of traumatic events have been widely studied. Rachman (1980) suggested

---

[1] After Garcia and Koelling (1966), who gave rats food with sufficient poison in it to make them ill, then when they gave them the same food some months later the rats would not touch it.

that it is useful to think of people as either successfully or unsuccessfully processing or absorbing their emotional reactions to stressful events. Conditioned fear reactions are one of many signs that the emotions associated with an event have not been processed successfully (other signs include intrusive thoughts, dreams, behaviour disruptions and the sudden return of fear). This provides evidence for a common process underlying PTSD and other anxiety problems such as phobias, which may have a traumatic origin but may not be treated until much later. The reappearance of fear after it has diminished in intensity cannot be explained successfully using traditional conditioning theory.

What separates PTSD from other anxiety disorders is the monumental significance of the traumatic event (Foa *et al.*, 1989). It is so important that – as we have seen – it shatters previously held beliefs and assumptions about the world. Foa *et al.* proposed a model whereby the memory for the fear network is held separately to normal memories. The associations between the elements of the memories are more powerful than normal memories, and they can be triggered by a number of non-conscious triggers.

Emotional processing theory is a more sophisticated version of the above. Foa and her colleagues (Foa and Riggs, 1993; Foa and Rothbaum, 1998) suggested that individuals with more rigid pre-trauma views would be more vulnerable to PTSD; that is, those with strong views about themselves as competent and the world as safe would be more at risk. They also suggested an increased emphasis on negative appraisals of the responses and behaviours that exacerbate perceptions of incompetence. Those beliefs present around the time of the traumatic event could reinforce the negative schemata – which involve incompetence, danger or fear – that underlie chronic PTSD. Exposure treatment, providing repeated reliving of the traumatic event, should lead to habituation of fear, and reinforce more positive aspects, such as safety information, eventually leading to the reintegration of dysfunctional and disjointed memories.

The dual representation of memory

There are two key memory systems with regard to traumatic stress (Janet, 1925; van der Hart and Horst, 1989; Terr, 1990; van der Kolk and van der Hart, 1991). These memory systems have been given various names that essentially refer to the same constructs, such as verbally accessible memory and situationally accessible memory (Brewin and Holmes, 2003), or implicit and explicit memory (van der Kolk and Fisler, 1995). Whichever terminology is used, there is a verbal system that is under conscious control, but is – crucially for traumatic stress – a relatively slow processing route. There is also a non-verbal system that is not under conscious control, and is very fast-acting. We use the verbal system for our everyday activities, remembering what we had for breakfast or discussing the latest happenings in the world, whereas we use the non-verbal system for dealing with automatic processing, such as how to ride a bike or bowl at cricket. Interestingly, many non-verbal skills are initially verbal but then become implicit as we become better at them, i.e. we develop automaticity. The difference for traumatic stress is that this learning takes place over a single trial – the traumatic event.

According to van der Kolk and Fisler (1995), what is remembered in explicit memory depends on the person's existing schemata. New to-be-remembered information is incorporated into existing schemata. Unfortunately, the traumatised individual is unable to incorporate the new traumatic information into the existing schemata, and hence into explicit memory. Traumatic recollections enter implicit memory, where they are not under conscious control. The contents of implicit memory, at least in the context of trauma, are the individual's initial conditioned reactions to the trauma, including associated emotional and behavioural responses. Implicit memory can be accessed via the individual being in a situation where they are reminded of the stimulus, leading to the appropriate conditioned response.

In practical terms, the traumatised individual will be able to live a normal life except when the contents of implicit memory are triggered. This can mean that the person who successfully avoids all reminders of the traumatic event can live a symptom-free life. Unfortunately, for some traumatised people, this activitation is almost constant (Chemtob et al., 1988). When this happens, the individual experiences traumatic recollections. These are memories of the traumatic event that are still 'raw'. The individual has not processed them (Creamer, 1995; Creamer et al., 1992) and has not incorporated them into explicit memory; they have not developed a narrative.

Memory has two main roles: it is a storage and retrieval system, and it is a functional system with affective, psychosocial and cultural uses (Barclay and Smith, 1992). As will be explored in Chapter 8, where the focus will be on the flexible nature of memory and the role of individual and social factors in changing memories, cognitive psychologists and clinicians have explored the malleability of memory. Explicit memory is an active and constructive process (Bartlett, 1932; van der Kolk and Fisler, 1995). Inputting new information into explicit memory depends on existing mental schemata. Once the new information is integrated, it is no longer available as a separate entity, but only within the context of the schemata. This has implications for the changes that may occur in memories over time, depending on individual circumstances. Memories can be confabulated, so presumably they can range along a continuum from being highly accurate to completely inaccurate. Davis and Lehman (1995) describe what they call 'counterfactuals' – memories of a traumatic event that are not true. This was explored in detail in the 1990s in the so-called 'false memory debate', where it was thought by some that patients were recovering memories of child abuse, which led to the prosecution of some people, particularly fathers. In the end, the debate fizzled out, with the general consensus being that these memories were fictitious and created during the therapeutic process (e.g. British Psychological Society, 1995). People coping with traumatic events appeared uninhibited in their ability to generate counterfactuals, i.e. false memories. The memories of traumatised individuals should be treated with caution, but not the individual's *responses* to those memories.

While 'ordinary' memories are not fixed, traumatic recollections often are. Weine *et al.* (1995), in a study of Bosnian refugees, quote one survivor who says that he has 'films of traumas that constantly play in his head; although he may look away from them, they continue to inhabit him' (p. 540). This is not an isolated case. Much of the work involving trauma survivors has indicated that individuals appear to relive the traumatic event, not just recall it. This reliving is one of the characteristics of PTSD. Koss *et al.* (1996), in a review of work on traumatic memories, conclude that there is a consensus of evidence which suggests that emotion facilitates accurate recall of central details of the event, though there is no similar increment for the peripheral details. They also concluded that emotion slows forgetting, and time may actually enhance such memories, because shortly after the trauma emotions may disrupt retrieval, but over time such disruption diminishes. Brewer (1992) suggests that the explanation for the durability of emotional memories is not rehearsal, but occurs at the encoding stage, which would suggest that it is a form of one-trial learning that is adaptive, in support of the work outlined above.

Perhaps the most prominent current theory regarding traumatic memory is Brewin's dual-representation theory (Brewin *et al.*, 1996; Brewin and Holmes, 2003), which proposes that there are two memory systems known as 'verbally accessible memory' (VAM) and 'situationally accessible memory' (SAM). The two systems operate in parallel, and one may take precedence over the other at particular times. VAM memories of trauma contain information that the person has attended to before, during and after the traumatic event, and contains sufficient information to be encoded and stored for later deliberate retrieval. These memories only contain what was consciously attended to. They may also contain the elaborated memories of the narrative, the elements which did not actually exist during the traumatic situation but which the person has added to the information, consciously or non-consciously.

In contrast with the VAM system, flashbacks and other trauma memories are contained within the SAM system, demonstrating that flashbacks are triggered involuntarily by external or internal reminders. The information is usually lower level, with more perceptual information from the scene of the trauma, i.e. information that has received no, or minimal, processing. The SAM system has no verbal code, and so the memories are difficult to access and communicate to other people. The memories do not interact with other memories and so are not processed. This is an important point, which explains why trauma memories are fragmented and uncontrolled, and why, in order to develop the narrative, a person must find ways of accessing the VAM.

The implications of the dual-representation approach are that PTSD is a hybrid disorder that has potentially two pathological processes. The first involves dealing with negative and shattered beliefs and assumptions and their accompanying emotions, and the second involves managing classically conditioned flashbacks or other intrusive thoughts (Brewin and Holmes, 2003). Full recovery depends on both being resolved, and perhaps shows why cognitive behaviour therapy is effective (at least for a proportion of traumatised people), as it deals with both elements. To resolve the VAM problems, the person needs to reappraise the information, and reintegrate it into their schemata. To resolve SAM-related problems will require exposure therapy.

In the end, the VAM/SAM model provides integration between cognitive understanding and learning theory. Both are critical to developing a full account of what happens when someone is traumatised. Now we have an effective psychological understanding, it is important to underpin this with a neuropsychological understanding of trauma processes.

Neuropsychological understanding

Until fairly recently, comparatively little research had been carried out on the biological underpinnings of PTSD and war trauma. This is interesting given that the early theories of war trauma implicated physiological systems, either the heart ('soldier's heart' during the US Civil War) or microscopic brain damage (shellshock during the First World War). The problem with developing neuropsychological understanding was that the appropriate methodological tools had not been developed. It is only with the introduction of imaging techniques that our knowledge about the brain mechanisms underlying trauma has rapidly developed.

There is a range of systems involved in the traumatic response, ranging from the limbic system to the cerebral cortex. Specifically, a number of areas have been identified, including the thalamus, which plays a role in sensory input, the hippocampus, which is involved in memory processing and perhaps the fear response, and the amygdala, which is involved in the conditioned fear response. Areas that focus on visuospatial processing and the assessment of threat include the posterior cingulate, and the parietal and motor cortex. Finally, the medial frontal cortex is involved in a number of cortical responses (Nemeroff *et al.*, 2008).

The biological effects of fear and stress in laboratory animals (e.g. LeDoux *et al.*, 1995) initially formed a key basis for our understanding of the neural pathways involved in PTSD, and this is now being supported by human studies, though, as we shall see, the findings are not consistent.

A primary focus of research with humans has been on the hippocampus – a limbic structure concerned with memory. The hippocampus plays a critical role in the development of explicit memories of trauma (Squire, 1992; Bremner *et al.*, 1995; van der Kolk and Fisler, 1995), and stress does affect this area, with high levels of glucocorticoids released during stressful events. Vietnam veterans show an 8% decrease in hippocampal volume compared with controls (Bremner *et al.*, 1995). Animal studies have also supported the relationship between stress, glucocorticoids and hippocampal atrophy (McEwen and Magarinos, 1997). Several studies have since reported reduced hippocampal volume in people with PTSD (for a review, see Bremner, 1998; Pitman, 2001; Nutt and Malazia, 2004; Bremner, 2005). The problem is that the evidence is inconsistent, because other studies find no hippocampal atrophy (Bonne *et al.*, 2001; Notestine *et al.*, 2002; Stam, 2007), though it may be that decreased hippocampal volume may be linked to chronic rather than acute PTSD, or that reduced hippocampal volume is instead a predictor of PTSD, with individuals with smaller hippocampi being more likely to get PTSD after a traumatic event. The link to the hippocampus does appear to be important, with further evidence coming from people treated with antidepressants, who show an increase in hippocampal volume linked to symptom reduction (Vermetten *et al.*, 2003).

Fear conditioning is mediated by subcortical mechanisms, involving sensory pathways that project to the thalamus and the amygdala. People with PTSD have increased activity of the amygdala to fearful or emotional stimuli (Bremner *et al.*, 2005; Williams *et al.*, 2005). According to

Stam (2007) the altered responsivity of the amygdala seems to support the idea that reduced inhibitory control by frontal cortical regions over the amygdala may underlie some of the behavioural hyperresponsivity in people with PTSD. There is little consistent evidence relating to laterality of function in the amygdala in people with PTSD (Stam, 2007).

Animal research shows that emotional memories established via pathways linking the amygdala and the thalamus may be relatively indelible (DeDous et al., 1989). LeDoux (1995) studied fear conditioning by pairing a foot shock with a sound; this elicited the physiological components of the fear reaction, such as freezing and elevated blood pressure. The animal becomes conditioned to respond to the sound alone after several pairings. The shock alters neurons in both cortical and subcortical regions of the brain, the central nucleus of the amygdala, the thalamus, and parts of the cerebral cortex (LeDoux, 1995). The thaelamic pathway may be the most useful for an immediate reaction, enabling a response before the organism fully realises what is happening. Christianson (1992) suggests that this pre-attentive pathway is fast, independent of context, independent of processing resources and able to carry out parallel processing of different inputs. It is this pathway where much of what we remember and forget (including presumably traumatic memories) is determined automatically. This clearly has adaptive value, as discussed earlier. Bremner et al. (1995a) suggest that memory is a survival mechanism during trauma; an organism will need efficient retrieval of memories in similar future situations.

Propranolol (an alpha-adrenergic antagonist) interferes with the recall of an emotionally arousing story, which suggests that activation of alpha-adrenergic receptors in the brain enhances the encoding of emotion-arousing memories. PTSD patients have more problems with ordinary stressful events than non-PTSD individuals. Acute stress increases the release of noradrenaline in the hippocampus, which becomes sensitised to subsequent stressors, so leading to an accentuation of noradrenaline release with an ordinary stressor. Southwick et al. (1999) showed that, under normal stressful conditions, the release of noradrenaline increases alertness and selective attention to significant cues, facilitating memory encoding of the stimuli, again having an adaptive function in preparing the organism for future stressful events.

The prefrontal cortex also plays an important role in the stress response. This area acts as an interface between internal and external experience, and is suited to the integration of sensory information during a stressful event (Bremner et al., 1995). This area also plays an important role in sustained attention. This links with the work of Christianson (1992), who focuses on the attentional elements of the traumatic situation, suggesting that, when individuals feel threatened, they experience a narrowing of consciousness, they focus on central details, and it is terror that prevents the integration of traumatic memories with ordinary memories. Many years ago, Janet (1925) suggested that, after trauma, memories become unconscious fixed ideas until they have been translated into a narrative; in other words, they are contained in implicit memory until they are processed and incorporated into explicit memory. There may be implications for the amnesia experienced by traumatised individuals. Individuals may not be able to recall all aspects of the traumatic event because the event itself may interfere with general attentional skills or the focusing of attention on details (Wolfe, 1995). With increased arousal the output of noradrenaline leads to increased activation of the posterior attentional system (Posner, 1993).

In this way we can see how an understanding of the underlying neurobiology of PTSD and traumatic memories reinforces current cognitive and behavioural theories.

Other biological associations

PTSD is also linked with a number of other health-related problems, and there may be longer term consequences, not only for psychological symptoms, but also for physical illness. Traumatised people often report problems with physical health. This is sometimes confounded by the traumatic experience itself. POWs report longer term gastro-intestinal problems, but these are often associated with the physical conditions of their imprisonment (Eberly and Engdahl, 1991; Hunt, unpublished data), though it is difficult to be certain of this, as the studies do not – of course – have appropriate control groups. Nevertheless, many studies indicate the presence of physical health problems in people with PTSD. The extent to which there is an underlying third mechanism which causes both PTSD and these physical health problems is unknown, but there may be linkages with personality traits such as hypochondria and neuroticism.

There is good evidence of the linkage between PTSD and the cardio-vascular system. There is a small but significant increase in basal heart rate and blood pressure in PTSD patients compared with controls, though there is an overlap between the groups, and the effect is stronger for chronic PTSD (Buckley and Kaloupek, 2001). There are a number of potentially confounding variables, such as smoking and drinking behaviour, which may themselves cause the increase in cardiovascular problems rather than the PTSD itself. If people with PTSD are exposed to combat sounds, then they have greater heart rate and blood pressure responses than controls (Stam, 2007). This can be a reliable diagnostic tool for the indication of PTSD. Finally, WWII veterans with PTSD had higher levels of angina and vital exhaustion than controls (Falger *et al.*, 1992), but again this may be the result of confounding variables.

While our understanding of the biology and neurobiology of traumatic memories and PTSD is increasing, there is immense variability in the findings because of the complexity of symptoms and the complexity of the individual response. There are also methodological problems owing to the relative newness of imaging and other methods, but the overall picture is promising.

Physiology and narrative processing

One area where there is relatively limited understanding of the biological substrate is that of narrative understanding. Current neuropsychological research has only had a very limited focus on this area, partly because it is difficult to break down the various linguistic components of narrative, but without an understanding we cannot have a full picture of how people deal with traumatic events. There are a number of brain regions that are associated with narrative, but the details are largely conjecture. Most language-based imaging studies are concerned with individual word processing rather than more complex linguistic structures. As Marr (2004) states, attempting to ascribe brain areas to the full range of cognitive activities associated with narrative is a daunting task, though it is possible to start by exploring those regions we know to be associated with lower level language tasks. Marr attempts to draw the literature together using three narrative components: memory encoding and retrieval, integration, and elaboration or simulation. As narrative is a high-level task, it is likely that the control of narrative processes is via the frontal lobe. Specifically, areas of the dorsolateral prefrontal cortex have been associated with language processing (Fuster *et al.*, 2000). Working memory is also going to be important for narrative processing (Baddeley and Wilson, 2002). The episodic buffer of working memory is thought to be associated with the right frontal lobe.

There are a limited number of neuro-imaging studies of narrative processing. The major methodological difficulty is the temporal nature of stories. Some studies have explored story comprehension. Fletcher *et al.* (1995), using PET, had participants read stories of varying complexity and found differential activity in frontal lobe areas. Maguire *et al.* (1999) also found frontal lobe activation linked to the complexity of story comprehension, though these studies are not explicitly examining full narrative processes. Studies of brain-damaged people suggest that a number of areas are important for story comprehension, particularly the frontal lobes (Novoa and Ardila, 1987; Hough, 1990) and the right hemisphere (e.g. Benowitz *et al.*, 1990).

There are very few imaging studies relating to narrative production. Braun *et al.* (2001) studied sign language using positron emission tomography and, when they eliminated the motor effects of signing, found that the frontal lobes were important in narrative production, similar to the findings associated with language comprehension. One of the problems with this study is that the narrative processes linked to sign language may differ from those associated with speech production.

Marr (2004) draws the literature together and summarises our understanding drawn from the studies described above and others. He concludes that there are a number of key brain areas associated with narrative. The medial prefrontal cortex is associated with both comprehension and production and with ordering; selection processes, in particular, take place here. This area is also probably associated with theory of mind, the ability of an individual to recognise the psychological characteristics of other people. The lateral prefrontal cortex, particularly the right hemispheric dorsolateral section, is important in the ordering of events within a narrative. This is also linked with working memory, particularly episodic memory retrieval. The temporoparietal, posterior cingulate cortex and the anterior temporal regions are also concerned with story comprehension and production.

This limited work begins to tell the story of narrative comprehension, but there is a long way to go to ascertain the specific systems involved and the role played at different levels of the narrative. The neuroscience of narrative is a very new area, so it is not surprising that relatively little is known.

Psychodynamic approaches

Psychodynamic theory has been used throughout the twentieth century to explain post-traumatic stress, and while such an approach is rarely accepted in mainstream psychology, at least in Anglo-Saxon psychology, it is important not to dismiss the contribution made by this perspective, particularly on the Continent. By exploring psychodynamic theory, we may find that it enhances our understanding. Emery and Emery (1989) related psychodynamic theory to the diagnostic criteria of PTSD and concluded that the distinction between psychoneuroses and traumatic neuroses should be retained, and that the aetiology of PTSD lies in the stressor itself. This argument is directly relevant to the debate regarding the role of the stressor. The critical distinction between explicit and implicit memory is partly analogous to psychodynamic notions of the conscious and the unconscious respectively. In Freudian psychology, the individual has little control over the contents of the unconscious, and uses defence mechanisms to deal with information contained therein. While the present approach does not make any claims regarding the structure of the unconscious, the analogy is acceptable, particularly as the behavioural effect is for the contents of implicit memory to be accessed via appropriate stimuli of which the individual may not be aware.

Freud's 'seduction theory' was one of the first formal theoretical approaches to describe how traumatic experiences can lead to psychological problems (see Wilson, 1994). One of the main differences between this and modern non-psychodynamic approaches concerns the role of repression and the unconscious. Freud suggested repression was an ego defence that suppressed traumatic memories. Once these memories were in the unconscious, neurotic symptoms might arise as a result of active forces being applied in the unconscious. Modern theory generally uses the concept of avoidance in place of repression, where the individual may actively avoid reminding situations. But once the traumatic memories are repressed, they do not change, but are retained in an inactive unconscious (implicit memory) and emerge via the activation of situational reminding cues. In this sense avoidance is an effective coping strategy as long as avoidance is effective, while repression requires the active avoidance of cues, a more difficult task for the traumatised person.

Existentialism and humanism

Individuals who experience trauma can experience growth through the way they deal with the memories. This is dealt with mainly in Chapter 6, but needs to be mentioned here in the context of integrating theory. Herman (1992) focuses on how psychological trauma is about disempowerment, loss of control and disconnection from others. She proposes that recovery is about empowering the survivor and taking on new connections. To Herman, recovery can only take place in the context of relationships (e.g. comradeship for veterans), but the only way for an individual to recover is to do the recovering themselves; there is no external cure. The survivor has to come to terms with the traumatic past and reconnect with life. Herman puts this in terms of mourning the old self and developing a new self. The resolution of the trauma is never completed; there is no full recovery in the sense of a return to the previous self. The humanist perspective considers the traumatic experience from the perspective of the individual in a holistic sense. Many

Vietnam veterans keep alive their memories of the war because they are significant and meaningful. Many continue to suffer from PTSD because of this (Bradshaw *et al.*, 1991).

Greening (1990) discusses PTSD in terms of a fundamental assault on one's right to live, on our sense of worth and on our sense that the world (including people) basically supports human life. This is similar to Horowitz's cognitive theory (Horowitz, 1986), whereby our world schemata are shattered by traumatic experiences, and in order to be 'cured' we have to reconcile these schemata with the evidence provided by the trauma that the world isn't as pleasant as we believed it to be.

Coping

Coping is critical to understanding how people respond to traumatic events. There has already been a discussion of some of the different coping strategies people use, but we can get bogged down when discussing coping. There are numerous theories, and 40 years of research has failed to generate any sense of coherence in the literature. Some theories have just a few coping strategies, others list ten or twenty. This is not the place to summarise this research, but to outline a simple model that will inform our understanding of war trauma. It links closely with the narrative approach taken in this book.

While there are complications, and many theories suggest a range of coping mechanisms, it is argued here for the sake of simplicity that there are two fundamental mechanisms for coping with traumatic recollections: avoidance and processing. These are the main strategies we use in everyday life, and the ones we use after a traumatic event. Most people do most of their coping through avoidance; it is often easier not to think about a problem and hope it will go away, and in the real world, it often does. With psychological problems, including PTSD, effective avoidance means that symptoms are rarely or never experienced, but there is the potential for future problems arising as any trauma-related information (e.g. cognitions, emotions) remains in the memory and is not dealt with. Processing – used by most of us for a minority of the time – concerns the active 'working through' of problems, in our case traumatic recollections. Traumatic memories that are worked through are turned into narrative-explicit memories. Through the narrative, the individual deals with the cognitions, emotions and behaviours associated with the memory.

Both strategies work, but if a person usually employs an avoidant strategy, traumatic memories may re-emerge many years, even decades, later. As discussed above, researchers, including Creamer, Horowitz and

McFarlane, have proposed that people resolve their traumatic stress by moving through cycles of intrusion (processing) and avoidance, dealing with traumatic information until it becomes emotionally too difficult, and then moving into a phase of avoidance until they are ready to process further information. In this way people work through their own traumatic information over time.

Processing can take many forms, from talking to friends and family, through writing books and journals, to having formal treatment with a psychotherapist. All are forms of narrative development and enable the person to cope more effectively with their memories. This will be discussed in Chapter 8.

There are important individual differences in coping. Processing information and developing a narrative requires significant cognitive resources. There is some evidence that more intelligent people are able to resolve their traumatic experiences more effectively just because they have access to these resources.

The single most effective means of helping people to cope with war trauma is social support. In my own research with war veterans, social support takes two distinct forms. First, veterans talk to their comrades about the detailed events of their wartime experiences, sharing the trauma with people who understand because they were there. Second, veterans use their families as social support in a different way, not talking to them about their traumatic experiences, but protecting them from the emotions associated with them, and relying on the home as a safe haven from the memories of war (Hunt and Robbins, 2001b).

Integrating theory

It should be clear from the above brief discussion that the different perspectives in psychology can all contribute to our understanding of traumatic memory and PTSD. While the core of the book is concerned with narrative – and we will move on to that area in detail in the next chapter – it is critical to acknowledge that an understanding of trauma from any perspective – including narrative – must involve integrating findings from other areas if we are to develop a coherent understanding of traumatic stress.

It is unfortunate that, in many areas of psychology, researchers focus on a particular theoretical perspective. The ease with which trauma can be explained in terms of several perspectives says a great deal about how trauma theory taps into the fundamental attributes of human functioning, memory, coping, emotions, beliefs, implicit and explicit functioning, and our response to stress, and how these are grounded in fundamental biological structures and mechanisms from which common behavioural responses emerge. In later chapters, the interdisciplinary perspective comes to the fore, and we can see how drawing on the expertise and knowledge of different disciplines can enhance this understanding of war trauma still further.

6   Positive outcomes of traumatic experiences

Our greatest glory is not in never falling, but in rising every time we fall

Confucius

That which does not kill us can only make us stronger

Nietzsche

The focus of most research on traumatic stress has, as we have seen in earlier chapters, been on the negative psychological and social consequences of the event or events – how many people experience PTSD, depression or problems with relationships or alcohol, and how many people take years to recover, if they ever do. The focus on the negative is a criticism that is true of much applied psychology, which has usually focused on what is wrong with people and tried to find ways of putting it right. While this is admirable, it is not everything.

Most people who go through traumatic or stressful situations are not traumatised. They come out unscathed, somewhat changed but easily able to cope, or having learned something about life. There should be a focus on more positive aspects of change that occur as a result of being exposed to massively traumatising stimuli, change which may take place immediately but which is more likely to take much longer, perhaps years. This positive focus can teach us a lot about the normal psychological processes that come into play during traumatic situations, but may also aid clinicians and others to assist people with problems. The experience of trauma can help people to develop their understanding of themselves, other people and the world. These ideas link to the existential ideas regarding the potential for growth and positive change.

Terminology

In the relatively few years since research began in this area, a number of terminological problems have developed. Researchers have used a number of terms to represent the positive outcomes that occur after traumatic experiences. Linley and Joseph (2004) list a number of these terms, including post-traumatic growth, stress-related growth, perceived benefits, thriving, blessings, positive by-products and positive readjustment. Many of these terms relate directly to the difficulty; for example, stress-related growth implies that a person must have had a psychological experience of stress in order to achieve growth. Similarly, the term 'positive by-products' suggests that a positive outcome is simply a by-product of the distress, and not really something significantly positive. Blessings suggest religion, and though religion can play a key part in positive outcomes, as we shall see, the picture is broader than that. Thriving suggests that not only has the person achieved a positive outcome, but that they are rapidly moving forward. Positive outcomes may not be that positive for everyone! Here we will use the term 'post-traumatic growth' as it recognises that there was a traumatic incident, does not require that the person experienced pathology, and recognises that there is some growth after the event.

For many people, the eventual outcome of a traumatic experience is significant positive psychological growth, though it may take years for the person to achieve this. While this approach is relatively new in psychology, it has a distinguished background in literature and philosophy, where the term 'suffering' is often substituted for 'trauma', e.g. Sartre's existential position that we interpret our experiences, and that interpreting them positively in terms of growth will enable us to improve our lives and our relationships in our own individual ways. An illustration of this is Sartre's 'Age of Reason' trilogy, where the events of M's life were described in extraordinary detail, along with his interpretations of those experiences. Those of us interested in war should read the final part of the trilogy where it is 1940, and M, now in the French army, is trapped on a church tower and the Germans are approaching.

Stories of growth go back a long way. Buddhism began because Siddhãrtha Gautama (Buddha) realised that people need to come to terms with the suffering in the world. He set out on a journey lasting many years to understand the origins of suffering, why people suffer, and what can be done about it. Other religions also focus on suffering, and the ways in which we can learn from difficulties. Christianity is another case, where Jesus died on the cross to relieve suffering – though this is rather a crude example that fails to show the thought processes behind tragedy and salvation. Similarly, tragedy as art has been used throughout literate times as a means of demonstrating how we can learn through suffering, be it the Greek tragedies, Shakespeare or more modern works.

There are examples dotted throughout psychology in the twentieth century that present evidence for growth. For example, the motivational theory of Maslow (1954) proposed that we have a hierarchy of needs, and that needs at one level need to be satisfied before moving up to the next level. At the bottom of this hierarchy there are needs for shelter and food, and at the top there are special moments in life called peak experiences, where, in words not used by Maslow, we experience positive growth. There are many cases from the horrors of the twentieth century that demonstrate growth, particularly from the Holocaust. Viktor Frankl (1963/1984), a Holocaust survivor who wrote extensively about his experiences and, in his terms, became a better person and a better psychologist because of his experiences, discussed growth and the way he managed to interpret his experiences over the following years and decades and use these interpretations to help others.

What do we mean by growth? Is it simply a change after a traumatic event that, in some cases, leads to a perceived better understanding of the world in some way, or do people actually become happier or more satisfied with life? Learning something about the world does not necessarily make someone happier, so growth is not about happiness. Fundamentally, the concern is with a changed perception regarding the self – a better understanding of self, others or the world. Growth implies change towards a different (and assumed better) structure of the personality and identity. The person who experiences growth after a traumatic event will look at the world differently, perhaps in a less naïve manner, recognising for instance that the world is more complex than they thought or less good, or that by seeing the vulnerability of people there is a recognition of the importance of living one's life to the full, of not wasting time on trivial activities, or gaining a positive outlook even when carrying out the most trivial tasks. Many people look on others in a different way, recognising them as people with rights and responsibilities.

There is no one area where people experience growth, but these are some of the key aspects. The traumatic event makes a person re-evaluate his or her life; that person tends to reflect on the traumatic event – how they and others behaved, thought and felt, and the implications of these. Through this, fundamental change relating to the self can occur. This may entail a changed philosophy of life, with the realisation – perhaps – that the acquisition of ever-more wealth is unimportant compared with having a good relationship with one's family and friends. The change of perspective is fundamental. The person may realise that the sound of birds in the morning, the rustle of the wind in the leaves, or the varying nature of the earth around us, is much more important than social status and wealth. This change occurs specifically because of the threat to life that has been experienced.

Much of this may seem to be stating the obvious, but in reality many of us living ordinary lives have a philosophy of life that is not thought through particularly well, at least not until the person is challenged in a fundamental manner, as with a life-changing experience such as a traumatic event.

Why is it that after a traumatic experience some people are traumatised, some people experience growth and some people appear to change very little? There is a range of personality factors that impact on outcome: factors relating to resilience, coping styles, perceived social support, cognitive abilities, etc. Which of these are important in experiencing growth? According to Lev-Wiesel and Amir (2001), who have studied survivors of the Holocaust, these differences result from the level of a survivor's personal resources in terms of sense of potency, self-identity and social support.

In my study of Second World War veterans (Hunt, 1996), veterans did see positive sides to their war experiences. Many experienced foreign travel for the first time, they got to use the latest technology, and, perhaps most importantly, they got to meet and mix with people from other social classes, people they would usually not get a chance to meet. For many, this was the most important positive aspect of their war experience and, it can be argued, it was the area to have most impact after the war, contributing to significant changes in the social class structure. Furthermore, people fought the Second World War for positive reasons: to remove Hitler and the evils of Naziism, to free the people of Europe, to protect their families and to create a better society. These factors are important in contributing to a change in outlook, and also contributed to the unexpected Labour election victory in July 1945. In these terms, we can see a socially constructed notion of positive growth after the war, at least at the societal level, if not always at an individual one.

Assessing growth

There are a number of ways to assess post-traumatic growth, both qualitative and quantitative. Most research has focused on questionnaire measures, designed to assess particular aspects of growth, though qualitative approaches are also used.

There are a number of quantitative measures available, and while this is not the place to review them, it is worth mentioning two that have been used widely and to good effect. The Post-traumatic Growth Inventory (PTGI) was devised by Tedeschi and Calhoun (1996) as a 21-item self-report inventory that measures the person's perception of positive change resulting from a traumatic life experience. People are asked to use a 0–6 rating scale to measure the extent to which their views have changed across a range of areas, for instance 'A feeling of self-reliance' or 'Appreciating each day'. The PTGI was validated using students, though it has been widely used on more appropriate populations.

The Stress-Related Growth Scale (Park *et al.*, 1996) is a longer scale (50 items), which again asks about change, this time in the specific areas of personal resources, social relationships, life philosophy and coping skills. The measure has a three-point (0–2) response choice. A typical item is 'You learned to be a more confident person'. Again, it was developed using students, though it was specifically adapted to stressful situations. Statistical analyses indicate that it is a single scale, and should be used as such, rather than broken down into subscales.

These two scales are just examples. Others are available, but these provide you with a reasonable idea of how positive growth is measured using self-report scales. There are, of course, numerous problems with such scales, from reporting bias to the relatively shallow information that can be obtained from such a measure. The main alternative is to use open-ended questions or interviews. The latter are more effective because they enable a greater depth of information to be obtained. This is important in this area because positive growth differs significantly across people, and we need to understand exactly what changes are taking place.

While these quantitative measures are well validated, there is a serious problem, in that the notion of growth is closely associated with meaning and meaning development. A prescribed questionnaire restricts the range and depth of responses that a person can give, and so may give a misleading idea about whether they have experienced growth. A qualitative approach, on the other hand, can enable a free discussion of the variety of areas that may be considered to have growth potential, and hence that may provide a more accurate picture of the extent and type of growth experienced. The problem with a qualitative approach is that it does not provide a measurable variable with which to determine the relationship between growth and other factors, so depending on the circumstances, it may be more appropriate to use a quantitative mea-sure. The close relationship between growth and narrative development shall be explored later in the book.

Evidence for growth

Rosner and Powell (2006) used a Bosnian version of the PGTI to explore growth after the Bosnian war. The original wording of the measure, relating to changes that have occurred 'as a result of your crisis', was inappropriate because of the complexity of the war experiences, so they changed it to 'in comparison with the period before the war'. The authors found a positive relationship between coping styles and positive growth, and concluded that post-traumatic or adversarial growth is something more than another coping mechanism, though the finding suggests that growth is closely associated with a particular coping style. It is difficult to conclude that the authors were measuring genuine change and growth resulting from war experiences, both because of the problems associated with the quantitative nature of the PGTI and also because of the nature of war. It is difficult to see how any measure that breaks down such a complex construct as 'psychological growth occurring as a result of traumatic experiences' to a series of simplified tickbox response categories can be accurate. The construct of growth has many facets and may need to be assessed using more complex and appropriate qualitative methods. The issue of war is also complex. Using a phrase like 'in comparison with the period before the war' is problematic. War is complicated. The participants will have had many experiences both during wartime and afterwards that will have impacted on their outlook on life. As many of the participants were young, maturity alone will have changed the way they think – irrespective of the war. Also, during the war they will have had many experiences that had nothing to do with war and that will have changed them. Rosner and Powell (2006) conclude that post-traumatic growth is associated with increased value given to relationships with others – in other words, a more effective use of social support. The study does not – because of the use of the measure it cannot – conclude anything more complex than that. We are left unclear as to whether these participants have genuinely experienced post-traumatic growth as a result of their traumatic war experiences, or whether they have simply matured in certain ways between the time before the war and the time they were tested. In fairness to the authors, they do conclude that the number of measures available hampers the research into post-traumatic growth, and that there is little conceptual overlap between the measures, making it difficult to compare studies. They also concluded that their study showed limited empirical evidence for growth due to war, and that there is no evidence that any growth that does occur is a result of specific traumatic events.

Research has been conducted that specifically examines the role of post-traumatic growth and war, though it is relatively limited. Elder and Clipp (1989), using a sample of 149 US veterans of World War Two (Korea and Vietnam), referred to growth through coping with adversity, discipline and learning to value life more; this was particularly the case for those who had experienced higher levels of combat. Fontana and Rosenheck (1998), interestingly, had only a single open question on growth, and showed a relationship between growth and perceived harm and threat – along with a relationship between education and growth, which may be an indicator of the relationship between cognitive functioning and growth. Maercker *et al.* (1999) were interested in both the positive and negative effects of the Dresden bombing in 1945, and found salutogenic factors resulting from the bombing.

Research on child Holocaust survivors has focused on two areas: firstly showing that Holocaust child survivors have great difficulty maintaining cohesive and independent self-identities, and secondly, that the resilience of many Holocaust child survivors has enabled them to develop successful careers and have good stable marriages and caring families (Lev-Wiesel and Amir, 2001). Sigal (1998) showed that there is a strong sense of resilience among survivors of the Holocaust. Similarly, Moskovitz (1983) interviewed 23 child survivors and found that they had a positive outlook on life, a strength ('durability') of character, and a desire to have a stable family life and be committed to the social world. Lev-Wiesel and Amir (2006) studied 97 Holocaust child survivors and used a range of measures to assess PTSD and post-traumatic growth. They found that the higher the level of the survivors' personal resources, the less they suffered from PTSD symptoms. There was also a positive association between social support and post-traumatic growth. (See Calhoun and Tedeschi (2006) for a good edited account of research into growth.)

Growth and psychotherapy

The concept of growth – under a number of different names – has been around within psychotherapy for many years. Carl Rogers (1980) founded the school of client-centred psychotherapy in opposition to the traditional schools of behaviour therapy and psychoanalysis. Rogers was influenced by existentialism and by humanism, and focuses on people being basically good and thoughtful, rational people. Building on work such as that of Maslow with his hierarchy of needs, Rogers assumed that there is a constructive force – the actualising tendency – which is within everyone and helps them to develop to become better people. According to Rogers, there is an innate ability or force that drives us to improve ourselves, to become better when ill. If this theory is correct, then the normal outcome after a traumatic event should be positive growth. Of course, others factors play an important part, particularly a nurturing environment. Without this, the person will not be able to fully use the actualising tendency. Psychotherapy is about helping individuals who, for some reason, are unable to draw on the actualising tendency. Rogers does not explicitly discuss the kind of post-traumatic growth considered in this chapter, but he does make a theoretical contribution to our understanding of why some people experience growth.

Victor Frankl, mentioned earlier, drew on his Holocaust experiences to develop his own psychotherapeutic approach. His approach, known as 'logotherapy', is based on a spiritually orientated approach to psychotherapy. According to Frankl, finding meaning as a source of strength was critical, as was finding the potential for growth amidst adversity. He used the term 'will to meaning', which, Frankl suggests, is present in everyone. It has a similar formulation to the Freudian notion of the pleasure principle (the will to pleasure) but is more important. There is a fundamental striving in people to find meaning and purpose in life (Frankl, 1969). According to this approach, there is the existence of a spiritual component in everyone. In a similar fashion to Maslow and to Rogers, this inner force enables people to transcend negative situations. Therapy is concerned with helping people with their quest for meaning. Frankl distinguished between present meaning, relating to particular situations in which the person finds himself, and 'supermeaning', which relates to the meaning of life – for the individual. Therapy focuses on the first of these, helping the person to find meaning relating to specific situations. The person will then be in a better position to find and develop his or her meaning of life.

Existential approaches are also concerned with the development of meaning, but focus more on the more fundamental existential questions, such as meaninglessness, death and freedom (Yalom, 1983). Yalom discusses the role of meaning-making that is important when a person is dealing with tragic or difficult events.

Spirituality

One area that is often neglected by psychotherapists and psychologists in general is the role of spirituality. The mainstream monotheistic religions, Christianity, Islam and Judaism, are rarely about personal growth and more about appropriate behaviours for a better future in heaven. Spirituality, on the other hand, while it is closely linked with belief in god, is also concerned with growth and the development of meaning in one's life. Spirituality is important for many people. It is notoriously difficult to measure, as it is a complex construct. Spiritual issues often come to the surface when people face serious crises. The link with post-traumatic growth can be seen in the work of Tedeschi et al. (1998), who include a new sense of spirituality or religion in their conception of post-traumatic growth. This is quite rare; notions of spirituality (and religion) are largely absent from, or peripheral to, most theories of psychology – let alone theories of personal growth. This is a serious omission, and it is interesting to speculate why it is so. While it is easy to ask someone if they are religious, whether they believe in some form of god, it is more difficult to determine spirituality. While some psychologists take religion into account – it is quantifiable in the sense that someone can report they are religious or not, or that they belong to a particular religion, it is very difficult to determine what people *mean* by god, or by spirituality – which are not the same thing. People will say they believe in god without necessarily having a clear idea about what god is. As soon as the word spirituality is discussed, it becomes more difficult.

Spirituality is, in essence, more difficult to explain than religion. The word's origins relate to the wind, and the meaning does seem to get lost on the wind in that it means different things to different people. For most, spirituality and religion go closely together, but there are spiritual people who do not believe in god, and religious people who are not spiritual. Most psychologists either fail to account for the distinction between religion and spirituality, or assume that spirituality can be accounted for by 'inner strength', 'improved relationships with people' or 'having a clear meaning as to the purpose of life'. While spirituality is concerned with these, it is also something more. As this is not the place to begin a religious and philosophical debate as to the meaning of words, we should focus on the role of religion and spirituality in post-traumatic growth. Many traumatised people will say that their god or their spiritual self plays an important role in dealing with traumatic events and in experiencing post-traumatic growth; this may take the form of feeling closer to god, or understanding the meaning of their god's world. Essentially, religion plays an important supportive and explanatory role (see also Dale and Hunt, 2008). People rely on religion for explanations of what has happened to them, and they rely on their god to help them through their problems.

Narrative growth

Narrative is a useful concept that can help us to explain growth. As we have seen in earlier chapters, if a person is going to resolve traumatic problems that have arisen because of the fundamental rift that occurs as a result of a traumatic event, then they need, if they are not going to use an effective avoidant strategy, to develop a narrative of the event. The strong argument here is that the development of an effective narrative more or less guarantees that the person will experience growth. The focus is on the word 'effective'. Many narratives are not effective, and do not enable someone to 'move on'. A narrative may lack coherence, and in so doing may be ineffective at helping the person come to terms with their experiences.

As noted, one of the problems with the literature on psychological growth is that it takes a relatively narrow focus, and attempts to quantify growth through questionnaires, when growth is, by nature, qualitative and personally meaningful. To measure growth is to ignore the key meaningful elements of growth.

Neimeyer and his colleagues (Neimeyer, 2005, 2006a, b; Neimeyer and Levitt, 2001) have discussed the notion of post-traumatic growth through narration. Post-traumatic growth is seen as a form of meaning reconstruction in the wake of crisis and loss (Neimeyer and Levitt, 2001). Neimeyer does believe that a narrative approach to understanding growth is little utilised, but is capable of being among the richest literatures in the field of growth. This is, in part, because of our natural penchant for both telling stories and for being an audience, as already discussed.

This kind of evidence should link the literature on social support and on narrative – as all stories need a listener – but there is little evidence for this link. Few authors have explicitly discussed how it is that social support is usually the best predictor of recovery from a traumatic event and the role of narrative in such recovery. This highlights a problem with the social support literature. Much of it is based on crude measures of support, whereas its effects may be best identified through the study of narrative. If this link was made explicit, then we are likely to provide a much better explanation for the role of social support. This notion is hinted at by Neimeyer (2006b) when he discusses how considering narrative at social levels can establish the context for post-traumatic stress or for growth not only at the level of the individual but also at the level of society as a whole.

Neimeyer (2006a) discusses several forms of narrative disruption, including *disorganised narratives*, where the individual is immersed in the perceptual elements of the traumatic experience and is unable to draw them together (this is the area most closely associated with work on post-traumatic growth), *dissociated narratives*, which are silent stories, those in which the person is unable to relate in the social situation, such as the suicide of a spouse, and finally *dominant narratives*, which are, in a sense, too cohesive in providing an explanation for the traumatic event. A healthy profile of a person post trauma is one in which such narrative disruptions either do not take place, or they take place temporarily, only to be displaced by a new, more effective and growthful narrative. According to Neimeyer (2006b), healthy profiles of post-loss adaptation concur with the view that resilient survivors are able to assimilate their loss into their existing narratives in a way that does not radically alter or undermine the way they look at life, the key themes of their life story. Neimeyer (2005), in a discussion on bereavement, argued that accommodation is also important, with bereaved individuals struggling to accommodate their self-narratives to integrate their loss, and also accommodating their lives to the changes necessary to adapt to the loss. According to Neimeyer, this interpretation of assimilation and adaptation may help as a heuristic by which we can understand the multiple pathways people negotiate bereavement.

There are a number of methods by which people have studied narrative and growth, e.g. repertory grid (Fransella et al., 2004), where biographical grids are constructed to help the person articulate their key life themes, systematically comparing critical life events. These critical life events are not just related to the trauma; they are other key aspects of life. For instance, if a person has a theme of helplessness/control, then by applying this to different events, e.g. getting married or being at work, and to the traumatic event, the person can work out the relationships between the key themes and these events, and see which events are linked, and how they are linked across themes. This may be of benefit in helping a traumatised person to make sense of how that person's traumatic events fit within his/her larger life story. Another approach, widely used in different forms, both in research and clinically, is to encourage the person to reflect on the key events within his/her life, and then to build a narrative picture of that person's life from this. Each key event is a narrative or a chapter of the life story in itself, and the individual is encouraged to link these together to establish important life themes and to enable the key events surrounding the trauma to be incorporated. A further approach, which has varying levels of support, is that of Pennebaker (1997), which involves the individual writing about their experiences for 20 minutes a day for 3 days. According to Pennebaker, this procedure is effective in reducing symptoms, and contributes towards the development of a meaningful narrative. The evidence for this is mixed, and different forms of the paradigm have been employed.

Clinicians and researchers regularly encourage traumatised or bereaved people to develop narratives about their experiences, to help them make sense of, and hopefully learn from, their experiences. Guidano (1995) has proposed a method whereby emotionally discrepant episodes in a person's life are replayed in a slow motion fashion, focusing on the difficult, emotional and painful details, and then panning out to consider the impact of these episodes on the person's broader life. The idea is that this method will help the client to make sense of his/her experiences, to close the gap between experience and explanation.

Resilience

According to Meichenbaum (2006), self- and group-narratives play a critical role in determining whether individuals and groups display persistent distress and PTSD or whether they will evidence resilience and post-traumatic growth. Meichenbaum takes a constructive narrative perspective of the concepts of resilience and post-traumatic growth. This perspective has five key points:

(1) People are storytellers.
(2) The type of story used by individuals and groups following a traumatic event determines the level of distress versus resilience.
(3) Research indicates the specific features of negative behaviour and thinking that lead to PTSD.
(4) Healing activities work because they enable individuals and groups to engage in 'non-negative thinking'.
(5) To move from resilience to post-traumatic growth, individuals and groups must find benefits, establish a future orientation and construct meaning.

This kind of model is helpful in demonstrating the processes that occur in people after a traumatic event. The concept of resilience is helpful because it shows how people can show positive adaptation and not break when exposed to adversity. Meichenbaum proposes that resilience is not an inbuilt personality trait, but a skill that can be developed. He draws on an American Psychological Association Help Centre that suggests 'ten ways to build resilience':

 (1) Make connections.
 (2) Avoid seeing a crisis as an insurmountable problem.
 (3) Accept that change is part of living.
 (4) Move towards goals, but stay flexible.
 (5) Take decisive action.
 (6) Look for opportunities for self-discovery.
 (7) Nurture a positive view of oneself.
 (8) Keep things in perspective and learn from the past.
 (9) Maintain a hopeful outlook.
(10) Take care of yourself.

Meichenbaum's constructive narrative approach builds on our understanding of narrative – that people live by storytelling and listening to others' stories – and incorporates the notion of resilience, building to a demonstration of what is meant by growth, which includes benefit seeking, finding and reminding for self and others, engaging in downward comparison ('it could have been worse'), establishing a future orientation and constructing meaning.

The assumption that, if someone experiences a traumatic event he/she will have a negative outcome, is often wrong. Bremner (2005) gave a presentation for a group that included some ex-POWs on the possible effects of the stress of captivity on heart disease, when an ex-POW challenged him and asked why there couldn't be positive effects. The veteran stated that there were positive effects of POW experience, including the knowledge that one could survive anything that life had to offer, having an increased tolerance for others resulting from sharing cramped quarters, and developing skills that were useful for later life. The example given by Bremner is memory. Several POWs developed mnemonic skills that were useful for finishing their education. One person said that he had learned the names of every POW in his block in the 'Hanoi Hilton' camp in Vietnam. Thirty years later, he could still remember all the names.

Issues surrounding post-traumatic growth concepts

As is the case for most trauma research, most work relates to the short-term outcome of traumatic experiences, and how positive change can occur over a period of a few months, or a year or two at the most. Positive growth may take many years. What is needed is research that demonstrates positive change over decades. My research with Second World War veterans shows that such positive change can occur, but that brings up another problem – that the relationship between the traumatic experience and later interpretation is complex and irreducible to a simple comparison between traumatic experience and current psychological state, so it is difficult to ascertain whether positive changes are a result of the traumatic experience, learning from the traumatic experience, or other events that occurred after the traumatic experience. In reality, of course, it will be a combination of all these things and more.

This leads us to another problem associated with the field – that most of the research focuses on self-report scales, reducing individual variation to simple numerical values. While such research is valuable, if we are to understand positive change then we need to take an idiographic approach, and to explore the experiences of individuals rather than groups. While nomothetic approaches may recognise that a range of variables impact on psychological outcome (whether positive or negative), they cannot reconstruct the complexity as experienced by the individual.

Linley and Joseph (2004) also recognise the over-reliance on self-report measures, but in terms of them not allowing for negative responses (to indicate both a negative outcome as well as growth). They also note other methodological problems, such as the need for prospective longitudinal designs, the need for collateral assessment of related behavioural and physiological indicators, and – importantly – the notion that adversarial growth is simply the adherence to some cultural script – that some 'people report growth simply because they have been led to believe that good things come from traumatic events' (p. 19). This last point demonstrates that memories are not simply a result of the individual, but also of the social world. It is not only universal psychological factors we must take into account, but cultural factors also.

There is some research relevant to the notion of very long-term growth resulting from traumatic experience, such as that relating to life review (Butler, 1963), and more recent work concerning reminiscence (Coleman, 2005). This research does not specifically focus on the outcome of traumatic experiences, but the theoretical approach is relevant and there is evidence resulting from war experience. Butler (1963), building on the life stage model of Erikson (1982), stated that as we age, we begin to look back on our lives and address any unresolved issues. This is likely to occur when we start having more time available, particularly after retirement, or when the children leave home or a spouse dies. This may be a preparation for death – that people have a drive or urge to sort out unresolved issues before they can die peacefully.

There is anecdotal evidence for this. A clinical psychologist colleague was treating ageing veterans with war trauma. Out of a group of eleven, five died within months of the completion of treatment. Is this because they had resolved their issues concerning their war experiences? Perhaps – or perhaps not. This is not empirical evidence one way or the other, but the ethical issues arising out of his treatment of such ageing veterans intrigued my colleague. If resolution did increase the chance of dying earlier, and if clinical techniques aid such resolution, was he indirectly killing them? Is this assisted suicide, or is it simply that he helped them die feeling more contented than they otherwise would have done?

Conclusions

The notion of post-traumatic growth has become very popular over the last few years, and research in the area shows no sign of abating. There is evidence that, after a traumatic event, people learn and experience growth. This is demonstrated in the novels that emerge out of war, or the non-fictional accounts written by people who have been through terrible events and have somehow learned to live with their memories. After a burgeoning of psychological work in the 1960s and beyond that looked at humanistic and existential approaches to psychotherapy there is, at least within mainstream psychology, a mechanical and reductionist approach to much of the work on growth. This is seen particularly in the various questionnaires that are meant to measure growth. They take a complex concept and break it down into parts that are less than the sum of the whole. The narrative perspective does enable us to address issues of meaning-making and story development within the context of growth, and enables a deeper understanding of exactly what we mean by growth.

Finally, we should note that many people do not experience growth at all, nor do they experience PTSD. Many, perhaps most, people just carry on with their lives. The factors that predict how and whether someone will experience growth are not well understood. Perhaps as psychologists, as clinicians, as academics generally, we should stand back and think about what happens to those people who neither experience deep distress nor narrate their experiences. They carry on with their lives, but perhaps with an enhanced wisdom that they have learned from their experiences. I spoke with a war veteran who had been captured at Calais in May 1940, served down the mines as a prisoner in Silesia, and been on the forced marches in 1945 away from the advancing Russian lines. He said that whenever he becomes emotional about the war, he will go out into his vegetable garden, tend the plants and realise that what is important about the world is the everyday things – growing onions, the changing seasons and life itself. Did he learn this at least partly through his traumatic experiences, or did he just know it because he was brought up and lived his whole life in a village?

7   Memory and history

This chapter and the next form the heart of the thesis in the book. This chapter focuses on the role history plays in understanding the psycho-social response to war trauma, while the next chapter focuses on the role social factors play in psychological understanding, building together to develop the concept of the personal narrative. The arguments can be expressed from a variety of cultural perspectives, but due to my own upbringing and background, the examples that are used to illustrate what is meant by memory, history, social discourse and narrative are drawn largely from my own experiences of being brought up English and European.

The focus here is on the psychological perspective. We are trying to understand at the level of the individual, but we are all socio-cultural creatures, so in order to understand the individual effectively we need to draw on broader social and cultural forces so as to understand how a person interprets the past and the present, and how that person looks to the future. If we want to understand psychological processes fully, we need to be able to separate the universal from the cultural aspects. What are the key universal psychological processes about memory, coping and the response to stressful events, and what are the cultural aspects of these? This is intensely relevant to trauma studies, but is also relevant to the ways in which all of us live our lives as social beings. There are two fundamental truths about humans that are relevant here. First, that without memory we are nothing. If we do not remember the past we have no structured life. Second, that we are social animals. If we lived in an isolated world we would not learn; we would not have any sense of structure in our lives. We would not have life.

Definitions

Definitions are necessary here because there is dispute about the meaning of many of the terms used. This largely arises because they are used in different ways across disciplines.

History. This is the non-psychological past that is defined and determined by the systematic research of academic historians. It also refers to that part of the past (the distant non-rememberable past, i.e. beyond about three generations) that has no psychological relevance because there is no-one around who remembers that time or who knew people who remembered that time. An example might be understanding the role played by King Henry VIII in the establishment of Protestantism in England. That is not to say that Henry VIII does not have a current impact on our lives (note the debate regarding whether a British monarch should be allowed to marry a Catholic), but that none of us has a psychological memory of that time.

Collective memory. This refers to the joint memories held by a community about the past. It can refer to any period in the past, but in the current context it has the more specific meaning of the collective memories held over about three generations. In order to have a collective memory an individual does not need to have experienced the event, but it must be of such importance that it is thought of in memory rather than in historical terms. An example might be someone born after the Second World War still thinking of it as memory, partly because the people around them experienced it and behave in ways that demonstrate their experience, and partly because the evidence of the war is in the environment.

Social discourse. This is the ways of thinking that are prominent in a society at a given time. These ways of thinking are brought about through the media, education and general social interaction. Social discourses relate to the important areas of interaction between people, and the beliefs that people hold. They relate to the relationship between the sexes, attitudes towards foreign countries and peoples, or views regarding supermarket shopping or the value of television. There are thousands of social discourses throughout society, some assuming more potency than others at given times but, as we shall see, they change dramatically over time. They are not agreed by everyone, but are generally accepted by most or many people, both explicitly and/or implicitly. There are, at any one time, conflicting forms of social discourses held by people within society.

Narrative. The narrative or story is at the heart of what it is to be a psychosocial human being. We naturally try to make sense of things, whether that is finding a good reason to go out for a beer or trying to understand the nature of the universe. Inevitably, owing to our social nature, our individual narratives are determined not only by how we think, our own memories of our experiences, but also by others, and by the social discourses that exist in society. Individuals do not have a single narrative; the narrative depends on the audience. A father narrating his day will talk to his small son in a different way to how he talks to his wife. A teacher will describe her career differently to a prospective headteacher and to her boyfriend. The narrative is at the heart of understanding behaviour.

The main focus in this chapter will be history and memory, which will then lead into the discussion of social discourse and narrative in the next chapter.

The relationship between memory and history

History is perpetually suspicious of memory, and its true mission is to suppress and destroy it. (Nora, 1989, p. 9)

Memory is now the focus of interest to people across a range of academic disciplines, far more than it was a few decades ago. It is no longer the sole remit of psychology. When we discuss collective memory, for instance, a number of disciplines become important, including sociology, history, political science and anthropology (Wilson, 2005). The new journal *Memory Studies* explicitly states that it is a journal that hopes to draw on a wide range of disciplines, and help academics to develop and present theories that are interdisciplinary in nature. As Olick (2008), writing in *Memory Studies*, put it, we now have sociologists interested in cognitive psychology, and cognitive psychologists interested in sociology. This interaction has to be a good thing, broadening our understanding of memory, outside the normal remit of a narrow academic discipline. Another journal, *Memory and History*, though it has an explicit focus on the Holocaust, is also concerned more with the general relationship between memory and history.

Memory is derived from the Greek work 'mnema', from 'Mnemosyne', the mother of the Muses. Before the invention of writing and other recording devices, memory was the poet's key skill. History is associated with logos and with narrative, i.e. a narrative rendition of the past. History gradually emerged from memory when it became a reevaluation of the past, particularly in written form – narrative and reinterpretable – and later gradually developed into a social science. The narrative nature of history is seen in Herodotus, the 'Father of history', who explicitly reconstructed and stabilised the past to provide a fixed story. According to Favorini (2003), we can distinguish between history as a chronological record of significant events affecting a nation or an institution, and memory (or collective memory) as a set of recollections, repetitions and recapitulations that are socially, morally or politically useful for a group or community. This is a useful distinction for psychologists. Whereas history is generated by an individual, is unequivocal and depends on systematic evidence, collective memory is generated by the group, is multivocal and is responsive to the social framework in which it is created, i.e. the social discourse. Psychologists usually focus on the individual rather than the collective nature of memory, the processes by which we as individuals remember and forget, and what we forget (or do not learn in the first place) is as important as what we remember.

Inevitably, when discussing concepts across disciplines, there are disputes about the nature and meaning of these terms. Halbwachs (1992), a French sociologist who worked in the first half of the twentieth century, eventually becoming part of history by dying in a German concentration camp in 1945, was interested in the relationship between collective memory and history, contrasting them as two contradictory ways of dealing with the past. According to Halbwachs, history begins where social or collective memory stops operating. He argues that there is only one objective history, but many collective memories. Collective memories are confined to the most recent past (the lifetime of the people in the society) and are valid only for people within that society. History is the academic objective study of the past, whereas there are collective memories of the past which are shared by communities and which are specific to that community, i.e. are subjective. Halbwachs takes the traditional view of history, as an attempt at developing objective and impartial accounts of the past. He also saw a distinction of time. History can consider both the recent and the distant past, whereas memories are restricted to the recent past, i.e. the lifetime of the individual, and are limited to individuals who lived through particular events.

Halbwachs makes a further distinction between *personal* and *historical* memory. Personal (or autobiographical) memory is the memory of things that the person actually experiences, whereas historical memory is about the world beyond one's own personal experience, and can include things that happened before you were born. Importantly, to Halbwachs as a sociologist, historical memory has priority over autobiographical individual memory. Historical memory provides a social framework for the functioning of individual memory. This creates the social context for remembering things peculiar to oneself. Individual memory processes will always depend on social factors that impact on what we remember and forget. According to Halbwachs (1992), 'the individual is dependent on society, so it is only natural that we consider the group in itself as having the capacity to remember' (p. 54). Halbwachs states the strong argument that, once the social aspect of memory is removed, there is nothing left that can be called memory.

As already stated, without memory we do not exist. Where there is no remembered past there is no present, because the present cannot be interpreted without knowledge of the past. How we read and write, how to walk, how to talk, knowing people, working, all require memory. There is neuropsychological evidence showing the difficulties that some brain-damaged patients can have leading normal lives if they have significant memory impairments. People with damaged short-term memories can no longer remember meetings they have had just a few minutes earlier, and they are doomed to repeatedly re-enact scenes. They cannot meet and remember new people, though their memories of earlier times may be intact. Others lose their long-term memories, and may no longer be aware that they are married or have children. These cases are each individually tragic, and wreck the lives of affected families.

It can also be argued that, without history, a society does not exist; history is intimately linked to the social and cultural world of which we are all a part and which has made us the people we are. Some authors argue that memory and history are not that different. Geary (1994) argued that both collective memory and history are memories *for* something, i.e. that any representation of the past has some political meaning, and that historians are actively trying to influence our past and our memories of the past. While this is true, the arguments can become muddled. Apart from the special case of oral history, the assumption is that historians are trying to develop a systematic understanding of the past. It differs fundamentally from memory, whether individual or collective, in that memory is subjective, and not necessarily constrained by a search for the truth.

In many traditional societies, i.e. those without a literary tradition, there is no real distinction between history and memory; cultural ideas are expressed through the oral tradition. Academic distinctions between memory and history are relatively recent constructions. In traditional societies, it is the role of specialists (often the epic poets) to remember detailed accounts of the past and to pass them on to future generations. Such historical knowledge and its perpetrators are revered in many societies. Now, it is argued by Nora (1989), as shown in the quotation at the beginning of this chapter, history is destroying memory. Nora argues that there are stages of memory collapse, such as the destruction of peasant culture, which was the repository of collective memory. As with Halbwachs, real memory is, according to Nora, social, and is retained in so-called primitive societies, where it is not recorded in history books, but retained in the minds of people. Nora (1989) draws his own distinctions between memory and history, arguing that memory is the living past (still reconstructed), whereas history is an attempt at reconstruction, which will always be incomplete. This is in accordance with the distinction used in this book. History is 'how our hopelessly forgetful modern societies, propelled by change, organise the past' (p. 8), while 'memory is life, borne by living societies founded in its name. It remains in perpetual evolution, open to the dialectic of remembering and forgetting ... vulnerable to manipulation and appropriation, susceptible to being long dormant and periodically revived' (p. 8). Further, 'history ... is the reconstruction, always problematic and incomplete, of what is no longer ... History is a representation of the past. Memory, insofar as it is affective and magical, only accommodates those facts that suit it; it nourishes recollections that may be out of focus or telescopic, global or detached, particular or symbolic' (p. 8). In other words, according to Nora, memory is, by its nature, multiple and yet specific, collective, plural and yet individual. History belongs to everyone and no-one, whence its claim to universal authority. While societies and individuals take responsibility for memory, who takes responsibility for history? In the end no-one, as it has a way – like science – of standing, or appearing to stand, outside society, applying the historical microscope and objectively interpreting and recording the past, irrespective of society. History annihilates the mnemonic past through the objective systematic record.

Nora presents a strong argument, if a little extreme to the eyes of a psychologist. According to both Hutton (1993) and Nora, the crucial rift between memory and history occurred in the nineteenth century, when historiography took possession of what had been memory's territory. History attempted to reclaim the past with the strong intent of forging national consciousness; that is, historians provide politicians with a means of providing a past that is the same for everyone in society, where there is no room for memory (the later popularity of oral history may be a claim to restore memory to the people). In the end, according to Nora, memory has retreated to what he calls '*lieux de mémoire*' – sites of memory. These sites are exemplified by everything from funeral eulogies to battlefield monuments, memorials and museums. Memorials are discussed later in Chapter 12.

Hutton (1993) argues that history's work of imagining and recollecting the past ultimately interferes with memory's work of holding the past close and repeating it. Furthermore, he argues that there is interplay between memory and history, with two key themes. The first is repetition (associated with memory) and recollection (associated with history). This is the foundation of the history/memory problem. The second theme is the impact of the shift from the oral to the literary tradition and the development of subsequent technologies regarding changing conceptions of memory. This shift is illustrated again in the work of Nora, who says that society has an obsession about remembering everything. We attempt the complete conservation of the present, as well as the complete preservation of the past. Nora has a good point. If we try to remember everything, we are likely to remember nothing, because remembering is not mainly about the input of information into the brain; it is about how that information is organised and used. If information is simply stored, it is of no value. Furthermore, the preservation of the past can be problematic. It creates a heritage society, one looking backwards rather than forwards. A heritage society means well in attempting to represent the past in a particular way, but the reality is that it is fixed, focused and depends on a particularly prevailing political viewpoint about the past, and takes away the ability of people in society to use heritage sites for today's purposes, rather than fixing them in aspic to provide a single view of the past.

As we shall see in Chapter 12, memorials can do the same but, used effectively through remembrance and commemoration, they can look to the present and the future – it depends on whether the focus is on living memory or dead history – the life of those doing the remembering, or the history that is the events where the remembered died. The heritage industry that preserves, for instance, ancient buildings is not looking to the future; it is historical fixation, or heritage. For instance, Wingfield Manor, a fifteenth century Derbyshire manor house built for the then Chancellor, Ralph Lord Cromwell, sits atop a hill, a ruin used mainly for film and television (though it contains a working farm). The heritage industry spent several million pounds on preserving the ruin in a ruinous state – a twenty-first century folly – rather than spending money on turning it into something useful for the present and the future. This can be contrasted with Spain, where the government, in 1928, set up the Paradores, a series of luxury hotels set in (often) historic buildings such as castles and monasteries. These ancient buildings are carefully restored to something of their former glory, but with modern conveniences such as comfortable bedrooms, air conditioning, central heating, swimming pools and excellent restaurants serving local and seasonal food. They look from a distance as they might have done hundreds of years ago, but inside is luxurious. If Wingfield Manor had been rebuilt, carefully retaining its fifteenth-century nature but including twenty-first century technology, as a hotel and restaurant, then society would have something functional and beautiful – still historic, but useful to modern society and looking to the future. This demonstrates the importance of the relationship between culture and history. British culture tends to favour heritage over the living past, and heritage enables history to dominate memory, fixing the past in aspic. From the example of the Paradores, Spain uses the past to look to the future, illustrating how memory (living, breathing, personal and social) has the ability to remember what is important about the past, and to make use of this in a way that is beneficial to the present and the future. History – in the shape of heritage - fails to do this. This does, to some extent, support the views of Nora (1989), who is very anti-history, arguing against the 'terrorism of historicised history' (p. 14), yet highly supportive of memory. Heritage should be contrasted with academic historians, who debate the meaning of the past in ways pertinent to the present, attempting to provide a historical context that is meaningful in the terms of both past and current society.

Shifting perspectives: from memory to the past to history

At several levels, the shift from memory to the chronological past and to history is important. The societal level, described by Nora, concerns how we now record more information in a written form, on-line, through photography and by other means. This ever-increasing archive of the past provides historians with so much information that they are unlikely to be able to organise, analyse and synthesise it all, even if such a goal was desirable. From this perspective, we can see how memory shifts to the past through increasing technology and on to history through literacy, the science of history and mass education. Once information is recorded in a book or on the Web, the epic poet has no further purpose. It is rather ironic that the more education one receives, the less value is placed on memory.

There is a transition from memory to a sense of the past (the term 'history' does not refer to the past, but to an interpretation of the past by historians) over about three generations. This is a normal psychological process, with the experiencing generation having a memory of what they have experienced, their children taking on those memories in a weaker but nevertheless still memoric sense, and their children perhaps still having a sense of memory from listening to their grandparents. After this generation, the events fade into the past as there is no-one left who experienced the event and can impart it directly or indirectly into the following generations. The memory, as it is transmitted through the children and grandchildren, may become a collective memory if it relates to a major societal event, or it may remain a familial memory if related specifically to the family.

A specific example may make this clearer. The First World War, as it had such a major impact on both the individuals who fought and on society as a whole, was remembered deeply by the soldiers who had fought and by their families at home. It became a central part of their narratives, their life stories. When these people married and had children, their memories of the war were passed down to the next generation – those who did not remember the war but lived it constantly because they were so close to the participants. These memories might be the stories told to them by their parents or others, or they might be in the behaviour of people, from the physically wounded (my own father, born in the First World War, told me of a man who used to stand in an alley in the village who would show the young lads his wound by sticking his finger through the hole in his arm) to the traumatised (I remember a veteran of World War Two who would regularly make loud grunting noises in the local pub; initially it was comical to we teenagers, but we found out it was a result of his wartime experiences and it stopped being funny), and include commemorative events such as Armistice Day, along with the living families who had lost a family member during the war. These children developed their own strong memories of the war, perhaps having an emotional reaction to the words 'Somme' and 'Passchendaele' in a similar way to their parents. To them the war was still memory, not the past, not history. When the stories pass down to the next generation, the grandchildren, they may still be called memories because the information is passed from the mouths of the participants, but this is also the period when memories of an event become descriptions of the past, something that has little immediate relevance to the current generation. It is also the time when academic historians and others, such as novelists, start to turn the period into history. That has now happened to the First World War, and it is beginning to happen to the Second World War. This chronological sequence occurs because memory is concerned with that which is relevant to the people living in society. Once the participants of an event are dead, the event usually loses its immediate relevance, though major events such as war can remain highly relevant. In this case, such events are remembered through commemorative events, museums and Nora's *lieux de mémoire*. In these ways societies continue to remember the past in a way that is significant and meaningful in the present. These key societal events remain in collective memory.

The transition from memory to history is important to psychologists, and has been little studied. The work on inter-generational transfer of memories has focused largely on traumatic events, such as the Holocaust or sexual abuse, but the basic psychological processes are the same whatever the event being recalled. The arguments regarding how the past is transformed into history, or how collective memory is transformed into history, or how these are all transformed into heritage are really beyond the scope of this book, though they have relevance for our understanding of the past.

An illustration of the transition from individual to collective memory can be seen in the ways that novels emerge. Immediately after major wars, many accounts, including fictional accounts, were written by the participants (not just soldiers). For about 15–20 years, very few novels emerge; then, once most of the participants are dead, there is another flurry of novel writing. This can be seen in relation to the First World War through novels written after the war by Erich Maria Remarque, Henri Barbusse, Rebecca West, Siegfried Sassoon and others. There was then a period when fewer novels were written, and it was only after most participants were dead that WWI novels again became popular, through work by Pat Barker, Sebastian Faulkes and others.

Social continuity

Collective memory ensures continuity in a community. It is the way in which we preserve our collective knowledge and pass it on from one generation to the next. This enables future generations to construct their own personal and social identities, constructing the present by building on the past. Having social or collective memories ensures that members of a community share a sense of unity. This can work at all levels, from the village in which all men once worked in the same pit, and so have shared experiences, to the country that has a shared memory of the role it played in the Second World War. Individuals are linked to social memories. Most people in England will have knowledge of individual members of their families who fought in the First and Second World Wars. Most communities have war memorials which show how individuals from that community shared in the common social goals represented by those wars.

This sense of social identity is important; it is more important than having accurate objective memories of the past. In terms of the Second World War, it is more important to have had a member of the family who fought in that war and so contributed towards the 'greater good' than to know that perhaps that person was a coward or a thief who stole from his comrades and ran away from the enemy. During World War Two, the British displayed the stiff upper lip, the ability to stand firm against all adversity. Of course, at one level this was nonsense – people broke down, they failed to cope – but at another it was a necessary idea, a necessary collective ideal that helped the nation through the difficult years of the war; and after the war it became a collective memory. People looked back and thought that they 'pulled through' those years at least partly because they had a 'stiff upper lip'. This was portrayed in many of the war films that emerged during and after the war, such as *Dambusters, Reach for the Sky* or *The Longest Day* (USA).

We reconstruct the past in ways we wish to reconstruct it, with little consideration for any objective truth. Collective memory does not involve testimony about the truth. This is even the case in a courtroom, which is an entirely artificial situation with regard to memory, where witnesses are expected to recall the past with a degree of accuracy and details that – as psychologists – we know is hardly possible. Witnesses' statements will also be influenced by the groups they are in, by the police officers and lawyers who question them, and by the narratives they have constructed about the events in question.

Our identities are tied up with memory and history. Without memory we have no identity. In order to create our identities we draw on cultural memories and historical understanding of our cultures. Remembrance of the past is important in terms of our socialisation into our culture. Family traditions are also important in this.

The nature of collective memory

There has been a lot of work on collective memory in a number of disciplines, though there is dispute about its ontological status. The construct has proved unpopular among many psychologists, perhaps because of concepts such as Jung's collective unconscious, which some have thought entailed some kind of spiritual connection between minds. Here, collective memory does not imply connectedness beyond the usual forms of social interaction.

According to Halbwachs (1992), all memories, except dreams, are social. That may be why it is difficult to remember dreams; they are always out of a social context, and so the cues for memory that may exist in waking life may be absent. The disorganised nature of dreams may be precisely their individuality, showing how the social is critical if we are to remember them – though there is limited evidence for this. Nora (1989) notes that the less that memory is remembered in a collective manner, the more the individual has to remember, unless there are the means of storing memories outside the mind. In technological society these storage facilities are widely available in, for example, books or the Internet. The problem is that such information, unlike memory, is not organised, and so, if we reduce the importance of collective memory by storing information on the Internet, then it becomes more difficult to establish both individual and societal identities. As an example of increasing disorganisation, 20 years ago a rock group would present an album in a structured, organised manner, listing songs that were intended to be played in a set order. With the advent of memory devices that can hold thousands of songs, the concept of the album (the structured) has been lost, and listeners are faced with playing songs in a random and meaningless fashion (the unstructured). The random shuffle means that music becomes fragmented, losing its identity and coherence, in a similar way to how individuals, without the support of their community through collective memory, lose their identity.

Collective memory is very similar to Nora's (1989) *lieu de mémoire*, a memory environment 'entwined in the intimacy of a collective heritage ... ceaselessly reinventing tradition and linking the history of its ancestors to the undifferentiated time of heroes, origins and myth' (p. 285). Whereas history is reinforced by writing, collective memory is reinforced by social occasions such as rites and commemorations (Favorini, 2003). Folklore and myth are particularly important in collective memory. We are all aware of our nation's folklore. This binds together the people within a society and aids the development of morality and behaviour deemed appropriate to society. For instance, in English society, Robin Hood is important to children's understanding of what is morally right and wrong. It is a simple argument – that it is right to take from the rich and give to the poor. This is expressed in society through taxation. The nation is lived through the internalisation of myths and ideas about the nation (Knox, 2006). The national community is developed and maintained through the practice of national traditions and acts of remembrance (Hobsbawm and Ranger, 1983).

Collective memory can be developed in a number of ways. Thelen (1990), having a concern about whether people remember accurately – and as research has shown they do not (e.g. Bartlett, 1932) – states that collective memory is developed by people in groups, discussing memories, debating, arguing, and coming to conclusions about what happened. That is, they debate over the meaning, and come to a collective decision, creating a collective memory. The debate continues. It takes place at all levels, from discussions between people in the pub, to the media. The information is considered from all angles, and a near consensus emerges (there will always be dissident minorities). When new events occur, these are discussed and integrated. Collective memory is a living process – in a way that history is not; though historians may disagree, their debates are essentially academic rather than functioning at the level of the individual in society. While historians' conclusions depend on current societal mores, they debate the past as history, not as memory.

The impact of collective memory on individuals

In some ways it is not possible to separate the past and the present, because the way the past is interpreted inevitably impacts on the present. An extreme example is the Soviet Union under Stalin, where people who, for whatever reason, had been declared non-persons were eradicated from the historical record, including being brushed out of photographs. This was well described by George Orwell in the novel *Nineteen Eighty-Four*, where Winston Smith's job was to alter past newspapers to provide a representation of the political leader's views in the present. This has a truth in all societies. Every reading of the past is in itself a narrative which owes its meaning to the ways we, in a community, wish to interpret the past. This is true of both history and memory, in the sense described above. Historians work within their society, and interpret the past in the light of the moral and ethical codes of the present, and the social mores and norms of society. Individuals do exactly the same thing, interpreting their past memories in terms of their present social experience (as will be explored in the next chapter). So, in a very real sense, the past is incorporated into consciousness, and the present and past are fundamentally linked. Within the study of memory it is pointless to discuss whether or not a particular memory corresponds to the actual objective past. What we should be concerned with is how and why the memory is constructed as it is. Two people who lived through the same 'objective' experience will have different memories of that experience, and the experience will have affected them in different ways. Unless there is a legal issue, or there is a reason to demonstrate that someone is lying, it is fruitless to argue who is right or wrong. The reality is that both are reflecting accurately on their memories, and both have a different consciousness because of their experience. Geary (1994) argued that, because of these factors, there is no sharp distinction between individual and cultural or social memory. In order to understand memory (and history), we have to understand the context of the present.

Oral history

Oral history hovers between academic history and collective memory in our attempts to understand the past. Modern oral history approaches are a shift back towards the tradition of collective memory rather than the objectification of the past in traditional academic history. It is an acceptance that what people actually say about their pasts is meaningful and relevant. The journal *Oral History* has done a great deal in highlighting the history of the 'ordinary' person, as opposed to the faceless but 'important' people in much social history – the politicians, industrialists and generals of traditional history.

Oral historians access the memories of participants to describe particular historical events from a personal perspective. In historical circles it is sometimes seen as a contentious and radical form of examining the past, focusing on the memories or narratives of specific individuals to make an important contribution to our understanding of history. Oral history helps us to understand the world of our parents and grandparents but has a limited contribution to make to our understanding of memory beyond confirming the constructed nature of memory. While oral history makes no claims to understanding the processes of individual memory, it does bring together individual memories to help develop collective memories of particular events or times, taking on a formalised role normally carried out by groups. Perhaps Nora sees this as another way in which memory is destroyed by history, though oral historians may contend that individuals' memories are worthy repositories of past events, which it is appropriate to reconstruct.

Derderian (2002) notes that, while official histories are losing their influence and legitimacy within modern society, private citizens are, through oral history, being required to do more memory work. For some traditional historians, the problem with oral history is that it is subjective, and so it is not a sufficient means of understanding the past. As shown above, memory (and hence oral history) is intrinsically subjective at several levels. People may choose to recall or not recall particular aspects of their past. For instance, if a person has been a perpetrator of war crimes, it is likely that they will choose not to discuss memories of these events. On the other hand, a victim of such crimes may focus on them in some detail. Subjectivity is selective, with people only being able to draw on elements of an event in the past, the elements they experienced and remembered.

While oral history is a legitimate discipline, we should not be over-reliant on it. Oral history can be a means of legitimising oneself and one's own beliefs and attitudes, by providing a justification for behaviours. This is exemplified by the experience of the Balkan wars of the 1990s, where nationalists justified themselves through relating selective discourses regarding events going back to the Second World War and beyond. For the Serbs, even back to the Battle of Kosovo Polye in 1389, which has a strong oral tradition (see Judah, 2000, for a discussion of Serbian discourses).

Politics, memory and history

The South African Truth and Reconciliation Commission set up after the end of apartheid, demonstrates how society can influence the kinds of memories that are recalled after crimes. The commission succeeded in drawing together the disparate elements of South African society in a way that many thought impossible in a very short time. By enabling perpetrators to admit their guilt through the commission in exchange for a form of societal forgiveness, the deep wounds engendered by apartheid were at least partially healed.

Memories are manipulated by the state and by political groups, often for what are generally seen as positive reasons, such as the binding together of people after a war (see Chapter 12 on memorialisation and commemoration). Sometimes there are less positive reasons. Graham and Shirlow (2002) describe how, in Northern Ireland, there is competition among the religious groups for the mythology of the Somme (in 1916 the 36th Ulster Division was one of the first divisions 'over the top' on the first day of the battle near Thiepval and suffered huge casualties). The Unionist narrative concerns how the Ulstermen were helping the British in their fight against the Germans, whereas the Loyalists take an alternative position, seeing the battle as a betrayal by the British. This betrayal, which initially involved an attempt by the British Government to kill off as many 'troublemakers' as possible on the Somme, is extended to the betrayal they perceive has occurred since 1969 in Northern Ireland.

It is difficult to generate political inclusivity in collective memory after a civil war. In Bosnia, since the Dayton Agreement in 1995, it has been very difficult for people to erect memorials because of the difficult political situation. The Bosniaks (Muslims), Serbs and Croats still effectively run separate statelets within the state, and there is little desire for memorials recognising the loss of life throughout the country. Even when memorials are set up to represent some aspect of the war, these may be quickly defaced. For example, this has applied to memorials set up by the Bosniaks commemorating the dead at Srebrenica, and to a memorial set up to commemorate the women victims of the Serbs in eastern Bosnia, an area within Republika Srpska that is still dominated by the social discourses of Serbian nationalism.

Another way in which memory and history are manipulated is how the victor in any war determines the past through official histories. There is selective 'forgetting' about the role of each side in the war. For instance, after the Second World War there was much written and spoken about atrocities committed by the Axis powers, Germany and Japan, but very little about allied atrocities. This selective memory is common not only in individuals, but also in 'objective' histories. Take, for instance, how histories of World War Two are written by British, French, American, Russian and Chinese authors. The story of the war is very different. The French experience something similar regarding the Algerian war

(Derderian, 2002). For the British, a current concern is the representation of the colonial period, the behaviour of British forces in India, Africa and elsewhere. Only when the participants are old or dead (and hence not a threat) do we reawaken old memories of war and attempt to develop a redress regarding biased remembering. It is unclear whether this is out of respect for the participants or out of a fear that releasing unpalatable memories will lead to social disruption.

The impact of politics and memory on the individual is vividly demonstrated in the work of Einhorn (2001), who described a generation of German women who were forced to change their life stories on several occasions because of historical changes in social discourse. They were brought up as Nazis in Germany until 1945, when they were ejected from Germany, only to return as Communists to East Germany in 1946. After the fall of Communism in 1989, they had to fundamentally alter their life stories again. Each change requires a fundamental rethink of the personal life story, and hence memories. Kamierska (2002) described how Polish land-owning women who survived the Second World War had a similar problem. Before the war, Poland was an independent state, and women played a particular role in society – as a crucial part of the family. After the war, under the Communist regime, the Communists encouraged the forgetting of pre-war memories and the establishment of new social structures where the family played a more minor role.

Memory, history and politics are also linked with memories of the English Civil Wars of the 1640s. These conflicts were remembered for longer than most because of the major impact they had on English society. It is estimated that around 200,000 people – 3.5% of the population – died during these wars. According to Carlton (1991), it was, in relative terms, the bloodiest conflict fought by the English. On the accession of Charles II in 1660, the anniversary of his father's execution (30 January) was to be remembered by society for the sins committed during the civil wars. Sermons praising the memory of the late king and condemning the 'rebellion' were preached in churches every year (Stewart, 1969). The second date that continued to be celebrated into the twentieth century was 29 May, the anniversary of the accession of Charles II. It became, and remained for many years, one of the high points of the festival calendar (Stoyle, 2004). People wore oak leaves, and decorated their houses with oak wood, to commemorate the night Charles had spent hiding in a tree to avoid the Parliamentary troops. Of course, the supporters of Parliament would have been unwilling to commemorate this date, and so the civil war rivalry was likely to flare up again between supporters of the opposing camps. In Tavistock, in Devon, rival groups would engage in mock street battles representing the opposing camps until the nineteenth century. Remembrance of the Parliamentary side often had to be kept quiet. In the eighteenth century, supporters of Cromwell, known as the 'Calves' Head Club', met secretly on 30 January every year to celebrate the anniversary of Charles's execution by eating a calf's head (Stoyle, 2004). Though there had been a lot of support for Charles I, and Oliver Cromwell was, for centuries, compared to the Devil, social constructions about historical memory do change; when New Labour won the 1997 election, several members of the Cabinet requested portraits of Cromwell to decorate their offices (Stoyle, 2004).

This is tied up with the importance of forgetting. In the above examples, the people were encouraged to forget about their previous status, and focus on the present and the future. This encouragement usually comes from within as well as externally. A good example was presented by Connerton (2008) in an article entitled 'Seven types of forgetting'. He discusses 'forgetting as humiliated science', showing how societies choose to 'forget' certain events. Around 130 German cities and towns were destroyed during the Second World War, and around 600,000 German citizens were killed, along with the loss of around 3.5 million homes, leaving 7.5 million people homeless. The occupying forces saw and described the survivors as being utterly lethargic, wandering around the ruins without purpose. But few people – German people – have written about these times, either immediately after the war or in the decades since. This is hard to explain, but Sebald (2003) wrote about how his teacher had seen the corpses in the street, and observed them in a similar way to how people view pornography, furtively and with a sense of shame. According to Sebald, the main emotions felt by the German public were humiliation and shame – probably for both the defeat in the war and the support, whether implicit or explicit, for the Nazi government, which had caused so many problems and represented something evil. Connerton (2008) notes that we cannot infer forgetting from such silence; just because people do not speak of a thing does not mean they forget.

Another example, also discussed by Connerton (2008), is that of the Great War, which led to massive memorialisation and commemoration – for the dead. It has been estimated that around 10 million mutilated men were walking the streets of Europe in the 1920s: blind, crippled, with gross facial disfigurements, mainly badly cared for. The commemorative events focused on the 'glorious' dead. Societies were ashamed of the living maimed; 'they were dismembered – not remembered – men' (p. 69). In more recent years, there has been a growing recognition that the beneficial purpose of commemoration is to remember the living as well as the dead, to remember the veterans who fought in wars and survived, whether wounded or not, and to remember the families who survived bereavement and loss. This notion of remembrance is perhaps easier when we are looking back into the more distant past. After the First World War, and less so after the Second World War, the shock of loss focused society on the dead. In recent years we do now recognise the need to remember the living.

Conclusion

The central constructs discussed in this chapter – history and collective memory – are interpreted in different ways by academics of a number of disciplines. The purpose of the chapter was to provide an overview of the constructs as they are used in this book, as they are used for the purpose of broadening our psychological understanding of the individual response to traumatic events. This chapter should not be read as a criticism of the discipline of history; no such criticism is intended. The intention was to highlight how history detracts from our full understanding of how memory works in the social world and across generations. Memory is crucial. People need to remember the past in order to have a successful present and future, in order to be able to interpret what has happened to them in the past. This is not just an individual process; it is, as Halbwachs would argue, a social process. We turn to this interaction between the individual and the social in the next chapter.

8   Personal narrative and social discourse

The previous chapter demonstrated the role and importance of the past in enabling individual understanding. This chapter moves to the present to show how the social world plays a crucial role in determining how we think about ourselves and the world. In order to develop a complete theory of the response to traumatic events, it is critical to consider the response, not only from the psychological perspective, but also the broader social world. War trauma is not an individual disorder. It arises out of a complex interaction of personal, social, cultural, historical and political forces – the relationship between the personal narrative and social discourse – building on the discussion in the previous chapter.

The personal narrative has already been touched on, but here it is considered in more detail, particularly with regard to the role of narratives and how they are developed. William James (1890, 2007) was one of the first to establish psychology as the science of the mind, which since has mainly been conceived as the science of the *individual* mind. More recently, researchers have recognised that the attribution of psychological traits is not the exclusive domain of psychology and the cognitive sciences (Wilson, 2005), and that other disciplines contribute to our understanding of the mind simply because the mind is socially and culturally situated, and cannot be seen outside of that social context. Attempting to understand the individual mind without recourse to the social aspect is always going to limit the efficacy of any theory.

The key point is that there is a constant interaction between individual (narrative) and social forces; the individual draws on the social context in order to make sense of the world, and the social context itself is derived from a range of sources, including the media, academic argument (e.g. in history or sociology), government policy and other sources where individuals interact. The flexibility and fluidity of narrative and individual narrative change is crucial. This relates strongly to the development and treatment of war trauma.

Narrative

As discussed in the last chapter, humans are prolific storytellers; it is what we do best. In low-technology societies, the epic poet would keep the past alive through reciting the deeds of great people in the society, providing the context for current discourses and showing how people within a society should live. Even now, we use stories in a vast number of contexts: from entertainment – whether telling a child a bedtime story or reading a novel – to developing understanding of the world by listening to news stories or reading magazine and journal articles, to gossiping to each other about the latest events and about friends and acquaintances, to the more detailed stories we tell ourselves and others about our lives, the stories that are our autobiographies – life stories should be pluralised because we have alternative versions for different people and situations. I have one narrative of my past that I would share with my students, but a very different one I might share with my close friends.

Narrative is necessarily complex; a good story has a number of elements. It must have a sense of time, with one event following another in a logical sequence; the events themselves play a key role. They are included because they have some importance. There is a context, with each event being set in a particular situation for a good reason. There is the format of the narrative – whether it is oral or written, and in which style it is presented. There is cohesion, so that the story hangs together in a meaningful way. And finally, there is the important notion of agency. The person who is telling the story owns it; it is that person's story to present as he/she wishes to whoever he/she wishes. This then links to the plurality of narrative. We all have numerous narratives, many interconnected, that we use with different audiences at different times.

The narration of experience is not only very widespread, it does appear to be essential for health, and that health gains can be made as a result of such narration (Pennebaker and Graybeal, 2001). Storytelling is not optional – it is something we have to do; we are compelled by our nature to create narratives. According to Gergen and Gergen (1988), we select and organise our personal memories to build a coherent sense of the self and establish and maintain our identities (see also MacIntyre, 1984). Wrye (1994) noted that personal stories are not just about telling stories; they are the means by which identities can be fashioned and developed. People need to make meaningful sense of their experiences through the use of language and stories. This relationship between narrative, self and identity is central to our understanding of the response to trauma, and links with the social constructions that help to build notions of self and identity. According to Squire (2000), narrative research helps us to explore how the self is developed out of our cultural resources (or social constructs, see below), and how we believe that our lives need to have a certain shape or structure (narrative) which has personal identity at the core. In this sense, narrative is the performance of the self in the sense of self-identity.

Kihlstrom (2002) argues that memories are reconstructed in accordance with our theories of self – our personal views regarding who we are and how we got to be that way. Autobiographical memory (how we remember our own past) is a part of the personal narrative, reflecting our views about ourselves. These views do not (as Freud claimed) necessarily derive from our childhood experiences; this is a naïve perspective given the importance of the social world. A more interesting perspective is that of Adler (1958), who proposed that memories of childhood can change if the current personal narrative changes. This is because childhood memories remind us of who we are now. In other words, as Ross (1994) argued, people, through narrative, reconstruct their personal histories around their tacit theories of the self, revising their histories as their self-concepts (narratives) change.

As we have seen, narratives are systems of personal knowledge (Crossley, 2000). The turn to narrative in psychology (e.g. Bruner, 1990), provided an important opportunity to develop our understanding of memory processes. Narrative involves the attempt to develop a coherent past, which involves over-emphasising the role of some events (memories) and under-emphasising others (perhaps memories about which we are embarrassed, or which do not fit our current conceptions of ourselves). Narrative is about making sense of our lives, integrating the past with the present with a view to how we intend to live our lives in the future. Because our lives can change, either dramatically, or in a slow evolutionary manner, we are constantly updating our personal narratives. This may involve confabulation (Bartlett, 1932), or selective remembering and forgetting. Other factors may also impinge, such as personality (Pals, 2006), coping styles, social support, our friends and family (Burnell et al., 2006), age (Coleman, 2005), personal experience and the social world.

Research into narrative can help us to develop our understanding of memory. Narrative researchers have explored how memory works in a number of fields. Psychologists have focused on the impact of traumatic stress, and how individuals learn to cope with their memories by cognitively processing emotional content through narrative, attempting to understand their trauma by making it meaningful (Linley and Joseph, 2006; Ness and Macaskill, 2003). Twentieth-century examples include Simon Weston's charitable work after being heavily scarred in the

Falklands War, Oliver Stone's dealing with his own Vietnam experience through the production of a series of Vietnam War films or Pablo Picasso's representation of the bombing of Guernica during the Spanish Civil War. Creating a coherent story about a traumatic event is essential to trauma recovery (Herman, 1992; Brewin *et al.*, 1996). Such narratives may provide positive benefits for the individual, particularly in terms of helping to resolve traumatic issues through narrative development.

Narratives may or may not correspond to reality. There was a debate in the 1990s regarding recovered memories, where it appeared that traumatised patients were, with the help of therapists, retrieving suppressed stories of child sex abuse which, it was claimed, was the cause of the person being traumatised. Many cases came to court, and parents and other carers were convicted of sex abuse largely on the basis of stories that emerged in therapeutic sessions. The therapeutic environment is one in which vulnerable patients can be induced, through discussion with therapists, to develop a rationale for their problems, and this rationale can be based on entirely fabricated memories. This is not to say therapists deliberately attempt to manipulate memories, but that, through conversation, patients find ways to explain their feelings, and these explanations can be non-consciously fabricated. The recovered memory debate is largely over, but is an effective demonstration of not only how trauma narratives may not be objectively true, but also how within the profession social constructions (in this case recovered memories) can dominate at a particular time.

Knapp (1988), discussing the context of biblical stories, asked why it should ever matter whether a narrative corresponds to reality. This is relevant to the current discussion because, except for certain contexts (e.g. law) where we do want a narrative to be accurate, in other contexts objective truth is irrelevant. It does not matter whether biblical stories are an accurate representation of the past; what matters is that there is, for Christians, a foundation for their faith. In the context of war trauma narratives the situation is complex. On the one hand, when treating victims of war trauma, it is more important to reduce symptomatology, and if this means some fabrication within the narrative, then that can be of little importance – though the case above of recovered memories shows how this can go wrong; on the other hand, if victims' narratives are potentially going to be used as witness testimony (e.g. narrative exposure therapy, Shauer *et al.*, 2005), then the narratives should be as close to the truth as possible.

In everyday life these errors and distortions are common. In a sense we all go around hiding the truth (though it may be portrayed as projecting the right image). This is the case in the narratives we call 'autobiography' and those we call 'literature', which obviously leads to problems in establishing an accurate record of the past. For example, Binjamin Wilkomirski (1995), in *Fragments*, provided an account – fragmentary, as in the title – of a young childhood spent in Nazi camps. The book initially received a great deal of acclaim, won literary prizes, and was later shown to be false. The account is entirely fictitious, based on Wilkomirski's reading about the Holocaust and others' experiences in the camps. Another example is the book entitled *I Rigoberta Menchú: An Indian Woman in Guatemala* (1983), which described a woman's life during the Guatemalan civil war. The book won the author the Nobel Prize, but again was later shown to be a fabrication, because the author could not have witnessed many of the things she claimed to have witnessed. This genre, which appears to be growing, is often known as 'non-fiction fiction', as it is often based on true stories that have been brought together in a single narrative.

We know that memory is complex, and that it is constantly reconstructive, focusing on the more salient features of life experience – importance, uniqueness, imaginative elaboration and confabulation (Bartlett, 1932). There are both personal factors (importance of event, distance in time, illness and disease, narrative) and social factors (social and cultural discourses, interaction with other people) which impact on what we remember.

An interdisciplinary approach is beneficial to understanding how memory changes. Freeman (1993) draws on psychology, philosophy and literary theory to examine the ways by which people reinterpret the meaning and significance of past experience. If we are to fully understand how memory works, we have to look outside of the psychological laboratory and research people living their lives. Freeman is partially right in looking at the contribution of other academic disciplines, but for a fuller understanding we need to look more broadly at memory function.

Trauma and narrative

Many, if not most, theories of traumatic stress discuss the important role of narrative, even if the term itself is not used. As previously discussed, Pierre Janet was one of the first to acknowledge its importance, with his view that resolving a traumatic experience was about turning a traumatic memory into a narrative memory, i.e. turning a memory that is disjointed and incoherent into one in which the memory of the traumatic event is integrated into the life story. This notion is at the heart of most theories of trauma, implicitly if not explicitly.

Many current theories of PTSD suggest that trauma is the result of enduring maladaptive responses which have impacted on the individual's autobiography or life story (e.g. Brewin *et al.*, 1996; Foa and Rothbaum, 1998; Brewin and Holmes, 2003; Nemeroff *et al.*, 2006). Autobiographical memory is organised primarily around narrative structures, so if traumatic events impact on autobiographical memory, they inevitably impact on narrative and narrative development.

As shown in Chapter 5, the core of trauma is the traumatic memory. While we integrate our normal life memories into our narrative, traumatic memories are not so integrated. Traumatic memories are dominated by sensory, perceptual and emotional components, components which are harder to integrate into the conscious narrative as they do not normally have verbal components. This means that they will have fewer interconnections and weaker organisation (O'Kearney and Perrott, 2006).

O'Kearney and Perrott (2006) reviewed the literature for trauma narratives in PTSD. They used two key criteria for selection. The study had to include a linguistic analysis of the narrative, and ratings of narrative or memory quality. Studies also had to have an appropriate control group such as people without PTSD, non-trauma narratives, or non-intrusive narratives; an examination of how an individual participant changes over time with or without treatment; and a study of the association between narrative measures and PTSD symptom severity or symptom change. This restrictive but appropriate set of criteria led to a selection of nineteen studies being included. As there was a great deal of heterogeneity in the studies, which would not allow any meta-analyses, the analysis was qualitative. The focus was on four areas of concern to the narratives: (1) sensory, perception or emotional dominance in the lexicon, (2) narrative disorganisation or fragmentation, (3) disrupted temporal context, and (4) the nature of references to the self. The results showed support for the prediction that sensory and perceptual elements are more highly represented in PTSD narratives, but there was relatively little evidence for PTSD-related disturbances in narrative organisation and self-referential themes. There was tentative support for PTSD disturbance in the temporal organisation of the trauma narrative, but the data were inconclusive. O'Kearney and Perrott conclude that there are too few high-quality studies on which to base any conclusions regarding self-referential themes. There were also similar problems relating to the fragmentation of memory. While clinicians argue for this fragmentation, and it is implicit or explicit in many theories, there is limited evidence either way. This is not because the theories lack potency, but because the studies are just not good enough. As we saw in the chapter relating to methods, there is a range of good narrative methods available. It is just that trauma psychologists are not using them, or not using them enough.

O'Kearney and Perrott (2006) also argue that part of the problem is theoretical, relating to the complexity of language structure (see also Martin, 2003; Graesser *et al.*, 2004). Fragmentation can be seen not as a simple breakdown of complex linguistic process, but as relating to two linguistic processes – narrative cohesion or connectedness, and narrative coherence or conceptual organisation. These demonstrate different ways in which narratives can be fragmented. Cohesion focuses on temporal and causal relationships, focusing on the relationships between sentences or clauses, i.e. the basic building blocks of language, whereas coherence focuses on the connections of goals, actions, topics and events, i.e. the underlying meaning rather than the surface structure (Sawyer, 2003).

Interpersonal and social discourse

Cultural stories and social discourses are cultural codes that shape collective processes and identities. These are, according to Baars (1997), related to deep-rooted narrative traditions, often literary, such as Ulysses, Don Quixote or Shakespearean characters. These embody the intelligence and wisdom of a society.

Cultural narratives are now transmitted through the media to a greater extent than through literary or oral sources (e.g. the Challenger disaster, the death of Princess Diana, ethnic cleansing in Bosnia), but this only focuses on social ideas about ageing. It is much more important to understand how individual narratives are developed using media discourses. Most people would agree that the media is important in shaping people's attitudes and beliefs, but we need to go further than that and recognise that memory and identities are also shaped by the media. We cannot understand memory without drawing on the social and cultural influences of memory.

Bornat *et al.* (2000) have studied family and change, examining ageing members of families who have experienced break-ups, and found that attitudes towards family break-up have changed over the years. She used respondents who worked with their own memories of family change, yet at the same time were negotiating public discourse recording such change. This is a good example of how individual memory and societal discourses interact to form a person's narrative.

According to Mishler (1995), we are continually re-storying our pasts, and changing the significance of different events, discovering and altering the connections between events, and repositioning ourselves and other people in our network of relationships. This is a point of intersection between the individual narrative and social discourse. Much of this repositioning takes place because of our social relationships, and because of the changing nature of the discourses (both interpersonal and societal) around us. Our narratives have key turning points, where we carry out this repositioning. The turning points are not generally 'aha' moments (though they can be); they are more usually related to people and events around us. When narratives and social discourses do not develop in tandem, then individuals can get left behind in society. As we shall see in Chapter 10, many older people still function with the social discourses of their youth, instead of adapting to newer discourses.

Memories belong to the individual at one level, but they are much wider than that. They are affected by how societal discourses impinge on individual experience. Individual remembering does not take place in a social vacuum (Zerubavel, 1997). Other people help us to remember some things and forget others. There are, according to Zerubavel, social rules regarding remembering and forgetting, which are termed 'mnemonic socialisation'. Whenever we enter a new social environment, whether it is a change of workplace, home or indeed a move to another country, we acquire new memories. Through this process of mnemonic socialisation we learn to remember things we never experienced, and to identify with a collective past. Memories are social and cultural constructions. We who were born after World War Two have memories of that war, obtained through talking to people who lived through the war, reading books and magazines, seeing films and documentaries, seeing battlefields in various countries, and seeing memorials – both small memorials to the dead of particular villages and the larger national memorials that serve not only to honour the dead but also to provide a cultural memory for the living (Halbwachs, 1992). Social discourses relate to cultural and social memory, and to both formal and informal approaches to history (e.g. academic and oral history). Historians who attempt to describe a past still being lived by participants in that past may influence the way those participants view their events. There is limited direct evidence for this proposition, but I have noticed that there are times, when interviewing ageing war veterans, where the veteran provides detailed memories about aspects of a battle that they could not have seen directly, but they have wide collections of books and films about their war, and it is quite likely (but this does need formal study) that their 'memories' are influenced by what they have read and seen. More directly, there is evidence that witnesses to an event can change their story according to the type of question they are asked (e.g. Schreiber *et al.*, 2001).

The social process of societal remembering and forgetting is based on a mechanism relating to our need for such remembering and forgetting. People are naturally tribal; they belong with other people, and depend on them for a successful life. In order to be successful in this, people must take on the behavioural codes and mores of the society in which they live, and in order to do this memory plays a crucial part.

Memories change because society changes its perceptions of past events through the media – by books, films, newspapers, discussion or news reporting – the whole plethora of information as we receive it. In order to understand individual memory we have to examine societal and cultural contexts (Hinchman and Hinchman, 1997).

Discourse impacts on individuals in different ways. There are accepted norms of society that affect how an individual interprets the social world. Of course, many people do not accept social norms and so may be outcast from society (e.g. racists or smokers in Britain), and so develop or use alternative discourses. This also creates a separation of groups and possible group conflict (e.g. Tajfel, 1981), which, at best, generates social debate regarding the benefits of each group, and, at worst, leads to war. There can be conflicts of memory within a society; there is often a dispute regarding the nature of societal memory ('mnemonic battles', according to Zerubavel, 1997).

There are many examples of chronological discourse change, which is related closely to historical interpretation. In Britain in the 1940s we had the German enemy, which soon after World War Two became the Russian enemy. Once the Cold War was over, the Russian enemy became the Islamic enemy, and suddenly the threat of Islamic terrorism is meant to be all around us. (It is as though there is an Orwellian need for an 'other' on which to pour out one's hatred, to blame for the ills in society.)

Kamierska (2002) explored the interaction between the social and the personal, and how past events are important in meaning-making, in WWII narratives in Polish civilians. World War Two is central to all Polish family histories. September 1939 was a turning point in the biography of the nation, and for all Polish people. It was the start of 5 years of occupation by Germans/Russians, followed by 45 years of Communist rule. An estimated 6 million people died. During the Communist era the authorities encouraged the people to forget about many things, for example the pauperisation of landowners.

The history of war trauma throughout the twentieth century provides another – perhaps more relevant – illustration of the ways in which individual memory, narratives and social discourses act together. This has already been discussed in Chapter 7, so only the key stages are described here. At the beginning of the century there was some awareness in the scientific community that traumatic neuroses existed, and that they could have a psychogenic rather than a physical cause. But this was not widely recognised in western society, as illustrated by the fact that more than 300 British soldiers were shot for cowardice or desertion in the face of the enemy in the First World War (Babington, 1983). They were seen as weak individuals who let their comrades down by refusing to fight. Initially there was a widely held view that shellshock had a physical origin – that individuals with the condition had experienced damage to the central nervous system. Later in the war, medical officers and psychologists realised that men were breaking down for psychological reasons (Rivers, 1922). The different views – shellshock and cowardice – were held simultaneously, and applied differentially to officers (who were more likely to be sent to hospital for treatment) and men (who were more likely to be court martialled and imprisoned or shot).

As we have seen, after the First World War traumatic stress was forgotten, unless you were one of the many thousands of men who were locked in mental institutions as a result of their war experiences. It was not until the Second World War that psychological trauma again came to prominence. In Britain this resulted from the experiences of Dunkirk in 1940, when many men came back from Belgium traumatised, and there were too few psychiatrists to treat them (Sargant, 1967). In the USA the realisation came after the invasion of North Africa in 1943, when psychiatric casualties were evacuated to the USA with physical casualties, and the infantry found itself very short of men. The term 'battle shock' came to be used widely. They quickly rediscovered the principles of 'PIE' (proximity, immediacy, expectancy; three principles on which battlefield psychiatry is still based). In Germany and Russia men who were traumatised were often shot, showing how different social constructions were held in different countries.

Contrast these views with those of the latter half of the century. From the 1960s, when the USA were becoming heavily involved in the Vietnam war, there has been a growing acceptance that traumatic breakdown is not a sign of individual weakness, but a genuine illness brought on by extreme environmental conditions. Acceptance of this view has accelerated since the introduction of PTSD in 1980 (American Psychiatric Association, 1980). We have now almost reached the stage where we expect people to break down after a traumatic event, and there is something wrong if they do not. In a single century we have seen views go from one extreme to the other, from the view that breakdown was a capital offence to the view that not to break down is a sign of a problem.

This demonstrates the importance of the social construction, and also how people's individual narratives are formulated within the context of these social constructions. Traumatised WWI veterans often displayed 'hysterical' symptoms, with paralysis of the arms or legs, the inability to speak or psychosomatic blindness. These symptoms were very rare after the Second World War, and are now almost unknown amongst trauma victims. Again, this demonstrates the power of social constructions. If a person is led to believe that they will have one particular kind of symptomatic response rather than another, they are much more likely to have that response.

That is the 'societal' discourse. Not everyone would agree with it. During the First World War there were people, such as Rivers at Craiglockhart, who believed that there were social and familial factors as to why men broke down in battle (Rivers, 1922). There were many psychiatrists in the Second World War who helped thousands of men recover from battle shock. On the other hand, there are still people in the British Army who appear not to recognise that people can break down psychologically as a result of battle experience. Social discourses are never agreed by everyone.

Example: the British Empire

As an example of how social discourses change, we can take the British Empire, attitudes towards the Empire and the implications of this. This remains relevant for therapists and researchers treating or studying older people. Older people will remember the years before the war when the British Empire was still (fairly) strong, and the early decades after the war when the countries of empire gained their independence, either through negotiation or war. Many older people remember the British Empire as a force for good, where the British exported their knowledge, understanding and benefaction to the poor ignorant savages of the world – where the cultured brought civilisation to the uncivilised. British people know these stories – they are part of our cultural memory. Younger people often have a different social discourse: the British Empire was oppressive, cruel and narrow-minded, and totally failed to recognise that people in other countries outside of the Empire had civilised societies – they were just different to ours. This applies to individual words. In the recent past, terms such as 'Paki' and 'nigger' were perfectly acceptable. They denoted the subjects of the Empire, the *untermenschen* who were somehow less human than we white Europeans.

Historians wrote about the Empire in glowing terms – how we brought wealth and civilisation to the world – and the social memories of white

British people were broadly similar. Now our social discourse of the Empire has led to changes in the representations of the past through both history and memory. Historians write of the tragedies which befell other civilisations when the white man came, and the social memories of younger people – if they include the Empire at all – look back negatively, and see a time of oppression. In this way we can see how memory and history develop together, how individual social memories of the past are built on current social representations, and how historians write using those same social representations.

We can go back 100 years in relation to the British Empire by looking at the Empire of the USA today. Social representations in the USA now are broadly similar to those in Britain 100 years ago. Then we thought we could export our culture to the world; now the USA does the same. Then we thought we were more advanced than other people; now the USA thinks the same. Then we used guns to support our position; now the USA does the same.

Narrative development

As we have seen (Spiro *et al.*, 1994), memories consist of individual recollections of the past, which may or may not be accurate, which may or may not be drawn together to form an individual narrative about the past that enhances, enlightens and supports an individual's personal self-image. Narratives consist of recollections of individual experience that has been affected by social and cultural influences such as the media, family and friends, and also by self-education and development. We deliberately choose to emphasise certain memories and try to forget others. This is in order that we have coherence in our lives (e.g. Singer and Rexhaj, 2006). We try to forget those things in the past which we perceive as bad and which do not fit our current concepts of the self (Kihlstrom *et al.*, 2002). Just as remembering is important in understanding our narratives, so is forgetting. It is as important to forget as it is to remember. Just as a novel does not display all the characteristics of the main protagonists, our sense of self does not incorporate everything we know about ourself, particularly when it involves projecting that sense of self outward to family, friends and work colleagues.

This life story, or autobiography, is critical to understanding memory, and it is conceptualised into a narrative (or narratives). We all have many thousands of memories, and many ways of interpreting our memories. We cannot incorporate them all into our life story. We deliberately select particular elements of our past that fit with the way we want to perceive and be perceived in society. There are many factors that will impact on the way memories are selectively remembered, interpreted and changed. As we have seen, Bartlett (1932) identified many of these factors, including the importance of a particular memory, its salience, and the context in which it is input and recalled. Bartlett focused largely on individual memory, but these factors are applicable in the wider context of the life story and societal discourse.

Therefore, in order to understand memory, we need to go beyond the discipline of psychology and draw on the works of sociologists, political scientists, historians, novelists and people in the media – people who record societal memories in different ways. Only then can we understand how and why people have particular memory networks or narratives.

Narrative development and trauma

Traumatised people lose the coherence of their life narratives; traumatic events fundamentally alter the way people think, their views about their own strengths and weaknesses, how they believe others should act and the nature of the world generally. It is as though the written words of their lives are jumbled up and made meaningless. Recovery from trauma means making sense of it all again, learning to understand the world as it is in the light of the traumatic event, incorporating the new trauma-related information into one's own narratives. Narrative development can occur in a number of ways, some of which are illustrated in later chapters. Narratives can be constructed through discussion with others, thinking it through for oneself, writing down one's interpretation of the traumatic event, drawing or painting, or seeing a clinical psychologist or other therapist. Some people do not succeed in developing narratives about their trauma; they may use avoidant strategies (as discussed in Chapter 5), and live symptom-free lives. Others may be unable to make sense and use alcohol or other drugs to deal with their troubled memories. Everyone is different in the way they deal with what happened to them, and it is not the role of anyone to suggest that one way is better than another. It depends on the person. Here we can see that there are universal and cultural aspects of how people deal with their memories. If a therapist is going to be able to help someone, he/she not only needs a good knowledge of the universal aspects of how people respond to traumatic events; that therapist must also take into account the cultural aspects – the social and cultural reasons why people develop the narratives that they have in any given culture and at a particular time point.

9 Illustrating narrative as a scientific technique: the role of social support

One of the problems with narrative is its psychological application in a practical manner. Describing narratives scientifically is a difficult task. A story, however presented, consists of a complex set of rules and statements, which do not necessarily lend themselves to a straightforward analysis, particularly if the analysis must be inked to other variables, such as scores on a measure of PTSD.

The narrative approach, as we have seen, was largely developed in the social sciences, particularly sociology, being 'brought over' to psychology in a number of ways by a variety of people. While this has added enormously to psychological understanding, there have been, and remain, issues regarding the scientific use of narrative approaches in psychology, approaches that are acceptable to the broader group of psychologists, many of whom are embedded in the quantitative tradition. For many quantitative psychologists, qualitative approaches are still anathema, so there is a need to demonstrate the utility of such approaches. One example is presented here. This chapter is based on the PhD work of Dr Karen Burnell, whom I jointly supervised with Peter Coleman.

As already discussed, narrative is key to our understanding of our lives, the ways in which we think and the ways in which we interact with other people. It is in our nature to (it is unavoidable to) talk to each other in story form, to explore our identity and to share experiences. As shown in Chapter 8, narrative is a way of making meaning of our experiences so that we are able to grow from them. Karen Burnell's work (Burnell *et al.*, 2006; in press) focused on the role of social support in the reconciliation of traumatic war experiences throughout life. My previous research has recognised the importance of social support as one of the most effective ways of dealing with traumatic life events (Hunt and Robbins, 2001b). Previous research has also indicated the importance of using narrative to develop a coherent story that enables survivors of traumatic experiences to come to terms with their experiences, and also to experience post-traumatic growth.

Social support is a vital element in reconciliation after a traumatic event, but reconciliation is often considered to be the result of the alleviation of PTSD symptoms. This research has indicated a more complex picture, with PTSD providing, at best, only a crude approximation to war trauma. Reconciliation, in the narrative context discussed here, is the integration of traumatic events into the overall life story, removing (or at least reducing) the threat of traumatic memories, and thereby increasing autobiographical coherence. As already discussed, we are in a continual state of creating our life story, so an appropriate approach to understanding how traumatic memories are reconciled is to study how war veterans integrate their experiences into their life story; that is, we need to study the meaning-making process that lies at the heart of narrative and narrative development.

Assuming that social support is an important aspect of reconciliation, how can social support resources aid or hinder this reconciliation? Drawing on a sample of war veterans, this research analysed the narrative form (the level of coherence) and the narrative content (in this case social support) resulting from semi-structured interviews with war veterans who were drawn from across all stages of the lifespan and across different stages of narrative development. If we can demonstrate the processes by which people develop effective narratives through social support, we may be able to encourage the resources to enable these narratives to be developed more quickly and more effectively. Through developing our understanding of the cognitive, social and physical resources that are important for effective narrative development, we may be able to enhance their use, particularly as such resources may be lost in later life.

The experience of trauma disrupts the creation of the life story, creating an incoherent, disorganised and fragmented narrative. This special nature of traumatic memory makes integration problematic for many people, but integration – it is argued – is vital for coherence and, in turn, reconciliation.

Traumatic memory is made of up two different types of memory. First, individuals who have been negatively affected by trauma may have very vivid and clear memories of the event. Second, the narrative account of the event is fragmented, disorganised and contains gaps.

The importance of narrative coherence is understood within therapeutic circles. For instance, in a study conducted with female rape survivors, Zoellner et al. (2002) found that ease of reading personal trauma narratives of rape decreased with increasing post-traumatic symptoms. Thus, the more symptoms experienced by an individual, the harder the narrative was to read due to its incoherent and fragmented nature. Additionally, traumatic memories are initially recalled as dissociated mental images of sensory and affective elements. It is only over time that the trauma narrative emerges as an explicit and integrated personal narrative, where the individual can make sense of their experiences and place them in the past. Many veterans will tell of their experiences, and recount the smells of the battlefield, sensations that were originally fragmented, or they will explain how they can now make sense of the reasons why something happened as it did and they know now that they could not have prevented it.

Narrative coherence

What makes a story coherent? Many people have highlighted the significance of coherence as a vital characteristic of a 'good story', both theoretically and empirically. Examples range from students of literature to psychologists. In all fields, a good story is a good story. Linde (1993) defines narrative coherence as a property of the text, which represents the relationship between parts of the text and, consequently, the overall text. Coleman (1999) takes this further by suggesting that coherence comprises subjective truths, interpretations, emotions, unity/integration, purpose and meaning as characteristics. Coherence is a 'social obligation that must be fulfilled in order for the participants to appear as competent members of their culture'. The necessity for an audience to understand the story has implications for identity, problem solving and sharing. In the case of war trauma, veterans must have an audience to provide support for the processing of traumatic memories, which leads to reconciliation.

The narrative coherence model

Despite past research on narrative coherence, it has not yet been fully operationalised, which has made the use of narrative coherence methodology problematic. A framework methodology was established based on the narrative content (what veterans talk about; in the present case social support) and narrative form (the way in which the narrative is expressed; narrative coherence) (Burnell et al., 2007). This two-level approach to narrative analysis allows us to address the research question regarding the potential relationships between social support and narrative coherence as reconciliation of traumatic war memories.

The model of narrative coherence is based on the work of Baerger and McAdams (1999) and McAdams (2001, 2006), who formulated the

Table 1 *Description of narrative coherence indices*

Index	Description
Orientation	The narrative introduces the main characters and locates the story in a specific temporal, social and personal context. The narrative describes the habitual circumstances that serve as the parameters for the action of the story.
Structure	The narrative displays the structural elements of an episode system. Thus, the narrative has at least one of the following: an initiating event; an internal response to this event (e.g. a goal, a plan, thought, feeling); an attempt (e.g. to reach a goal, carry out a plan, remedy a crisis, resolve a state of emotional disequilibrium); and a consequence. These elements are presented in a causally and temporally logical way (e.g. the initiating event precedes the response, which in turn precedes the attempt).
Affect	The narrative reveals something about the narrator, or about what the events described therein mean to the narrator; the narrative makes an evaluative point. The narrative uses emotion in order to make this evaluative point, employing explicit statements of feeling in order to create an affective tone or signify emotional meaning. Thus, the narrative uses tension, drama, humour or pathos to communicate and emphasise the evaluative point.
Integration	The narrative communicates information in an integrated manner, expressing the meaning of the experiences described within the context of the larger story. Discrepancies, contradictions and inconsistencies are eventually resolved, and the various narrative elements are synthesised into a unified life story. Although complexity, ambiguity and differentiation may be used to indicate suspense, conflict or growth, the narrative ultimately reconciles these disparate story elements with one another.

Note: This is an adapted version of the original table presented by Baerger and McAdams (1999).

only coding structure for quantitatively measuring coherence to include orientation, structure, affect and integration criteria (see Table 1).

Baerger and McAdams's orientation and structure indices are based on the work of Stein and Glenn (1979), who argue that a narrative must have specific storytelling characteristics, such as orientation to main characters and temporal information, and the presence of an event – an internal response, a reaction, a consequence and resolution.

A sequential story is not enough to render it coherent. According to Singer and Rexhaj (2006), a story must have a point, an emotional evaluation and a moral lesson. Also, Baerger and McAdams's (1999) affect index posits that narratives exist to convey emotionally significant information. In this way, a good story will be organised around a high point when the action or emotion (either positive or negative) will be at its most intense. After relating this position, the emotional content is either resolved or diffused by the narrator.

Finally, the integration index refers to the integration of experiences into an overall life story, and is seen as an important element of coherence. Many psychologists have written on the importance of integration in later life.

An evaluation of Baerger and McAdams's (1999) operationalisation of narrative coherence draws parallels with other concepts of narrative coherence. Habermas and Bluck's (2000) work on coherence as a developmental task highlights the importance of global coherence within the personal narrative (i.e. a narrative understanding that incorporates all or most elements of a person's memory cohesion and identity). Global coherence is split into categories of temporal, biographical, causal and thematic coherence. Temporal, biographical and causal coherence complement the concept of structure as an element of coherence. Causal coherence also extends to coherence of personality traits, attitudes, etc., to provide an explanation for contradictions within the narrative. Thematic coherence is similar to the concept of integration because it suggests that coherence must be based on a credible theme which unites various experiences throughout life into one life story. Thus, the concepts of linked events and chronological order are of importance in assessing coherence.

Whilst global coherence is identified as being important within the personal narrative, this type of coherence is applicable to the local coherence (within sections) of the narrative; that is, these principles apply if, for instance, a person is attempting to make sense of their war experiences.

Habermas and Bluck do not refer explicitly to emotional coherence, but they argue that consistent affect is an important element of the narrative. Androutsopoulou *et al.* (2004) support the work of Baerger and McAdams. In their study, the authors assessed the types of coherence seen during consecutive sessions of narrative therapy. Although only focusing on local coherence, they placed importance on comprehensibility and evoking empathy at both the manifest and latent levels of the narrative. In their criteria, comprehensibility included the relatedness of events and explanation of contradictions, which echoes the elements of integration and thematic coherence cited above. Evoking empathy referred to acknowledging and responding to the needs of the audience and being in touch with emotions, which was defined as not venting or ignoring emotions, but acknowledging and processing them as part of the overall narrative. This component is therefore in line with the affective element of Baerger and McAdams.

Habermas and Bluck also introduce the concept of integration, but they argue that it is in adolescence that we begin to integrate the different experiences of our lives as part of the overall coherent life story. This conforms with work relating to the importance of adolescence as being the period during which people establish their identity independently from their parents. In line with previous research, integration is important when communicating our experiences to others. According to Linde (1993), there can be many explanations within a story as long as they do not contradict one another. This is important from a therapeutic point of view, as it demonstrates the potential complexity of a coherent narrative, a point that should be remembered by individuals involved in helping people to make sense of their traumatic experiences.

Development of the narrative coherence model

The narrative coherence model presented here is a synthesis of previous research. Habermas and Bluck do not provide adequate depth of information regarding narrative coherence for their model to be applicable. Also, the criteria of Androutsopoulou *et al.* are not sufficient. Finally, Baerger and McAdams's criteria do not focus on reconciliation, which is critical to the current study, though it is used as a basis for the current model.

Participants

The model was tested using samples of British war veterans. It was first applied to narratives of ten Second World War veterans. After this initial test, in which it did not need to be modified, it was applied to the narratives of twelve post-war veterans of wars and conflicts, including Suez, Korea, Aden, Cyprus, Northern Ireland, Falklands (Malvinas), the Gulf and Iraq. The use of different war veteran groups demonstrates the applicability of the model to different groups.

Transcripts

The interviews were transcribed in full, including non-verbal utterances (such as 'ah', 'oh', 'er'). Brief intervals between utterances are marked with ' ... ' and longer intervals marked in seconds, e.g. [3]. All quotations are anonymous, but each participant is identified by his/her initials, and quotations note the line number(s) of the transcript.

For further details of the analysis and coding, please refer to Burnell *et al.* (2007).

Table 2 *The narrative coherence model*

Type of coherence		Coding criteria
Basic storytelling principles	Orientation and structure	**O1** Introduction of main characters (scene setting)
		O2 Temporal, social, historical and personal context
		S3a Structural elements of an episodic system presented with causal and temporal coherence (does not include contradictions). Structural elements include an initiating event, an internal response, an attempt and a consequence
		S3b Explicit recognition of temporal coherence, e.g. 'I've jumped the gun/where was I?' Explicit recognition of storytelling
Emotional and thematic evaluation of lived experience	Affect	**A4** Past or present emotional evaluation of what described events mean to the narrator communicated through explicit statements of emotion
		A5 Consistency of verbal and non-verbal elements within a meaning unit
	Integration	**(f) I6** Meaning of events/experiences is expressed within the context of the larger story. This includes a coherent theme linking all the events (theme may be explicit and/or implicit).
		(g) I7 Contradictions between events or the narrator's personality traits or values, emotional evaluation or changes in attitudes are acknowledged and explained in a causally coherent manner.
		(h) I8 Presence of fragmentation of the narrative defined as long pauses and broken speech, and unfinished sentences. Also, defined as incongruent information within the context of the larger narrative. (Unless otherwise stated, the narrative is fluid.)

Coding

Table 2 describes the proposed coding criteria.

Orientation and structure

The orientation and structure criteria (O1/O2, S3a, but not S3b) relate to local coherence and were taken from the work of Baerger and McAdams (1999) in order to recognise basic storytelling principles within the narrative. Emphasis on specific types of coherence (temporal and causal), which added depth and detail to the analysis, was influenced by Habermas and Bluck (2000). Criterion S3b was an original addition to the analysis due to the Second World War veterans' explicit awareness of temporal coherence found in the interviews, such as 'it broke part of the hinge of the ramp [2] ah [4] but I've jumped a gun' [IH].

These principles must be identified within the analysis because, without them, the audience cannot be captured or entertained, and all narratives are created at least in part for an audience. This social element is vital if veterans are to have a supportive environment in which to process their memories. Whilst the content of stories may differ, the basic elements that constitute a story should not. For instance, the following quote from an Iraq veteran contains this story structure; it has an event, an internal response, an action, a consequence and resolution.

so ... shortly after that ... the pressures that caused me to get divorced ... [KB: right] ... and then ... having to start life again with er ... basically a back pack ... like being in the jungle as I call it ... and trying to get onto the ladder again ... which was very difficult ... and then ... I got myself together and ... I went to work as a civilian on the Army camps ... cos obviously being ... and I was attached to the Army aircorps ... for 2 years ... up in [town] ... and being an ex-regular ... and no ... chefs up there ... I used to go on helicopters ... down training in down in ... [town] ... with all the paras ... I even had my own uniform ... enjoyed the drops ... really ... well ... and I lasted over 2 years ... and erm ... thought ... one of the guys says why don't you get back to uniform ... so I thought ... don't want to go back into regular ... so ... join the TA ... so I went through all the fitness again ... passed it ... at the age of ... 30 odd ... [PH L23:34]

Affect

Affect and integration are vital aspects of narrative coherence because they highlight complexities of the narrative. If stories are perceived as being too simple, they cannot realistically reflect lived experience. Emotional evaluation also reflects the ability to express congruent emotion of traumatic events, which is especially indicative of reconciliation.

The affect criterion (A4) was influenced by Baerger and McAdams (1999), which captures the emotional evaluation contained within the narrative. A4 is only applied to explicit statements of emotion. A5 represents Androutsopoulou et al.'s concern with unreconciled emotion displayed either verbally or non-verbally. From initial application of these criteria to the interviews, a number of emotional inconsistencies within the narratives were found and the inclusion of criterion A5 became necessary. Both affect criteria are applied at the local level. Taken together, these two affect criteria allow for a holistic evaluation of the emotional content of the narrative.

An example of consistent affect and emotional evaluation came from a Second World War veteran. In this quotation, he talked about taking the salute from currently serving troops on a recent Remembrance Day parade in Canada. The meaning of the event is evaluated and communicated, and verbal and non-verbal affect is consistent:

... the Burma Veterans [1] those who could were asked to join in the erm ... and also Hong Kong veterans ... because that was the other group of veterans ... the ones who were imprisoned in Hong Kong [1] erm ... were asked to join in the march so we marched around the ... and yeah you felt good there ... and the Governor General took [1] the salute and you could even straighten your shoulders and [puffs out chest] [laughs] and it felt [2] it felt good [1] but then ... er [1] after we'd done that ... er ... which wasn't a very long march thank goodness ... but erm ... they put us all on the side of the road ... and then they had all the Canadian [tearful] present day troops [tearful] march past and salute us [4] that made you feel good too [5] [DS]

Integration

Integration represents the last element of narrative coherence, and is split into three levels: the presence of a uniting theme (Criterion I6), explanation or absence of contradictions (Criterion I7), and absence of fragmentation and disorganisation (Criterion I8).

Criterion I6 is a necessary criterion as it relates to the presence of a theme within the narrative, which brings elements of the narrative together in a meaningful way, and advances lived experience in a way that could provide a meaningful message for future generations. From the perspective of reconciled war trauma, a theme is necessary because it gives meaning to events that challenge the coherence of the life story. Criterion I6 represents global coherence, and provides a means of determining the extent to which war experiences have been integrated into the life story.

This criterion was present across age groups and cohorts as demonstrated by one Falklands (Malvinas) War veteran. Aged 40 years at the time of the study, this veteran explained how his experience in the Falklands had a positive impact on the way he felt about everyday life, and in this sense the experience is integrated as a beneficial experience. There is emotional evaluation in this excerpt. However, it falls into the I6 category rather than the A4 category because he indicates how his Falklands War experience has affected subsequent perceptions of life:

I often say [2] I say to people that know ... and who would have some kind of understanding having been in the ... in similar circumstances [2] that it was the best and the worst time of my life [5] erm and I say that because [3] the worst time because of [3] people getting killed erm [2] erm ... things that you see [1] but the best of times because erm ... life is so much simpler [5] it really doesn't matter whether you [1] whether you're all overdrawn thousands of pounds ... what kind of car you drive [2] erm [2] whether you're married ... that's different ... no [1] but material things and the [1] minutiae of sort of daily life ... it doesn't ... it doesn't even come into it [1] it's life or death ... and that makes life very simple ... it's very pure [3] and each day is [1] fantastic ... you know ... you can wake up and it can be absolutely chucking it down [1] and er [3] you know you feel it may be cold [1] but ... you think ... well ... you know ... it's another day ... everyone is around me ... and [3] and you have that comradeship [3] but ah [1] it made [3] life that much sweeter ... [DW]

Some veterans integrated their narrative with a theme that is negative and maladaptive in nature. For instance, for one Iraq veteran, who was undertaking therapy for PTSD at the time of the study, the overall theme was 'but ... every day is a battle ...' [PH]. Kilshaw (2004) studied the narratives of Gulf War syndrome (GWS) and found that poor health was associated with narratives that revolved around the perpetuation and terminal nature of GWS, which was central to the life story of Gulf War veterans. Consequently, for the current criteria, the integrating theme was required to be positive in nature. Reconciliation is not making a negative narrative central to the life story, but rather integrating it as one coherent chapter of the life story. This way, and in accordance with Brewin's theory of VAM/SAM, the memory loses its threatening and unconscious nature, can be recalled explicitly as an important and perhaps emotional memory, but also relates to other experiences that have occurred in one's life.

Analysis of contradictions within the narrative (Criterion I7), at both the global and local levels, was included in order to assess the consistency of integration within the narrative. If there is contradiction within the narrative, traumatic war memories have not been fully integrated and therefore remain unreconciled. Causal coherence was assessed to indicate the completeness of the story, including logical and functional contradictions that may make the narrative incoherent. The following example demonstrates contradiction between the personal beliefs of a WWII veteran at two points within his narrative. The reason for, and feelings towards, serving in the RAF are incongruous, but this is not explained or recognised by the veteran in the narrative, resulting in contradictory personal beliefs:

... yeah ... I enjoyed flying ... it never bothered me ... it's a job ... just a job ... work which I was being paid for ... ah ... it wasn't my main love ... my main love was football ... ah [2] but the RAF hadn't paid me to play football [1] [laughs] [1] [WS]

... I joined up to fly for here ... from Britain ... to defend my Mum ... and Dad ... that's ... the reason behind my joining up [1] I thought if people's going to drop bombs on Mum ... I'm going to ... do my damnedest for them ... and that's my simple thinking in 1940 ... [WS]

Finally, Criterion I8, which identifies fragmentation and disorganisation within the narrative, was included in order to combine findings from clinical trauma narrative studies within the narrative analysis. This criterion represents symptoms of unreconciled trauma. At the local level, veterans were perceived as having a fragmented narrative if there was broken speech, unfinished sentences and long pauses, or if it contained incongruent, but not contradictory, material. At the global level, I8 was also defined as incongruent (but not contradictory) information within the context of the larger narrative.

In order to be considered a *coherent narrative*, all criteria must be present within the narrative; no one criterion was perceived as being more important than another. While this may seem contentious, all elements of the narrative must be present in order for it to be classified as a narrative. Future research can identify which elements are relatively more important for a coherent narrative. Here, if a criterion was absent, the narrative would be considered incoherent. Without the narrative orientation and structure, the veteran cannot capture a supportive audience to aid reconciliation, and without this audience, consistent emotional evaluation and integration are more difficult to achieve. As noted earlier, after applying the model to narratives of Second World War veterans, all criteria within the model were successfully applied to the post-war veterans' narratives without needing to be adapted or supplemented with additional criteria. This demonstrates the model's transferability and effectiveness in assessing narrative coherence across age and cohort.

The model was able to differentiate between coherent and incoherent narratives; both coherent and incoherent narratives were present in the sample. The differentiation of coherence linked to the thematic analysis of narrative content concerning the presence or absence of traumatic war memories. The overall pattern in the data indicated that narrative content of coherent narratives explicitly stated that there was no trauma, whereas the content of incoherent narratives contained themes of battling with traumatic memories, or struggling to come to terms with traumatic experiences. The study does not enable us to test this empirically as there were no measures used to measure PTSD or war trauma – the focus was on developing the narrative coherence model.

Case studies

In the broader context of the data analysis, narrative coherence was presented within qualitative case studies for each participant. These case studies included thematic analysis of perceptions and nature of war experience, and analysis of experiences of social support (as well as the presence of traumatic memories). The combination of these two levels of analysis allows for the exploration of potential relationships between the types of social support that are associated with narrative coherence. This potential causality has interesting therapeutic implications.

By interviewing veterans of different wars and age groups, knowledge about the ways in which traumatic war memories are reconciled at different stages in life, and by different war cohorts, can be developed. Also, the generic model can be applied to the reconciliation of traumatic memories resulting from other traumatic experiences, not only war.

Conclusions and implications

The ability to understand the ways in which social support aids and hinders the reconciliation of traumatic war memories is of particular concern for theorists and therapists, because the lack of narrative coherence has implications for the wellbeing of the storyteller. This does not just apply to trauma; it applies across a range of mental disturbances, relating to anxiety and depression, and a range of other issues concerned with an inability to cope effectively in the world, whether in a generic sense (e.g. generalised anxiety or depression) or in relation to some specific target (e.g. eating disorders). Indeed, many such problems can be seen as a failure to hold and express a coherent narrative.

Another issue arising out of the current study is that of whether, and how, veterans manage to reconcile their war experiences before critical resources, such as cognitive ability, social networks and physical health, become depleted since these resources are vital for processing experiences into a coherent narrative. This will be explored in more detail in Chapter 10.

The narrative method described emphasises the importance of narrative devices in producing a coherent and reconciled narrative. This is also related to the dual representation theories presented by numerous authors (e.g. van der Kolk and Fisler, 1995; Brewin *et al.*, 1996), with narrative development transferring sensory-activated memories to verbal-activated memories, thus increasing voluntary control over the memories (similar to Janet's description of trauma resolution consisting of turning trauma memories into narrative memories). This approach brings together Bruner's distinct narrative and paradigmatic cognitive ways of knowing within one research approach – narrative affects cognition, and vice versa (Bruner, 1986).

There are several benefits to this approach. The main one is that it is a systematic procedure applied to interview transcripts that appear to predict the effectiveness of narrative development in the light of social support. Much more work needs to be carried out in this area, but it is a substantive framework for further research, both with war veterans and other traumatised groups, and with both the role of social support and other key variables. In the end, this should help to provide more effective ways to facilitate reconciliation than can be carried out using the natural process of meaning-making. Equally, it can contribute to an initial assessment of veterans in therapy sessions, which can provide knowledge of the veteran's social support networks, and aspects of the narrative coherence that are absent.

10   Ageing, trauma and memory

I used to think what landmines have I tripped over now . . . There's nothing to be seen but if you tread on the bugger it goes up.

Normandy veteran, 1994

This chapter examines the very long-term effects of war. Central to this is a study I carried out a few years ago with WWII veterans (Hunt, 1997; Hunt and Robbins, 2001a, b). It addresses the extent and nature of war-related distress experienced by the veteran population, and the factors that predict such distress. The effects of traumatic stress on the older population are exacerbated by developmental changes, which in themselves are stressors. These include diminished sensory capacity, reduced mobility, frailty, reduced income and social status due to retirement, loss of friends and subsequent isolation, ill health and reduced self-care (Cook, 2001), though many people do not experience significant decline in their cognitive abilities, and many develop special expertises. Major physical and mental decline often does not occur until very advanced age (Coleman, 1999).

War has very long-term or permanent effects (Hunt, 1997; Spiro *et al.*, 1994; Bramsen and van der Ploeg, 1999), though some of the symptoms may be less marked than in younger people (Fontana and Rosenheck, 1998). For instance, dissociation may be less persistent over time (Yehuda *et al.*, 1995). There may also be complications involving coexistent syndromes, or different patterns of symptoms; for instance, Goenjian *et al.* (1994), in a group of earthquake survivors with PTSD, found higher arousal levels and lower levels of intrusion, though the overall PTSD severity was similar. There is also some evidence of older adults having protective mediating variables, for example appraisals of the desirable and undesirable effects of trauma respectively decreasing and increasing the relationship between combat exposure and PTSD (Aldwin *et al.*, 1994).

People who experience war often claim that the memories they have when they get old are as strong as they ever were, or even that they become stronger. This links with Butler's (1963) notion of the life review. As we age we look back on our lives, particularly the key areas, and attempt to make sense of it, i.e. we actively work on the narrative of our lives. Inevitably, we focus on the more difficult areas, which, for many old people in the UK now, are the war years. This links to Erikson's (1982) need for personal integration as part of normal ageing. Many people still have problems many decades after their war experiences, it being estimated that in the 1990s up to 10% of the older population may still have been suffering from earlier (mainly war-related) traumatic experience (Hunt *et al.*, 1997). What we don't know is whether treatment at the time of the war would have been of any long-term benefit, or whether these problems would have continued to emerge as the veterans got older.

Various treatment models have been developed or adapted for older veterans. For instance, Robbins (1997) developed a treatment model based on his experiences treating Second World War veterans. Robbins recognised the emotional power of the traumatic memories, and their potential to overwhelm the therapist. The framework for treatment was developed to enable the therapist to cope with these emotions and his/her own responses to them. The treatment consists of four phases. The first phase, disclosure of events, is carried out in two stages – getting an overall picture of what happened, followed by a detailed review of events to clarify any confusion and identify dysfunctional cognitions and the emotions associated with them. The second phase is an exploration of the cognitions and emotions associated with the events. The therapist and the individual work together to identify specific key issues or themes, and the link between past events and current thoughts and feelings is established. The third stage is behavioural change, working with the individual to establish ways to enable change and improved coping. This might involve discussing problems with relatives or learning anxiety management techniques. The fourth and final stage – critical to the process – is termination. This is partly about the end of treatment, but is also about the individual taking responsibility for future planning. Issues around loss, future contact and follow-up are discussed and agreed. This treatment model is not dissimilar to other models, but takes into account the special circumstances of traumatised people, and also the impact of ageing. As Robbins (1997) notes, the impact of ageing and loss of work status (see also Ehrlich, 1988) can lead to feelings of helplessness, which is reinforced by infirmity. Such helplessness, for those who were ex-POWs, can reawaken emotions associated with captivity (see also Elder and Clipp, 1989).

WWII veterans, memory and coping

Data were collected from over a thousand veterans using a variety of methods, including questionnaires, depth interviews and obtaining narratives of battle in various forms, e.g. unpublished journals and published books. During this time I have also collected material such as photographs and mementoes. All are relevant to the overall narratives experienced by British WWII veterans in the late twentieth century (Hunt, 1997; Hunt and Robbins, 2001a, b).

Questionnaire

The questionnaire consisted of several sections: biographical informa-tion, which asked questions regarding history of illness and details of war service; combat experience, which was developed to provide a valid and easily completed measure of the amount and severity of combat an individual has experienced; the Impact of Event Scale (IES) (Horowitz *et al.*, 1979); the General Health Questionnaire (GHQ) (Goldberg, 1978); and several open-ended questions.

Participants

There were 731 veterans from the Second World War ($n = 657$, 90%) and the Korean War ($n = 22$, 3%), with $n = 52$ (7%) taking part in both wars, with a mean age of 72.4 years (range = 59–89, sd = 4.2) when the study was conducted. Nearly all (97%) were retired. They represented the range of armed forces: 53% had served in the British Army, 11% in the RAF, 27% in the Royal Navy, and 6% in the Royal Marines. Veterans were asked to provide their highest rank. This was recoded in three categories: officers ($n = 125$, 17%), NCOs ($n = 346$, 47%) and Privates ($n = 234$, 32%). Many of the sample were ex-POWs ($n = 105$, 14%).

Findings

Nineteen per cent (139 individuals) scored above the cut-off points on both the GHQ and the IES, indicating possible war-related psychiatric caseness. No claim is made regarding the PTSD status of these individ-uals, as the measures are self-reported ones. While there are problems with the interpretation of self-report measures, these findings are inter-esting simply because they show that people – many decades after their war experiences – still have psychological symptoms relating to those experiences.

Officers experienced less psychological distress than NCOs and Privates, and retired veterans experienced higher distress than those still working (though the number of non-retired veterans was small (22)). Veterans with war-related illnesses have higher levels of intrusion and GHQ, perhaps indicating that those maimed by the war think about it more often and are now experiencing more physical problems, perhaps due to the ageing process.

Importantly, combat experience was only slightly predictive of psychological distress decades later, even for those with particularly traumatic experiences, such as prisoners of war of the Japanese. This demonstrates the limited relevance of the actual traumatic experience after many years have passed. The way someone thinks about their experiences, rather than the experiences themselves, seems to be more predictive of longer-term problems. It was not clear whether veterans had war-related problems ever since the war, or whether they emerged only in old age or after retirement. Retirement is a life event which is potentially traumatic but which may provide more free time to think about the past, about the more important times in one's life, about a need to review one's life (Butler, 1963) and about the general effects of ageing.

Open-ended questions

The veterans were asked general questions about what they found 'interesting' and 'disturbing' about the war. The most disturbing aspects of their experience were: battle/combat experience, physical conditions, the effects on others and the government.

It is perhaps inevitable that many of the strongest memories veterans have is of battle experience. For many, the horror of such experience was still strong after 50 years, and it is the type of memory that is most likely to lead to psychological difficulties on the part of the veteran, though it should be borne in mind that the strength of the memory may not correlate closely with the traumatic nature of the original experienced event. The next most common response involved the physical conditions under which the men lived, both during battle and at other times during the war. The cramped conditions of ships, the weather and the poor food – all were mentioned on numerous occasions. British Second World War veterans suffered these conditions for up to 6 years. Apart from worrying about themselves, veterans would consider the worries they had about their loved ones at home – parents, wives and children – whom they knew to be suffering through German air attack or food shortages. Family separation has received little attention in the post-war years, along with the consequences such separations might have on the longer term functioning of such families. This was perhaps particularly the case for those married with young children. It is also only recently that research has considered the effects of war experience on those too young to have been involved in the fighting, or the women left at home (Waugh, 1997).

Another common response was the veterans' attitudes towards the government. There was bitterness towards the present-day government that stems from a sense of unfairness at the government's refusal to assist ageing veterans. People who had spent their early years defending the country were now getting a poor deal regarding the health service and pensions. Their present problems may be exacerbated by this bitterness. These issues are similar to those arising for current veterans of Iraq and Afghanistan, who have similar problems relating to obtaining help for their problems. This illustrates the importance of accounting for the relevant socio-cultural factors.

Many veterans thought that the novelty of their experiences was the most 'interesting' memory they had of the war, particularly meeting new people both from the same culture and from cultures around the world, and seeing new places. The majority of this generation would not have had the opportunity to travel as many of these veterans did. Most would never have been abroad before, and would not have done so had the war not occurred. With regard to meeting people of different social classes in their own culture, this had a major impact on the changing social attitudes of the wartime generation, an impact that would last a lifetime and change the nature of the post-war country.

The next major response to the question concerned comradeship. While none chose to define what they meant by comradeship, it was clearly important to very many veterans. It was concerned with the unity of people (whether battle unit or nation), and people's reliance on one another. Veterans felt that comradeship has gone from modern society. This may also have had an impact on their present psychological state.

The interviews

Twenty-five respondents were interviewed. The first ten were Normandy veterans. The rest included veterans who were ex-POWs and others who had experienced high levels of combat or other war experiences, and who either scored very high or very low on the self-reported symptom scales.

The veterans were asked in detail about their memories (the ways they have changed, what was most important, intrusive recollections, etc.), and also about the ways in which they coped with their experiences, including social support, both at the time and later, and about any effects they felt they still had.

Findings

A large number of themes emerged, only a sample of which is included here. The veterans experienced three main types of memory, of which the first two are particularly important for the general argument of the book:

(1) *Intrusive recollections.* These are implicit, uncontrolled and associated with strong emotion and/or perceptual elements, the memories usually associated with traumatic stress.
(2) *Consummate memories.* These are detailed, likely to be confabulated, and may in the past have been intrusive recollections. The veteran has learned to deal with the emotions attached to the memory and developed a narrative. He may still experience anger or sadness when recalling the event, but these emotions are under control. These are important memories when dealing with distant retrospective trauma, as they indicate which memories were problematic to the person.
(3) *Ordinary decayed memories.* These are memories that were never traumatic, which the individual remembers in the ordinary kind of way, and which are subject to the normal processes of decay. The individual is likely to remember aspects of an event, but not with emotion.

As these memories are retrospective of a time many decades prior to their recall, no attempt was made to verify them through other means and no comment is made regarding their accuracy. By definition, some of the memories will have been adapted and changed; consummate memories are likely to consist of elements of what really happened and elements that the veteran has incorporated in order to make sense of the memory. There is also the issue of the audience. Veterans are likely to tell different stories to a researcher (me) than the stories they tell to each other or to their families. The audience for the narrative affects the narrative that is told, as all narratives depend on there being an audience.

Intrusive recollections and other memories

I don't think you ever forget anything. I am convinced of that. It's just that the bloody thing won't bow down ... if something triggers them off.

Wartime intrusive memories intruded on some veterans' everyday life; they assume such importance that they are unable to stop thinking about particular memories. There is a build-up over time and the memories eventually intrude into consciousness:

You bottle it up. Then of course you bust every now and then ... it's a safety valve really. I bottle it up for so long then the lot comes out. It's a good thing I think really. But all that stems from the war, from the war experiences.

Though their effects may be temporary:

Occasionally something will happen and, oh dear, that reminds me of so and so and then I think I go a bit moody for a while. My daughter says 'He's got one on him again.' But it blows over. It blows over.

What kinds of memory are potentially traumatic?

Veterans experienced different kinds of traumatic memory, as shown below. Unlike many people who are traumatised, they did not report flashbacks. This may be a function of the distance in time between the war and the memory.

Nightmares

I dream a lot I'm shooting them, I tweak things off the bed table, I dream about it ... it's like all silly dreams. It's like I say, I'm shooting Germans but they don't go down and they chase me and I can't get away from them. I'm running and running but the beggars are still behind me. I can't get away. Most peculiar, silly dreams.

Many veterans still regularly experienced war-related nightmares. One still had them weekly, and has experienced them ever since the war. He now experiences them with no greater or lesser frequency than at any time since the war. Another has dreams about battle, and once (on an anniversary) reported experiencing a physical response. On waking, his wound scar was red and inflamed.

Dreams and nightmares are common among these veterans. Most mentioned dreaming about the war; for some the dreams have occurred ever since the war, for others they were more frequent in the early years, for others they are more frequent now. There is no consistent pattern, but such dreams play an important role in many veterans' lives.

Guilt

Many veterans describe the experience of battle:

[driving in a tank, the driver said] 'There's a wounded German officer', [and the commander said] – well I won't tell you what he said – and we drove on. The only ... point about that was – we weren't squeamish – I had a quick look, but of course the first

thing in harbour at night was you had to clean your tank down. Fetching pieces of German officer out of your tracks which wouldn't have been bad if he'd been dead but you realise you got him [speaking quietly] . . . That stuck in my mind, though it is 50 years ago next February when it happened.

This recollection has been through some cognitive processing, but remains traumatic. The veteran was experiencing difficult emotions as he was talking. It may be the guilt that is causing the problem – that the memory itself is manageable, but the guilt cannot be reconciled. This demonstrates the complexity of the problems experienced by people with these kinds of memories.

Others discussed the loss of friends, both at the time and seeing the graves. Again there were feelings of guilt:

Why am I standing here looking at him [in the grave] and not the other way round?

Many traumatic recollections involve feelings of guilt, where the veteran dwells on a particular action and goes over and over it in his mind. This phenomenon has been studied by Kubany (1994) in relation to Vietnam combat veterans, and by Davidson *et al.* (1990) in relation to the feelings of guilt still experienced by WWII veterans. Going over the information in the mind is not the same as processing. It is rumination, and is associated more with depression than with PTSD. In constructive processing the memory and the emotions are changed, yet with guilt they remain difficult to reconcile. To have a feeling of guilt the veteran must have processed the memory at one level, so why doesn't the feeling of guilt get processed? Either the veteran did do something wrong for which he cannot atone – such as guilt at others dying – or he is incapable of thinking at another level and addressing the guilt. This is where the veteran may require assistance, a means of providing a justification for his actions.

Atrocities

Other veterans describe atrocities that they witnessed:

I was with a sergeant one day and a German came out of a trench and this sergeant killed him because – he was crying – because [his friend had been killed]. Of course he was so upset and in fact he ran forward and killed two more Germans who were giving themselves up.

Atrocities were undoubtedly committed on both sides, often in the heat of battle, but most veterans were unwilling to discuss them. Atrocities were either only committed by the enemy, or they had heard stories of atrocities but had rarely witnessed or taken part – or at least they rarely admitted to witnessing or taking part.

Oh no, I never did that.

Although I've a feeling it was done and I'm not going to suggest it wasn't, because in the heat of battle if you are disposed to violence in a group of six or seven people and you have the opportunity of dealing with the men that did that what are you going to do? These are the men that killed your friends . . . Well, we went a little berserk, that's the only way to describe it because anything that moved, German or otherwise, they had no opportunity ever. We never called on anyone to surrender . . . we just pushed and pushed and pushed and that was the end of it, and eventually invariably they got killed.

It is difficult to put these kinds of memories – emotions associated with death, with being in battle – into a coherent narrative, which is why these kinds of memories continued to cause problems for traumatised individuals. Again they may relate to guilt. The individual at the same time feels angry – the same emotions at present recall as when in battle – and guilty, knowing that such acts are criminal.

How do memories change over time?

I notice as you get older, memories get stronger and stronger for some reason. You do think more now.

I can remember those things more easily than I can remember what happened a fortnight ago. I suppose this goes with old age anyway. You tend to dwell on these things because to you they were important then and they're important now.

These quotations show the effects of age. People focus on what has been important to them through their lives, and for many veterans this was the war. It is important to distinguish between traumatic recollections and the simple remembering of things past. Many of the war memories these veterans focus on are not necessarily traumatic, but they are among the most important events in their lives.

Coping with traumatic memories

They don't know they don't know they think it's crazy 50 years, you should be all right now . . . They ask you questions, they don't understand at all like what anybody thinks or what they've been through.

The psychological impact of wartime memories depended on the ways in which older veterans coped with them (both during the war and since), and on their general wellbeing, personality factors, social support, life events and any age-related effects. Veterans' present coping strategies are partly the result of the strategies that they employed during and after the war. This is particularly the case for avoidance, which was used when veterans were in situations where they could not express emotion, and soon after the war, when they were encouraged to forget about their experiences. Avoidance may be an effective coping strategy for many years, when the veteran has a structured life, with work and family commitments, but when this structure goes, it can lose its efficacy.

Coping during the war

The following are all strategies that veterans reported they adopted during the war. Of course, there is no way of verifying these, and their interpretations are likely to have changed over the years due to adaptations and changes to the life story.

Avoidance

Avoidance was used as a coping strategy during the war, partly because of training. Soldiers were trained to respond automatically to particular situations, to avoid thinking about the potential personal consequences of their – or the enemy's – actions. The individual who responds in such a way in battle is more likely to perform effectively than the individual who becomes distressed at the sudden death of comrades. Even after battle there was usually little time or desire to think about, to grieve, these deaths. This use of avoidant thinking may have led veterans to continue the use of the strategy after the war via keeping busy with work and family commitments.

As we saw in Chapter 5, behaviour that is adaptive in a traumatic situation, that helps someone survive, may be maladaptive outside of that situation, but the person is conditioned to respond in a particular way – they have no choice in the matter.

Fatalism

Associated with the concept of avoidance is fatalism, where the individual accepts what is going to happen as inevitable, so there is little point in worrying about it. There is a sense of acceptance with one's lot, that there was no alternative to what would happen and what had happened. This indicates a sense of helplessness with the situation, that the soldier cannot have an effect on the situation. This is a passive coping strategy that may have affected post-war coping responses, making it more difficult to actively process the traumatic information, leaving avoidance as the best strategy available.

No choice

This is different from fatalism. Veterans felt there was no way of escaping from battle. During the war people experienced many different difficult situations that they were forced to either cope with or die. POWs had to cope with particular difficulties. One ex-FEPOW (Far East prisoner of war) kept himself together physically by eating the rice polishings – chewing slowly, then regurgitating at the point of swallowing to chew again. This would both ensure maximum nutrition and stave off the pangs of hunger. Others cut cigarettes in half to make them last longer and to make them less hungry. For others the sense of comradeship in the camps was important. Veterans also mentioned the lack of choice when one is being shelled, that there is nothing one can do about it.

Problems can arise when individuals do not have a means of actively dealing with stressors. As Foa *et al.* (1989) showed, those who cannot actively deal with stress often develop more psychological difficulties than those who do actively deal with it. For instance, shooting at the enemy is perceived to be less stressful than being shelled. In the former situation the soldier is in control of the situation; in the latter he has no control.

War as a justifiable cause

For many, the simplest form of coping was that the war was justifiable. The idea of killing people was justified by claiming it was a job like any other. It was sometimes linking it to the Nazi atrocities and propaganda relating to what the Germans would do if they defeated Britain. Hitler was seen as evil, and needed to be defeated.

Comradeship

As one of the most effective strategies for coping with the traumatic events of war, comradeship is a sense of belonging to a group of people who share similar experiences. Comradeship is difficult to define. Some suggest it only existed between small groups of men fighting in the same unit, others that the whole country was in comradeship. Comradeship is not the same as friendship; it is deeper in the sense that comrades share experiences and lifestyles friends normally wouldn't. Because it involves sharing hardship and danger and that training prepares soldiers to depend on one another for their lives, there is a very strong bond that ties people together. On the other hand, comradeship is weaker than friendship because of the nature of how the bond is created; one does not choose one's comrades. It is not appropriate to consider comradeship as weaker than friendship because of the ability to virtually ignore the death of a comrade in battle.

Something to live for

One FEPOW, held for 3½ years by the Japanese in various camps, described how he survived imprisonment using a picture. He was very young when he was sent to India, and he took with him a picture of his childhood sweetheart. In India he had it enlarged. He then went to Malaya where he fought through the jungle, retreating to Singapore, seeing some horrific sights along the way, where he was captured. He had a typical FEPOW experience – beatings, torture, tropical diseases, overwork and not enough food. I asked him how he thought he had survived. His main reason, he said, was that his girlfriend would be waiting for him when he returned home. I asked him whether he ever doubted that she would be waiting – after all, it was a very long time, and there was no indication of when it would all be over.

I was about 17 when I fell in love with my wife and then she was 13–14 . . . I've never been with anyone else . . . I had her photograph with me all the time and I brought it back, the same photograph that I've had. It was a photograph I'd had enlarged in India, only an ordinary photograph, it was with me all the time . . . [Down in the] coal mine, 12-hour shifts, but it was the thought that the wife would be here, knew that she would be here when I came back . . .
NH: Did you ever doubt that she would wait?
No no.
NH: Never in the camps?
No.
NH: Even at your worst moments?
Never, never, never entered my mind that she wouldn't be here.
NH: Was she the main reason you survived?
Yes.

While I was interviewing him, she was cooking his dinner in the kitchen.

Unfortunately, we do not have the stories of those who failed to survive, and the reasons they lost their lives, and of course there are many stories where girlfriends or wives did not wait.

Coping in the immediate post-war years

Veterans discussed the immediate post-war years in terms of the difficulties they experienced with their memories and how they received little psychological assistance to help them come to terms with their memories. After the war they were told that the memories would fade over time, and their families were told not to discuss the war as this would create problems. Both are now shown to be erroneous pieces of advice, for which the long-term consequences are, for many, devastating.

There was no psychological support for most people. This itself may have created or exacerbated many of the problems that came later. Perhaps if they had been able to process the memories through counselling at the time, then there would have been fewer traumatic recollections now.

Just after the war I got blackouts you see, I had blackouts for a long time, I got dizzy . . . They couldn't get me around . . . I had it very very bad . . . When I think of the daft things, any noise of a car, something like that, I'd be under the table, covering my eyes, shivering with fright.

This lasted for 7–8 years. Fortunately, his wife helped him come to terms with it. His wife helped him through years of psychological suffering. She was his main source of support. Unfortunately, she died not long before I interviewed him and this has led to a re-emergence of war-related problems. If veterans have relied on their wives for many years as social support, then the loss, whether through death or infirmity, may affect their ability to cope – at a time when they have fewer physical resources themselves.

Coping in recent years

Many veterans have not learned to cope with their memories, or they are experiencing problems for the first time in years, and there are situations that arise where they have great difficulty. For one, the actual interview was one of these situations:

[Just before you came I] nipped to the toilet and had a tranquilliser just to stabilise myself, they would take about half an hour to work just to say to myself I could speak to you, [otherwise] I would have probably been effing and butting and shouting.

Is processing an effective coping strategy?

As we have seen in Chapter 5, there is a debate regarding the nature of cognitive processing. Research to date suggests that processing is an adaptive coping strategy, but there is an argument for discriminating between effective cognitive processing, which changes the nature of the traumatic memory, and rumination, which is simple repetition of the memory without inducing change. There is evidence for effective processing.

One example is a veteran who explained how, whenever a 'difficult' memory came to mind, he would sit with a blank piece of paper and write a poem. Afterwards, he reported, his memory would cease to be problematic. Here are two examples:

The Camp

The Corps centre line ran alongside
Beech Wood. The leading division
Paused. Urgent calls crackled
Demanding medics, food, ambulances pronto.

Behind barbed wire skeletons with skins
Stared out from shaven skulls.
Around us neat piles of
Dead and dying, like logs
Layered criss-cross with dangling heads.

Bursts of fire from pale soldiers
Ended the slouching arrogance
Of guards who failed
To leap to instant orders
Officers turned a blind eye.

In this camp, poised on the tips
Of bayonets, hate and madness swayed.
Outraged love burst from the barrel of a gun.
There remained only tears
For the dying in Buchenwald.

After Falaise

His men, flung like discarded dolls,
Lay close around the young captain.
Old in war beyond his years he lay
Tranquil.

Ghouls, stealing through the bloated dead
Emptied wallet and holster and hacked away
His ring finger.

On his grey tunic, tight with corruption
Campaign medals and an Iron Cross flashed
Indifferent pride.

Around the corpse letters and snapshots
of a young woman and two fair children
Lay scattered.

Larger than death his sex had risen,
Still yearning for the new, young
Widow.

Another veteran provided further support for narrative development. He was a Polish citizen caught up in the fighting in 1939. He was captured and tortured by the Russians, before escaping to Hungary, where he was sentenced to death by his compatriots because he refused to go back into Poland. Saved from this by a passing relative, he was put on a ship for Canada and Spitfire training. In the middle of the Atlantic his ship was sunk, and he spent 17 days on a life raft. He reported that he managed to survive because of two reasons: he had not said goodbye to his mother, and he did not want to die a virgin. He made it to Canada, trained as a pilot, and spent the rest of the war fighting the Germans. He did not discuss this period, only the torture and the life raft – they were his traumatic times.

He still experiences some difficulty with his memories, as evidenced by the emotions he displayed during the interview. On the one hand this shows that processing does not eliminate traumatic recollections, just makes them easier to deal with on a day-to-day basis, but on the other this is a highly sensitive and emotional individual who is aware of what he calls his 'emotional immaturity', his tendency to become emotional in many situations. This shows that caution should be observed when drawing conclusions if individual characteristics are not taken into consideration.

During the interview he explicitly stated that, when reporting events, there was a change from the reliving of experiences to memory:

I can tell the story of it but [I am] not reliving [the] experience. It becomes memory, in consciousness. Unless something triggered me it is just a story I remember.

Processing of the traumatic information has occurred here:

I think it is now more of a story and less of the actual experience.

This veteran is a sculptor and a poet (not the one who wrote the poems above), a man of great imagination, a veteran of some horrific experiences that caused him a lot of psychological distress, particularly in the immediate post-war decade, including an over-dependence on his wife that led to her temporarily leaving him, and to psychiatric treatment in a hospital. In the first instance, traumatic recollections were experienced as actual reliving of the event and, over time, the memories are translated into a 'story'. The story develops over time, with new elements of the traumatic memory being recalled at different times, and then being incorporated into the ever-changing narrative:

There are variants in what seems important at particular times.

Has avoidance become less effective in recent years?

Give sorrow words, the grief that does not speak
Knits up the o'erwrought heart and bids it break
Macbeth

The first ten years after coming out of the army. I never told anybody, the wife and daughter knew nothing about being a prisoner of war and all that.

This veteran never discussed his problems. When his memories emerge, he still avoids them:

I try to do some little jobs you know like in the basement, I do a bit of joinery work and things like that. When I get something I'm interested in I can take me mind off that and put it to that, that's how I cope and if in a morning I'm having my breakfast about what I've been thinking in bed I go walking for two or three hours, that's how I cope . . . people keep lending me military books like D-Day and all that. I'd take it off them but I never read it, I'd say it were a good book but don't ask me what was insider I won't read them now.

This policy of actively doing something different helps veterans to avoid war-related thoughts. It is also something they may be less likely to be able to do after retirement, or with increasing infirmity due to age. The veterans interviewed in the present study all seem to suggest that avoidance is an active strategy.

Avoidance stops a veteran from processing traumatic memories. Many used avoidance as an effective coping strategy for many years, perhaps the whole of their working life. It is only after retirement that for some it ceased to be effective. It is a passive coping strategy with limited effectiveness. It doesn't enable the veteran to live a symptom-free life.

War-related psychological difficulties may increase with age. The loss of work structure associated with retirement means the individual has more time to think, and if Butler's (1963) notion of a life review is accepted, then individuals as they age will tend to dwell more on the past. The problem is also in the changes that occur in ageing individuals' cognitions. Older individuals are less able to formulate newer memories, and so dwell more on memories of the more distant past (e.g. Fromholt *et al.*, 1995).

The avoidant coping strategy veterans have used for many years becomes, after retirement, much less effective. As they do not have other coping strategies to rely on, their traumatic recollections emerge and create psychological difficulties. Avoidance has succeeded in keeping traumatic recollections out of consciousness, but this has prevented the individual from dealing with them – unlike those who use processing as a coping strategy.

What role does social support play in veterans' coping?

Another common way of coping with the experience of war is to rely on social support (Barrett and Mizes, 1988; Turner and Marino, 1994). Social support is one of the most effective ways of dealing with stress and trauma (e.g. Hassan, 1997). The Spanish Civil War provided evidence that a situation of common danger reinforces morale (Hargreaves, 1939). Evidence for the use of social support here arises in three separate examples: wives, comrades and veterans' associations, with veterans using such support in different ways according to whether they are with family or other veterans.

Wives/family

The support received by veterans from wives has rarely been officially acknowledged. Many took – and take – an important role in the care of their husbands for many years, providing both practical assistance and emotional support. The FEPOW described above, who took the photo to India, says:

She's been marvellous, marvellous like anything. I worship the ground she walks on.

Wives have not only provided the emotional support that veterans have needed in the post-war years; many have had to provide their husbands with practical help throughout marriage:

She's more or less a nurse you know, I told the pension people she ought to get assistance. If I had to go to hospital they'd pay for that but because she's here we don't get anything. Millions of people in this country look after a mother or father for 50 years and get nothing. Not fair really is it?

If the veteran loses his partner – the person he has depended on – then it may be very difficult to cope if he has depended heavily on her over the years. This is another reason why war memories may emerge. This becomes more likely to happen as the veteran gets older. If he has depended on his wife for emotional and/or practical support since the war, then the joint effects of losing wife and losing support can be extremely traumatic. This veteran got over his problems through the support of his family, but not all veterans have such a family.

Comradeship

Comradeship helped veterans to cope with war, and it still exists for some, often in the form of veterans' associations. While comradeship may be a source of social support, it may also function as a reminder of traumatic recollections, which conflicts with its social support role. Whatever function it provides, it is a bond that is difficult to break.

Comradeship is still important today for many veterans. While there are differences in the ways that comradeship is perceived by different individuals, it is generally seen as something that cannot be destroyed by time. Comradeship was formed during the war years, initially in training, and then in battle. It has continued to be important for many veterans. Comradeship is seen as deeper than ordinary friendship, the depth of the relationship arising because of the shared hardships, the shared personal lives, and the sense of dependency for one's life on others. Many veterans are still dependent on their comrades.

Veterans' associations

For many veterans, these associations formed an important part of their lives. They became more popular as time went by, coinciding with veterans reaching retirement age. Veterans' associations served as a means of retaining or regaining comradeship, and providing practical help.

Associations provided a means of remembering the war and the comrades who were killed:

Next Sunday we go to Leicester for a commemorative service there. I suppose I've got to be honest we like to march and we love a good band to march to. A commemorative service to try again to remember the pals you've lost, it doesn't do them any good, it doesn't hurt you to remember them.

Meetings are generally regular, perhaps once a month, and veterans get together to have a drink and a chat – often about the war:

[We] get together and chat on wartime activities more than anything. We do go to different places. It's a social evening really.

Veterans' associations provide more than this; they have a supportive role for veterans who are retired and in physical decline:

It's a question of welfare first of all.

Concluding remarks

Some veterans still experienced problems with their memories many years after the war. There was evidence of both traumatic and consummate memories, the former still causing emotional problems, and the latter appearing to be resolved traumatic memories, or narratives. Veterans have several ways of coping with these memories, via processing, avoidance and social support. The results show the complexity of narratives, the integration with social constructs common within society, and how it is difficult to simply say that someone has 'resolved' their traumatic memories through the development of a narrative. It is more complex than that. People may have developed their narratives, yet still experience problems when they are faced with reminders. Others – perhaps most – use avoidance as a strategy, and one that works in many circumstances, though sometimes less so once the veteran retires.

The most frequently used coping strategy is avoidance. Many veterans learned to use this strategy through their war experiences, where it was an adaptive strategy, enabling the individual to carry on. After the war it ceased to be adaptive, but veterans could, because they were very busy working and building families, successfully avoid their traumatic recollections. For many, this strategy has been successful almost to the present day. It is retirement that has led to an increase in difficulties. The veteran has more time to think, more time to dwell on his past life, and if the war was the most important time of life, as many claim, then they are more likely to dwell on that era. Perhaps it is retirement when more people start to need narrative development, and when it is more effective, than immediately after the event.

As shown in the previous chapter, social support is a complex phenomenon. Wives and families provide both practical and emotional support, but not as individuals with whom the war could be discussed. On several occasions during the interviews, veterans would explain that they were telling me things they had never told their wives. Why? Perhaps wives are not appropriate audiences; they provide a safe and protective environment, one which the veteran does not want to endanger by discussing the emotional issues surrounding the war. Veterans believed comrades understand their problems. Veterans who wished to discuss the war find it easiest to discuss it with people who have had similar experiences. This highlights the role of the researcher or clinician. If the veteran is going to discuss his traumatic memories with somone unknown, then it helps that he is not emotionally attached, as the sharing of the memories does not endanger anyone, and it also helps if the researcher or clinician has some understanding and awareness of what the person has been through. Again, social support demonstrates the important role of the audience in the expression of narratives. A veteran has one narrative for his family, and another to share with other people.

The permanent effects of war experience can be mitigated by appropriate coping strategies, but for many older veterans these strategies are only partially effective. Wartime memories, even when processed into narrative form, remain powerful, and can still generate intense emotions, even after 50 years. Successful coping still means having to cope throughout life. For many, this is becoming difficult due to the extra problems created by ageing.

To best understand the interwoven processes of individual narrative and social discourse, we should look at an ageing population, one in which there have been many competing and contradictory social discourses over time, and one in which individuals will have developed and changed their narratives many times.

Baars (1997) argues that chronological time is overemphasised in gerontological research. This is as true for veterans as for anyone else. Veterans' life stories often focus heavily on the war and the impact of the war on their lives. According to Baars, we need to focus on comparative concepts of time, which signify change but which also recognise the importance of continuous identity. Changes are normally classified according to people's ages, but this is problematic as, in reality, an individual's identity is a mixture of constancy and change, continuity and discontinuity.

This demonstrates the usefulness of the narrative identity, which focuses on the important events in a person's life. In order to understand a life story, we can begin from a key event (for veterans, the war) and build from that to understand the whole of life.

Currently, reminiscence theory tends to focus on the importance of older people telling stories in order to keep themselves busy (e.g. Coleman, 2005), but we should be using those stories in order to improve our understanding about our culture, in order to remember the past, and in order to have an impact on the world, for example through educating younger generations. Narrative gerontology is a relatively new field that explores this area from a narrative perspective (Kenyon and Randall, 1999).

The importance of social discourses is important here. Second World War veterans fought in an era where it was not generally acceptable to break down, where the stiff upper lip remained fixed in British soldiers. If you were upset by your experiences you did not show it; you did not share your emotions with others. Many of the veterans recognised this problem, and drew a distinction between the way they see the world and the way younger people see the world. Problems can arise as these men age. Veterans' views often remain the same, but society changes around them. As society starts to believe that people should express their emotions, veterans should discuss their problems. But the veterans may find it difficult or impossible to change. Their upbringing was that of the stiff upper lip. Hence we have a disparity between the memories of the individual and current societal discourse.

Studying older people and their war experiences shows that memory is useless without meaning, without the social context. This has been understood at least since the time of the Ancient Greeks. It is only recently that psychologists have begun to acknowledge the importance of meaning in memory (Hunt and McHale, 2008). Memories are developed and changed through the use of individual narratives (this is a normal human process) and an integration of these narratives with social discourses. If we wish to understand memory we must understand the social context in which people live and have lived. In order to do this psychologists should consult with historians, sociologists and others to build the social world through which people have lived, in an attempt to integrate personal memories and the social world. Individual memories form key components of individual narratives; whether and how these memories are recalled ultimately depend on these narratives. Without the narrative there is no memory. Clinical psychologists and other therapists must move away from only trying to understand individual traumatic memories and incorporate the use of narrative approaches when they are considering the impact of traumatic memories on their clients.

11   Literature and trauma

The use of literature (novels, poetry) can both support the psychological evidence we obtain regarding the impact of war, and, in some circumstances, help to develop our understanding. A common way for many people to deal with their traumatic memories is to write them down as a story; this, for some, is an effective way of dealing with memories. It is not just literature, but also films and plays. Perhaps the best-known example of a film director dealing with his own nightmares is Oliver Stone, with his series on the Vietnam War, in which he fought. Several books could be written about the different ways in which traumatised people have dealt with their traumatic experiences by getting their work published. Many other books could explore all the manuscripts that have not been published.

Psychologists have traditionally ignored literature as a potential source of data. Analysis of literary sources can potentially provide psychologists with rich data from which to develop and test psychological theories. The traditional scientific approach of psychology has occasionally been unscientific in focusing too much on methods and too little on examining the theories they are interested in testing. After all, the nature of psychological data can include all behaviours of people, including writing.

Our understanding of the psychological effects of war benefits by a detailed consideration of literature published in the area. Apart from a means of validating theory, it provides an opportunity to explore responses to war trauma in other times and cultures. For instance, Hanley (1991) reviewed the literature regarding women and war, interspersing this with her own short stories – fictionalising accounts of real experiences (see Cobley, 1994) – and provided the reader with an understanding of the trauma of war from a woman's perspective.

Literature has provided countless examples of how soldiers cope with war experience. Wilfred Owen was shellshocked during World War One and was sent to Craiglockhart hospital outside Edinburgh for treatment. Through his work he describes instances of many concepts current to psychotraumatological theory. Re-experiencing, a key component of

PTSD (American Psychiatric Association, 1994), is described in Owen's poem *Strange Meeting*, where he describes in detail a soldier's nightmare. Another key symptom of PTSD – avoidance – is described:

Why speak not they of comrades that went under?

Elsewhere he describes the battle that won him the Military Cross:

I can find no word to qualify my experiences except the word SHEER . . . it passed the limits of my abhorrence. I lost all my earthly faculties, and fought like an angel. (Hibberd, 1992)

Losing all his 'earthly faculties' shows how in battle soldiers can fight automatically, as highly trained warriors without conscious thought.

We know that trauma research has demonstrated the importance of developing a narrative or story about the traumatic event (e.g. van der Kolk and Fisler, 1995; Hunt and Robbins, 1998). Shay (1994) provides a poetic example of the importance of these narratives for veterans. It is a means by which they stay sane:

> *I will tell you something about stories . . .*
> *They aren't just entertainment.*
> *Don't be fooled,*
> *They are all we have, you see,*
> *all we have to fight off*
> *illness and death.* LM Silko, 'Ceremony' (in Shay, 1994, p. 183)

This encapsulates the role of writing in dealing with traumatic memories at least for those who write.

Jonathan Shay (1991, 1994) produced an excellent contribution to our understanding of the importance literature can play in helping psychologists to understand more about war trauma. Shay is a psychiatrist who had been heavily involved in the treatment of US Vietnam War veterans. He found that the veterans were experiencing problems that were beyond the scope of PTSD, that they were describing things that had happened to them in war, and symptoms they experienced, that were just not in the clinical textbook. Shay made a comparison between the experiences of these veterans and the experiences of Achilles in the *Iliad*, and showed that a reading of Homer would educate the therapist about what to expect from war veterans. Shay argued that Homer, through the experiences of Achilles, managed to convey the complexity of the response to war trauma – that it is not just about symptoms of PTSD, but also about comradeship, guilt, anger, antipathy to leaders who make poor decisions, and the madness ('berserk') that happens to men on the battlefield. Any clinician wishing to understand war trauma should read both the *Iliad* and Shay's interpretations.

Tragedy

The concept of the tragedy has been used in drama throughout history. Drama is often about traumatic events and the ways in which people deal with them. Krook (1969) looked at tragedy in literature and identified four stages: (1) Precipitant: the act of shame or horror – tragic circumstances always arise from the fundamental nature of humans; (2) suffering: this is only tragic if it generates knowledge or insight or understanding of the fundamental nature of humans; (3) Knowledge; and (4) affirmation; of the worthwhile nature of human life and the dignity of the human spirit. Tedeschi *et al.* (1995) used this to consider how traumatised individuals can benefit from the insights gained after a traumatic event. War trauma can be considered in the light of these stages. Effective processing of emotional traumatic memories is directly analogous to the model of tragedy. There is a traumatic event which involves suffering, and the individual who successfully processes the information gains knowledge and understanding of themselves and also of the 'true' nature of what it is to be human.

The construct of post-traumatic growth was discussed in Chapter 6. Tragedy provides good examples – demonstrated through tragic literature – of how people, after a traumatic event, learn from the event in terms of increasing wisdom (processing and growth).

If trauma victims believe that their suffering has no meaning, if it cannot be interpreted in terms of saving civilisation or doing a worthwhile job of work, then it becomes despair (Frankl, 1963/1984). In order to successfully process the traumatic recollections, trauma victims must recognise the meaning of their suffering. This is not a matter of reverting to a former state, but an acceptance that things are permanently changed, and thus a learning experience. Many veterans acknowledge the beauty of the simplicity of life, the value of others and of relationships, in a way that they did not prior to combat experience. It could be argued that they would have learned this anyway with increasing age and wisdom, but it is very likely that their experiences enabled them to alter the ways in which they look at the world.

All Quiet on the Western Front (Im Westen nichts Neues)

A generation of men who, even though they may have escaped its shells, were destroyed by war. Erich Maria Remarque

All Quiet on the Western Front (AQOTWF) was written by Erich Maria Remarque and published in 1929. It was written in 6 weeks, became an instant success, and was translated into English by A. W. Wheen (Barker and Last, 1979). For many people it is the best work of fiction ever written about war. Remarque served on the Western Front in 1917, and it is commonly accepted that AQOTWF (along with its sequel, *The Road Back*) was written as a semi-autobiographical account of Remarque's experiences.

We can examine AQOTWF in terms of the experiences of the main character, Paul Baumer, and his comrades, to show how greater psychological understanding can be obtained by using works of fiction as psychological data.

Method

The data source is AQOTWF, the Wheen translation (Remarque, 1929). The book was analysed using a grounded approach (Strauss and Corbin, 1998). Appropriate quotations were coded, typed into Word and coded. Concepts arose out of the initial coding. These codes were then grouped under conceptual headings which could then form the basis for developing a theoretical model. This type of model is not developed here but it is used simply to illustrate the use of literature.

The resultant conceptual structure is presented in the 'Results' section below, with the main category headings presented as subheadings. For a more detailed explanation of this method, see Hunt (1999).

Results

The following is not a comprehensive analysis of AQOTWF, but focuses on a restricted number of themes: battle experience and understanding, memory, the past and the future, and coping.

Battle experience and understanding

Remarque tries to provide the reader with an understanding of what soldiers experienced. This is difficult because, as he indicates, it is not possible to put into words the experiences that the soldiers had:

Attack, counterattack, charge, repulse – these are words, but what things they signify. (p. 88)

This demonstrates the difficulty with understanding verbal accounts (of any kind). The words used may not fully describe the meaning the writer wishes to portray.

The lack of understanding in non-combatants, i.e. civilians, is best illustrated when Paul is at home on leave:

Suddenly my Mother seizes hold of my hand and asks falteringly: 'Was it very bad out there Paul?'

Mother, what should I answer to that! You would not understand, you could never realise it. And you never shall realise it. (pp. 107–8)

He recognises that others are willing to try and understand, but they cannot do so:

They understand of course, they agree, they may even feel it so too, but only with words, only with words, yes, that is it, they feel it, but always with only half of themselves, the rest of their being is taken up with other things, they are so divided in themselves that none feels it with his whole essence. (p. 113)

While Remarque recognises the divide between those who have and those who have not experienced the traumatic event, he does attempt to show what battle was like. For instance, the bombardments they regularly endured:

The shelling is stronger than everything. It wipes out the sensibilities. (p. 49)

Each man lays hold of his things and looks again every minute to reassure himself that they are still there. The dugout heaves, the night roars and flashes. We look at each other in the momentary flashes of light, and with pale faces and pressed lips shake our heads. (p. 73)

The wounds on the battlefield:

We see men living with their skulls blown open; we see soldiers run with their two feet cut off, they stagger on their splintered stumps into the next shell hole; a lance-corporal crawls a mile and a half on his hands dragging his smashed knee behind him; another goes to the dressing station and over his clasped hands bulge his intestines; we see men without mouths, without jaws, without faces; we find one man who has held the artery of his arm in his teeth for two hours in order not to bleed to death. (p. 91)

Memory

In order to understand psychological trauma we have to understand traumatic memory, though relatively little of the novel is concerned with memories. AQOTWF is set during the war. Paul and the others are not looking back, they are living through the traumatic experience of war.

Remarque demonstrates that the soldiers avoided thoughts of the past, of civilian life, because this led to problems. In extreme cases this could lead to desertion, such as in the case of Detering, who was finally broken by the sight of blossom on a tree that reminded him of his home on the farm. He disappeared and was not heard of again, with the implication that the military police had caught and shot him.

Traumatic events do lead Paul to think about the past. An example is when his school-friend Kemmerich has died:

Thoughts of girls, of flowery meadows, of white clouds suddenly come into my head . . . I feel my joints strong, I breathe the air deeply. The night lives, I live. I feel a hunger, greater than comes from the belly alone. (p. 27)

The suddenness of his friend's death makes life suddenly become more important again. Most of the time Paul accepts the reality of the battle-field, but this death acts as a reminder that in civilian life things are peaceful and life is secure. When soldiers are reminded of these times it creates difficulties, because the memories will not go away easily, as when Albert asks Haie about what he will do when there is peace:

Haie looks at him sadly and is silent. His thoughts linger over the clear evenings in autumn, the Sundays in the heather, the village bells, the afternoons and evenings with the servant girls, the fired bacon and barley, the carefree hours in the ale house – He can't part with all these dreams so abruptly; he merely growls: 'What silly questions you do ask.' (p. 57)

The soldiers know the danger of allowing themselves to be taken over by their memories:

[Memories] are always completely calm . . . It is the alarm of their silence that forces me to lay hold of my sleeve and my rifle lest I should abandon myself to the liberation and allurement in which my body would dilate and gently pass away into the still forces that lie behind these things. They are quiet in this way, because quietness is so unattainable for us now. (p. 82)

These memories create difficulties for Paul. Perhaps the worst occasion is after coming back from leave, when he finds it difficult to come to terms with being in the front line again:

What is leave? – a pause that only makes everything after it so much worse. (p. 119)

These examples illustrate how the soldiers have problems with memor-ies, that memories of other times can intrude and make life difficult or impossible to bear. In order to succeed at the front the soldiers have to relinquish much of what makes them human, the ability to look into the past and the ability, as we shall see, to explore the future. They have to live for the present, because when they realise that the past and the future exist, they may break down.

The past and the future

Remarque pessimistically suggests that the future is lost to this genera-tion. He believes that the older soldiers will survive psychologically because they have homes to return to, lives already established, but the younger ones, those who were adolescents when they joined the Army, had laid down few roots and so there is nothing for them:

They have a background which is so strong that the war cannot obliterate it. We young men of twenty however have only our parents, and some, perhaps, a girl – that is not much, for at our age the influence of parents is at its weakest and girls have not yet got a hold over us. (p. 19)

Memories of the past give an indication of how the future might be if only one could survive the war. But once one begins thinking in this way then one cannot perform effectively as a soldier, for instance becoming unwilling to go over the top because of the fear of death becoming predominant.

This way lies the abyss. It is not now the time but I will not lose these thoughts, I will keep them, shut them away until the war is ended. My heart beats fast: this is the aim, the great, the sole aim, that I have thought of in the trenches; that I have looked for as the only possibility of existence after this annihilation of all human feeling; this is a task that will make life afterward worthy of these hideous years. (p. 128)

The war has fully taken over for the young men – there is no future other than the war because there are no memories of adulthood from before the war:

He is right. We are not youth any longer. We don't want to take the world by storm. We are fleeing. We fly from ourselves. From our life. We were 18 and had begun to love life and the world; and we had to shoot it to pieces. The first bomb, the first explosion, burst in our hearts. We are cut off from activity, from striving, from progress. We believe in such things no longer, we believe in the war. (p. 61)

The loss of purpose appears to be known to Paul and the others while they are still in the trenches. It is confusing; on the one hand we are led to believe that the soldiers do not think about the past or the future, on the other that they do – and have done in great detail, thinking through the consequences of the war years. Do we have here an example of dissociation?

Remarque is concerned with how the men will be unable to do anything in the future because:

Through the years our business has been killing - it was our first calling in life. Our knowledge of life is limited to death. What will happen afterwards? And what shall come out of us? (p. 173)

This destruction of a generation is a very important theme throughout the book. Erikson (1982) proposed that there are seven stages of life, and that the transition from adolescent to adulthood is critical. This is when we develop our identities independent of parents. Remarque's argument is that this stage transition was shattered, and that – as Erikson proposed – this will have profound effects on the abilities of the soldiers to adapt to post-war life.

Had we returned home in 1916, out of the suffering and the strength of our experiences we might have unleashed a storm. Now if we go back we will be weary, broken, burnt out, rootless, and without hope. We will not be able to find our way any more.

And men will not understand us – for the generation that grew up before us, though it has passed these years with us already had a home and a calling; now it will return to its old occupations, and the war will be forgotten – and the generation that has grown up after us will be strange to us and push us aside. We will be superfluous even to ourselves, we will grow older, a few will adapt themselves, some others will merely submit, and most will be bewildered;- the years will pass by and in the end we shall fall into ruin. (p. 190)

This has implications for recent work on long-term effects of trauma (Hunt, 1997). Remarque is showing that this shattering of lives shall be permanent for many of the soldiers, that what is being destroyed on the battlefield shall never be rebuilt.

Coping

Through much of the book Remarque shows how Paul and his comrades use various coping strategies, including avoidance, comradeship and dehumanisation. These strategies concur with psychological research (e.g. Elder and Clipp, 1989; Hunt and Robbins, 1998).

Avoidance is perhaps the most important means of coping used by the soldiers on the battlefield. Soldiers are trained to fight battles. Through training, they are prepared for their traumatic experiences. Training develops both unit cohesiveness and the ability to respond automatically in given situations (Watson, 1978). During wartime these skills are adaptive. The individual who is part of a unit where he can trust his comrades and who responds automatically to life-threatening situations is more likely to come out of battle alive than the one who does not have these advantages. Avoidance also stops men from thinking too much.

There are many examples of avoidance in AQOTWF, relating specifically to avoiding particular subjects such as thinking about a recent battle:

Often we lay aside the cards and look about us. One of us will say; 'Well boys . . .' Or 'It was a near thing that time . . .' And for a moment we fall silent. There is in each of us a feeling of constraint. We are all sensible of it; it needs no words to communicate it. (p. 12)

It can occur during the battle itself. In a bombardment the soldiers are close to breaking down because there is nothing to do except wait to see if a shell falls on them. Having an active task enables the soldiers to avoid thinking about the danger to their lives. At one point:

We are buried and must dig ourselves out. After an hour the entrance is clear again, and we are calmer because we have had something to do. (p. 74)

Avoidance has to be employed:

Habit is the explanation of why we seem to forget things so quickly ... They are too grievous for us to be able to reflect on them at once. If we did that, we should have been destroyed long ago. I soon found out this much:- terror can be endured so long as a man simply ducks;- but it kills if a man thinks about it. (p. 93)

The same attitude is used in regard to friends and comrades who have been killed. The soldier is not allowed to grieve, and uses active strategies to avoid thinking too much about such people:

The terror of the front sinks deep down when we turn our backs upon it; we make grim, coarse jests about it, when a man dies, then we say he has nipped off his turd, and so we speak of everything; that keeps us from going mad; as long as we take it that way we maintain our own resistance. (p. 94)

Avoidance is not about forgetting, and it can only be an effective strategy for a limited length of time:

But we do not forget. It's all rot that they put in the war-news about the good humour of the troops ... We are in a good humour because otherwise we should go to pieces. Even so we cannot hold out much longer; our humour becomes more bitter every month. (pp. 94–5)

Avoidance is not always effective:

rarely does an incident strike out a spark. But then unexpectedly a flame of grievous and terrible yearning flares up. Those are dangerous moments. They show us that the adjustment is only artificial. (pp. 178–9)

Dehumanising the enemy is essential to ensure that the soldier can perform effectively. If Paul treated the enemy as fellow human beings, they would not be effective soldiers, and they would be unable to go out and kill the enemy if they, for one moment, perceived they were human. But this can happen:

Under one of the helmets a dark pointed beard and two eyes that are fastened on me. I raise my hand, but I cannot throw into those strange eyes. (p. 78)

The breakdown of dehumanisation is best illustrated in the scene where Paul is trapped in a shell hole in no man's land with a French soldier he has wounded:

You were only an idea to me before, an abstraction that lived in my mind and called forth its appropriate response. It was an abstraction I stabbed. But not, for the first time, I see you are a man like me. (p. 147)

Paul feels guilt for having killed the man:

His name, it is a nail that will be hammered into me and never come out again. (p. 147)

This man is bound up with my life, therefore I must do everything, promise everything in order to save myself; I swear blindly that I mean to live only for his sake and his family. (p. 148)

But this feeling does not last. Paul, in order to survive, must again become an unthinking soldier:

I think no more of the dead man, he is of no consequence to me now. With one bound the lust to live flares up again and everything that has filled my thoughts goes down before it. (p. 149)

The idea of dehumanisation extends also to one's dead comrades. Paul describes visiting the mother of his dead friend:

Why doesn't she stop worrying [about how Kemmerich died]. Kemmerich will stay dead whether she knows about it or not. When a man has seen so many dead he cannot understand any longer why there should be so much anguish over a single individual. (p. 46)

Conclusion

This analysis illustrates how literature can be used as data to enhance our understanding of the response to war trauma. As Shay used the *Iliad*, we can use AQOTWF. Remarque (1929) demonstrates a depth of understanding about the consequences of battle experience, the memories, the problems associated with the family, or of coping through avoidance. Two areas that are not dealt with well in the psychological literature are: (a) dealing with war through dehumanisation, and (b) descriptions of battle experience and the immediate impact on participants. AQOTWF is an eloquent expression of the use of narrative in coping with memories. It deals with notions of past and future, and the ways in which men experienced dissociation with regard to these concepts, at the same time rejecting both and yearning for both. AQOTWF describes in great detail the ways in which men dealt with the suffering on the Western Front.

The concepts of processing (narrative development) and avoidance are well described in the literature (Creamer *et al.*, 1992; van der Kolk and Fisler, 1995), but descriptions of the experience of battle and dehumanising the enemy are rarely discussed. Neither is there a clear understanding of how and why verbal descriptions are inadequate to describe traumatic experiences, though this has implications for all psychological work involving linguistic data.

Remarque's personal experiences can be interpreted using Krook's (1969) four stages of tragedy. For Remarque the precipitant was the war and the suffering the trenches. Through this came knowledge about the nature of people and how they deal with difficult situations. Affirmation is concerned with Remarque's post-war life, how his books, including AQOTWF, illuminated facets of people's lives, far beyond simple notions of trauma. Could Remarque have been a novelist had he not experienced the trenches of the First World War?

While literature should not be considered as a substitute for the scientific analysis of the consequences of trauma, it is useful to use such writings to triangulate with our psychological theories. A note of caution, though: novels are not designed to be data – they are stories about aspects of the world from the perspective of the writer. In the case of writers with battle experience, they may tell us something about what it is to be traumatised, but there are dangers of over-interpretation. Literary theory is full of interpretations of what writers are trying to say, but as Umberto Eco points out, there are limits to what we can make a text mean (Eco, 1992). There is the danger that we may be claiming more from a novel than the author actually intended. Nevertheless, our understanding of war trauma can be enriched by the study of works of literature, novels and poems written by war veterans and others.

12   Memorialisation and commemoration

The purpose of this chapter is to show how memory, narratives, social discourse and history are interlinked via the remembrance of war, and how people have a psychological need and a social duty to remember those who died in past wars.

Societies have always used memorials to help them to remember past events or people. Commemoration is probably the most heavily trafficked point of intersection between history, sociology and political science (Wilson, 2005) and the place of commemoration in the construction of group, particularly national identities. Psychology also has an important role to play here, as it is concerned with the role of individual memory and how the individual fits within the social context of such events. Memorials can be instituted by the state or by private individuals; they can be public or private (e.g. Quinlan, 2005b). British war graves, instituted in their present form after the First World War, are uniform except for the message at the base, where families are permitted to add a short message (even these employ a common social discourse, with the same phrases occurring repeatedly). The graves are institutional and public. In old battlefields such as the Somme, new memorials, privately funded but in public positions, are still being erected, long after the participants in the event are dead. These are attempts to ensure that the memories of particular individuals or groups are remembered by later generations, perhaps with the fear that they are being forgotten? The other main type of public memorial in Britain is the village or town war memorial, individually designed and erected shortly after the First World War, usually paid for by local subscription. There are very few villages in Britain that do not have such a memorial. (These are the so-called 'thankful villages', which did not experience any deaths; there are estimated to be fewer than thirty such villages.) War memories are kept alive through the Remembrance Day events held throughout the country in November each year. What we do not know is how these memories of war are held by the generations that come after the war is over.

Memorials help us to remember the wars and the people they commemorate. They are society's way of reminding us of war. According to Nora (1989), who was discussed in Chapter 7, memorials are examples of '*lieux de mémoire*', 'meaningful entities of a real or imagined kind, which have become the symbolic elements of a given community as a result of human will or the effect of time' (p. 7). Such *lieux de mémoire* are 'ultimate embodiments of a memorial consciousness that has barely survived in a historical age that calls out for memory because it has abandoned it'. We have commemoration because 'it is the nostalgic dimension of these devotional institutions that makes them seem beleaguered and cold – they mark the rituals of a society without rituals' (p. 12). This is a rather harsh assessment of the role of memorials and commemoration in society, but Nora has a valid point. His position is that, as we now have no spontaneous memory, we must deliberately create archives, maintain anniversaries and organise commemorative events because these things no longer occur naturally. As Nora states, 'without commemorative vigilance, history would soon sweep them away' (p. 12). As discussed in Chapter 7, we have lost our sense of memory, replacing it with history and, because of our psychological need to remember, we create specific – perhaps artificial – memorials to use for commemoration.

As Thelen (1990) argues, memory exists along a continuum of experience, with one end being the individual and private memories, kept alive in part by the development of individual narratives, and the other end being the collective cultural and public memories, which are kept alive at least in part through memorialisation.

Ritualisation and commemoration

Durkheim (1947) developed his theory of ritual and collective representations through an analysis of commemoration. There is a strong need within people to have ritual, a series of fixed behaviours that are agreed by people in society and that represent, in terms of commemoration, a formal way in which we remember something of the past. Perhaps the best example in the UK is the two-minute silence, which was introduced shortly after the First World War and quickly ritualised into society, so that, at 11 a.m. on 11 November every year, everything would stop. People would stand with heads bowed, vehicles would stop, work would cease, while everyone remembered the dead of the war. The ritual of the silence means that there is a shared memory, a social discourse that ensures society will not forget the dead.

Heritage and commemoration

Heritage was discussed in Chapter 7, where it was considered, rather negatively, as being a means of preserving a fixed idea of the past, rather than enabling and allowing reinterpretation. Here we can look at heritage in a little more detail. Knox (2006) argues that the relationship between tourism and war has received little attention. While this is probably true regarding tourism academics, Lennon and Foley (2000) discussed the importance and interest of so-called 'dark tourism', the attraction of sites of battle and sites of death, particularly in relation to the recent history of war. This is an example of how there is a development from memory (personal and collective) to history (impersonal and argued) to heritage, which is where events in the relatively distant past become fixed and unchangeable according to the ideas of the present. The heritage industry is massive, with a large proportion of heritage sites being related to battles (e.g. Bosworth, Hastings) or to war-related structures such as castles, particularly those ruined by distant wars. More recent battles, such as Normandy and the Somme, are not yet heritage sites. They are still picked over by the people who fought there, and their immediate descendants. They are argued over by academic and amateur historians, and they have not yet attained the status of 'heritage site'. That is, they are not yet sites dead to memory; they are not heritage sites. This is because they are still remembered, there are still survivors, and there are still people whose fathers and grandfathers fought at these sites.

Knox (2006) discusses the memories of the massacre at Glencoe, and how these memories dominate the heritage visions and interpretations of the valley. 'Performative acts and utterances make and remake the sacralised landscape' (p. 185). These events become concrete as they become heritage tourism. Knox is intrigued by how events that appear to have little connection to modern life continue to have a resonance beyond what we might expect. I have already discussed this in relation to the English Civil Wars of the 1640s. Knox provides the example of Glencoe, which has lost much of its emotive and terrorising power of a site of remembrance but which still retains a force among some groups. Glencoe is important to Scots as it helps to differentiate Scottish from English culture, which is important for those Scots who wish to obtain independence. More interestingly, on 13 February each year, there is a gathering at the MacDonald Monument to commemorate the 1692 massacre. Interestingly, the locals have little interest; most of the attendees come from the USA – is this demonstrating the need for heritage, for a past, by people from a heritage-free nation?

Heritage involves manipulations and untruths for the benefit of a good story. Mythology is often about telling deliberate lies or half-truths. On other occasions we construct the story because we do not know what really happened. When we get to the stage of heritage, it can be argued that we do not commemorate in the same way as we commemorate events in living memory. When we remember the Civil War, we do not think of particular individuals in the same way as when we remember the dead of the World Wars. But the question is not if, but when, will the latter events slip into heritage?

The WWI example is probably the largest scale memorialisation and commemoration in the world. It was the start of how we commemorate and has continued to the present day. While remembering wars and battles has occurred throughout history, most of the memorials we see, at least in Europe, date from the First World War or later. There are memorials to other wars and battles, such as at Waterloo, or to some of the sites of the English Civil War, and there are memorials to the Crimean War and to the Boer War, but these are relatively rare. There are probably two major reasons why memorialisation and commemoration did not occur on a very large scale before the First World War: first, that most wars involved relatively few people, so there was no national need for a national memorial, and second, that up to the First World War there was little regard for the ordinary person, so if several hundred or several thousand men die, then it is of little concern for the ruling classes or those who could afford memorials. Pre-WWI memorialisation – with notable exceptions – is more often about a single officer from a rich family than a memorial to all the dead. Memorials representing the men were often erected many years afterwards.

The Commonwealth War Graves Commission

The Commonwealth War Graves Commission (CWGC) was set up by Royal Charter in 1917, during the First World War. As stated on its website (www.cwgc.org) it was established to commemorate the 1,700,000 people of the Commonwealth forces who died in the two World Wars. It has around 1,500 cemeteries in 150 countries in the world. The largest cemetery, Tyne Cot in Belgium – at the site of the battle of Passchendaele in 1917 (where one of my own relatives died on the first day; see Chapter 13) – has about 11,000 graves; the smallest, on the Isle of Skyros, has just a single grave. There are also memorials commemorating the three-quarters of a million who have no known grave, the two most memorable being the Menin Gate at Ypres, and the Lutyens-designed monument at Thiepval on the Somme (see Stamp, 2006).

The CWGC keeps records of all the dead, and there is a searchable database where relatives of those who have died, and anyone else with an interest, can find details, including place of burial (if any).

The Cenotaph

Much of this and the following section is based on the book *Remembrance* by Mark Quinlan (2005a), which provides a detailed account of many of the key memorials for the CWGC, along with some fascinating background about how they came to be erected. There is also a series of short biographies of some of the key figures who worked on the memorials. He has also written another volume, *British War Memorials,* focusing on the British memorials. Remembrance relating to the First World War is a fascinating case of bringing together the need to remember the dead through memory and commemoration. At the end of the war the British Government wanted a day of celebration to mark the signing of the Treaty of Versailles in June 1919. At this point, there was some nervousness about the attitudes of serving and demobilised soldiers, and also unrest within the labour force. As so often after a war, there were many discontented and often unemployed men. The Victory Parade was, in part, an attempt to draw the nation together to both celebrate the successful (or so it was thought) end of the war, and to commemorate the dead. The French were arranging to have a march past the Arc de Triomphe, where a temporary catafalque was to be erected and which the soldiers would salute. The British Government thought this was a good idea and commissioned Sir Edwin Lutyens to design the Cenotaph. This was to be non-denominational, and he had two weeks to design it and get it built. Lutyens met with the Principal Architect of Works, Sir Frank Baines, and sketched out his design. Lutyens gave it the name 'Cenotaph', which was simply an empty tomb on a high pedestal. The word derives from the Greek words 'kenos' (empty) and 'taphos' (tomb). The origin is from the importance the Greeks attached to burying their dead, even if there was no body. This links neatly with the memorials to the dead who have no known grave at Thiepval on the Somme, and the Menin Gate and the remembrance wall at Tyne Cot Cemetery.

The Cenotaph was built and used for the victory celebrations, and it caught the public's imagination. It was temporary, and meant to be removed after the parades, but the public wanted a permanent memorial. After discussion in Parliament, it was agreed. Westminster Council initially objected to its site, but there was public acclaim for it to be on the site in Whitehall that was occupied by the temporary structure.

After some debate, Lutyens was commissioned to design the permanent stone structure that still stands. The structure cost £10,000 to make. It was this expensive because of the subtleties of design. Apart from its simplicity and lack of decoration, the stones have the smallest joints seen since the Parthenon was built. Neither does it have a single vertical or horizontal line. Lutyens drew on the Greek principle of entasis, where curved surfaces give the impression of being straight. All of the surfaces are spherical. The verticals would converge at a point over 1000 feet from the ground; the horizontals are part of a circle that has a centre 900 feet below ground. The height of the Cenotaph is 35 feet, and it is constructed from 120 tons of Portland Stone. Initially, the only writing on the Cenotaph was: 'The Glorious Dead' and the dates of the war, MCMXIV to MCMXIX. After the Second World War, the dates MCMXXXIX and MCMXLV were added. The Cenotaph deliberately avoided any religious symbol, because it was intended to commemorate all creeds and none.

The Cenotaph was unveiled on 11 November 1920, taking place on the same day as the funeral of the Unknown Warrior in Westminster Abbey. Since then, it has formed the national focus for the UK's remembrance services. It led to many copies being placed around the country.

The Unknown Warrior

One of the biggest difficulties for people who have suffered the loss of a loved one, whether in war or in other events, is when there is no body to grieve over. This happened a lot in the First World War. There were several solutions to this. The biggest were the memorials at Thiepval (over 72,000 names) on the Somme, and those at the Menin Gate (nearly 55,000) and the Tyne Cot wall (nearly 35,000) in Belgium. These monuments contain the names of all those killed with no known body across the two battlefields. An alternative, and perhaps more personal, idea derived from a British Army chaplain, David Railton MC, who noticed a grave near Armentières in France, with the words, 'An unknown soldier of the Black Watch' written on the cross. After the war he raised the issue of a grave for the Unknown Warrior, where a body would be chosen to represent all those who had died and which would be a memorial for all the grieving relatives, as no-one would know whose son was buried in the grave. After some debate, the idea was accepted.

The body was to be chosen from one of four unknown British servicemen who were exhumed from the battlefields of the Aisne, the Somme, Arras and Ypres. Each was taken from a grave marked as an 'Unknown

British Soldier'. The bodies were selected from the early years of the war, so decomposition had taken place. Proof of Britishness was the wearing of a British Army uniform. The remains were transported to a chapel at Saint Pol near Arras. The bearers arrived at different times and were immediately sent away so they would not know if 'their' body had been selected. Two British officers, Brigadier Wyatt and Lieutenant-Colonel Gell, entered the chapel alone at midnight and chose one of the bodies, each of which was covered by the Union Flag. The other bodies were taken for re-burial, and the chosen body was transported, with due ceremony, across the Channel on the British Destroyer HMS *Verdun*. The funeral in Westminster Abbey took place on 11 November 1920, with full ceremonial. The grave was filled with earth brought from France. The French Unknown Warrior was interred the same day under the Arc de Triomphe.

The burial brought back memories. A blinded veteran, Herbert Thompson, described how the atmosphere was impregnated with meaning, and the occasion brought back the most poignant memories. 'I felt with my comrades almost ashamed that I had given so little, while he who was sleeping by us had given all ... I came to the Abbey glad that I had been chosen from among so many, I went away sorrowing, but with the message of hope in my heart' (quoted in Quinlan, 2005a, p. 22). This moving quotation draws out the best in memorialisation – how it stirs memories of the war and comrades who fought and died, yet also looks forward to a better future. It is also interesting that a blind man felt that he had given so little compared with the soldier who had died. This shows the inherent contradictions in any war memorialisation; the men who were maimed are not the ones who are remembered. In some way it is thought that they have not contributed as much as those who died, they are not as important as those who died; because they did not die, they should not be remembered.

Commemoration in Leningrad

The siege of Leningrad lasted nearly 900 days. Around 670,000 people died, a third of the population, with up to 8,000 in a single day – mostly of starvation. In the first winter of the siege, 1941–2, with temperatures dropping as low as $-40°C$, the daily bread ration went as low as 125 grams. Commemoration of the Great Patriotic War, particularly the siege of Leningrad, started very soon after the Germans invaded in June 1941.

Lisa Kirschenbaum (2004) has described how, days after the Germans invaded the Soviet Union, it was reported by the Leningrad Komsomol (youth organisation) that efforts to chronicle the war had already begun.

Shortly afterwards, when the siege began, exhibitions started to take place that commemorated the war. These exhibitions, in commemorating the present, merged the personal and public lives of the people taking part in the war. Personal effects, such as letters, diaries and photographs, were used in these displays. The *Komsomol'skaia pravda* newspaper emphasised the importance, if not the necessity, of immediately commemorating 'life that becomes history'. Visitors to the exhibitions were encouraged to think of their lives in historic or mythic terms. The materials used in the exhibitions included artistic works, flyers and other documents relating to the defence of Leningrad, materials that the organisers assumed would later be of great value to historians.

The state played a central role in these commemorations, drawing on personal stories and memories to encourage the citizens to see themselves as part of the bigger struggle. This is not a particularly Soviet behaviour; all nations perform this kind of state control. Workers at the public library began collecting published artefacts of the siege shortly after it began in the autumn of 1941. The collection's director, Vera Karatygina, argued that every document they collected would enable the people to realise and recognise the past. The group of workers who put this collection together worked closely throughout the war, and all bore the loss of friends and family. Karatygina deliberately merged personal memory and public commemoration. Kirschenbaum (2004) describes how Karatygina, in a 1942 talk at a library conference, discussed the role of the propaganda posters, claiming that the posters roused the same feelings of patriotism in everyone, and that they were an exact representation of how Leningraders lived during the siege. She wanted the propaganda posters kept to help stimulate the personal memories of the survivors. After the war, the photographs that had been collected were published in a Russian book entitled *Leningrad Under Siege*, which has recently been reissued and which provides a very visual account of the siege. In 1943 an exhibition was presented displaying everything from the guns used by the Soviets and captured German tanks to the letters and diaries kept by the population. It even included a piece of bread, demonstrating the size of the bread ration in the winter of 1941–2. This made the exhibition memorable to everyone, as it evoked their personal memories, even if they had not seen the German weaponry at first hand. The museum, though it closed in the 1950s, reopened on the same site in 1989, and focuses largely on the everyday objects of the siege. It is still run by people who took part in the siege, who are there to answer visitors' questions; the personal commemorative element is still present.

What are the psychological benefits
of memorialisation and commemoration?

In one sense people have always memorialised war. It is just that, over time, we forget. The important wars at any given time are those where there are living veterans, or where there are people living who remember the veterans – their children and grandchildren. Once these people die, then the wars they fought become less important, and eventually irrelevant. That is one reason why we don't consider memorialisation for wars such as the Crimean War in the 1850s; it is just too long ago, even though 100,000 British servicemen fought in the war, and around 20,000 died. It was fought at a time when the recording of births, marriages and deaths was in its infancy. There were no death certificates issued for those who died. There were no commemorative services for the ordinary men who died – no Remembrance Sunday or Cenotaph. That is not to say that people did not have a need to remember their loved ones, but life was cheaper then. Attitudes towards people have changed. A few hundred years ago, individual life was relatively unimportant. A woman might give birth to a dozen or more babies, perhaps half of whom would survive to early adulthood, and most would be dead by the age of 40 years. It was normal to lose children. Life used to have a different value. We now assume that a person *should* live until they are 'three score years and ten', as the Bible suggests – if not quite a bit longer, so if a person dies, or if a lot of people die, we as the relatives and friends, and we as a society, consider it more important.

A further reason why we now memorialise more than in the past is the sheer scale of the deaths. During the First World War nearly 10 million people, mostly soldiers, died in a few short years. The industrial revolution had given us the technology to kill in vast numbers. During the First World War this was particularly represented by the machine gun. Though this was around in some form or other since the US Civil War in the 1860s – when it was known as the 'Gatling Gun' – it was not very efficient until Maxim patented his model. The Maxim machine gun, along with the Vickers' one on the British side, caused very many of the casualties on the Western Front. The machine gun was much more efficient than shelling, as up to one-third of shells did not explode (creating problems for farmers on the Somme to this day), and those that did tended to be more effective at causing psychological distress to soldiers hidden deep inside bunkers than at killing – at least in comparison with the machine gun.

Memorials and commemoration
in the defeated countries

In the defeated countries, memorialisation is difficult. There are far
fewer memorials to the World Wars in Germany than there are in Britain
and France, and the WWI cemeteries to the Germans are not given over
in perpetuity, unlike the British cemeteries, which effectively become
part of Britain but which remain part of France or Belgium. There are
far fewer cemeteries, with the German dead often buried in mass graves.

The Second World War was particularly difficult for the Germans to
commemorate. They were seen as the perpetrators, not only of the war
itself, but also of the atrocities associated with the war: the killing of
millions of Jews, homosexuals, Communists, gypsies and Soviet prisoners. There have been attempts to show that the *Wehrmacht* should not
have had the same war guilt as the members of the Nazi Party, but this
has had little success, especially when evidence emerged regarding the
role of the Wehrmacht in the killings in eastern Europe. Other attempts
have been made to expiate the ordinary Germans, whether soldiers or
civilians, as ordinary people who were as much victims of Nazi Germany
as others. Some Germans have claimed that the allied troops were
liberating Germany in 1945, but in fact the country continued to fight
until the very last moment. There were few mass defections and surren-
ders before the last few days.

The German experience demonstrates the important role of the state
in developing memorials and commemorative events. The German state
was destroyed in 1945 and the new states of East and West Germany did
not particularly want to look back on a war for which they were guilty.
Interestingly, even though there was an apparent complete break
between the old and the new states, inevitably the new states were run
mostly by the same ex-Nazi Party officials who had previously run the
country. These people only wanted to keep quiet; there was no cause to
commemorate, so the individual millions did not have a chance to share
in national mourning.

The Japanese have successfully managed to mourn their dead, though
not without controversy. Though they were subjected to unconditional
surrender in the Second World War, as was Germany, they were allowed
a continuation of the state in the form of the Emperor, Hirohito, though
he was forced to lose his godhead. The Japanese have a national memorial
to the dead of all wars, and the dead of the Second World War are
commemorated there. Ever since the war, there has been controversy
when high-ranking officials have attended to mourn the dead, such
mourning being seen as inseparable from the role of the nation in the war.

A detailed example: the Falklands War

Burnell and Jones (2005) have argued that, in order to understand commemoration, we need to break down artificial disciplinary boundaries and develop a research methodology that incorporates elements from different disciplines. Karen Burnell is a psychologist, and Rachel Jones is an historian. Together they discuss how both disciplines feed into our understanding of private and public commemoration of the Falklands War. They examine public commemorative practice through memorials that, they argue, reinforce a socio-cultural public narrative of the conflict. They also argue (as I argue throughout this book) that the reconciliation of traumatic memories occurs through the creation of a personal narrative as an example of private commemoration. According to Burnell and Jones, memorials and public commemoration in the latter half of the twentieth century became examples of aesthetic post-modernity, resulting from the rise of subjectivity and the end of the post-war historical certainty. This arose due to a change in the perceptions of war, from the 'just' Second World War to many of the later wars in which Britain has been involved, from Korea to Iraq and Afghanistan, where the aims and purposes of these wars were far less clear and, for many people, unjustified. According to Burnell and Jones, the Falklands is a difficult case study, belonging to the 'just' group rather than the 'unjust'.

There are many memorials to the Falklands War. Just like those commemorating the First and Second World Wars, they take many forms – from plaques to statues – and are situated in different parts of the country. They are not necessarily erected in response to grief and mourning, but are, like any other narrative work, the result of more complicated 'politically centred ceremonies and ritualistic behaviour... Within these complex languages of mourning we see death as a patriotic force, binding the individual with nation' (Burnell and Jones, 2005, pp. 2–3). They present evidence of this social narrative by using examples of Falklands' War memorials. One of these examples is the Gosport Hard mosaic and ceremonial garden. On the twentieth anniversary of the war, there was a dedication ceremony attended by Baroness Thatcher, who was, according to the authors, 'a former political leader attempting to reinstate and renegotiate the political spectrum of the conflict within the discourses of commemoration, essentially all these acts are framed by remembrances' (p. 3). The authors note the importance of the dead soldier being perceived as a hero and a militaristic image, which are key components of most war memorials.

Further to this, the memorial at Gosport Hard forms a direct link between the Falklands and D-Day. The two wars are aligned geographically, which suggests that the viewer is being encouraged to draw assumptions about the legitimacy of the two events.

The second example of a Falklands memorial used by Burnell and Jones is the Sallyport plaque. This is engraved with an image of the Falklands and the names of every British soldier killed (memorials never commemorate the enemy). This memorial serves a different purpose to the previous one; it is used as a site of pilgrimage by veterans and families. Items such as personal notes and photographs are left throughout the year, not just on Remembrance Day.

Burnell and Jones argued that the Sallyport memorial is used more than the Gosport memorial because the latter is not part of the 'organic narratives of memory that seek to commemorate the conflict' (p. 5). Instead, the Gosport memorial is an example of 'dominated memory', one which does not have a personal touch and is not relevant to private narratives.

The authors argue that memorials are complex texts or narratives which are open, as any other social discourse, to interpretation and reinterpretation by both veterans and mourners and wide public audiences. In this way, individual memory is responsible for the hegemonic public constructions of memory which may be utilised to reinforce the established narrative. According to Burnell and Jones, memorials can bridge the gap between public and private memory, and public and private commemorations are joint endeavours, not mutually exclusive.

The National Memorial Arboretum

The National Memorial Arboretum (NMA) was created in the 1990s as a site for remembrance (Childs, 2008). It consists of a large 130-acre site, deliberately placed in the centre of the country, away from London, for memorials and commemorative events relating to wars from the First World War to the present day. It has become the site for the national memorial to those who have died since the Second World War. This is a poignant memorial as it contains vast spaces of stone, as yet uncut with the names of those who have not yet died in the service of their country. That is a change from previous memorials, which have only looked to the past; this one looks to the future. In this way the NMA is a memorial not only to the past, but to the present and the future, and is attempting to be so through not only commemorative events, but also the education of younger people.

The site has many memorials to battles, to units of the armed forces, and to individuals. There are many trees planted as memorials, which will, in the near future, create a memorial forest, with clearings for the larger stone and brick memorials. It is interesting that it was thought necessary to create a new site of remembrance and commemoration in Britain, when nearly every town and village has its own memorial. Is there a greater national need for remembrance, or is it that we are now learning how to use remembrance and commemoration as an effective means of educating future generations about the past? Instead of memorials being inert and inactive, as many were becoming at the end of the twentieth century, perhaps we now realise that commemoration is not just about ageing veterans marching past the stones and flags, but about helping younger people, and those without experience of war, to understand something and to realise why we commemorate past wartime events, and remember those who fought, i.e. it serves an educative purpose. It certainly draws the experiences of war throughout the twentieth century and beyond together at a single site, which inevitably makes it more attractive to visit, not only to get a sense of remembrance for a specific person or group, but also to understand the wider context of war.

Conclusions

Memorialisation and commemoration are experiencing a growth in the West. It is difficult to determine whether this is because we are reaching the endpoint of commemoration for the dead of the World Wars, with most of the participants dead and the rest very old, whether it relates to the breakdown of the nation state and an attempt by the nation state to unify the nation again, and to draw on unknown reserves of patriotism, whether it is a result of the increasing publicity of current wars and the relatively large-scale casualties, or whether there is a psychological need that has not been fulfilled in previous decades. It is likely that there is a combination of factors. The state could not force individuals to commemorate, and individuals, though they do carry out small-scale memorialisation and commemoration, need the state to take part in the large-scale events.

Memorialisation and commemorative events are yet another way of demonstrating and creating narratives that are linked to the social discourses of the time. Both memorials and commemorative events tend to be public, and they tend to be aspects of a discourse that is accepted by most people within the country. In reality, many people from families who have immigrated to the UK in the last few decades may not feel anything about such rituals – they may not feel part of it – but remembering the dead of the World Wars and conflicts since then has become an important part of remembering the history of Britain. It is almost unheard of for groups to protest at a commemorative event. Anti-war demonstrators do not demonstrate at the Armistice Day service, perhaps partly because we have modernised the reasons for the service – if not the service itself; it is almost universally recognised as a series of events that remember the dead, and does not glorify wars or victories. As the Second World War generation dies, it will be interesting to see how important these commemorations remain. There is an attempt to make them valid for the more recent wars fought by our troops, but it is not clear that the key commemorative events will remain in place for long, or whether smaller, more individually focused events will take their place. The social discourse moves on, and narratives follow.

13   Battlefield tours

This chapter is a little unusual in a book about the psychology of war. One purpose of the book is to try and understand something about how humans behave in response to war, with a special focus on exploring the role of socio-cultural factors and memory. People's understanding of war – if they are lucky enough not to have genuinely experienced it – is largely derived from books, television and films. The aim of this chapter is to take a more active approach than just reading, but one where the danger has passed – to walk around the battlefields themselves, in the footsteps of the soldiers. In this way, one can improve one's understanding of war, and try to understand something more of what people go through when they fight. This is addressing the van der Kolk statement: 'the body keeps the score'. War trauma is about bodily experience as much as emotional or cognitive factors, so walking the battlefields adds something to one's understanding. The chapter does not provide the detail for specific tours, but instead gives some guidance on how to organise a tour, and on how what you put in to such a tour can enhance what you get out of it.

The chapter uses a single example: to Ypres, for Passchendaele. I make no excuses for choosing this site. It has been described many times before and is familiar to many people interested in war. Its woods and fields have been trodden over by many thousands of people since the battles took place. Many other battlefields could have been chosen, but I chose Passchendaele for personal reasons: because my father's cousin, Charles Hunt, died there on 1 August 1917, and is remembered on the Menin Gate. I know very little about him, as those who did know him are now dead. Those I could have asked when I was a child I did not ask – because I was a child. My father, who was born the year after Charles died, was named after him. My middle name is also Charles, so there is a clear link.

A brief outline of the battles

If you intend to do these walks, then you should do some prior reading, and find out about what happened during the battles, and where important or interesting events took place. There are numerous excellent books available about the battle.

Passchendaele

'What Jerusalem is to the Jewish race, and what Mecca is to the Mohammedan, Ypres must always be to the millions who have lost a husband, son or brother, slain in its defence, and now sleeping their eternal sleep within sight of its silent belfry.'

These words were written by Lieutenant-Colonel Beckles Wilson, the Canadian Town Major until October 1919, who was fanatical in his desire to preserve the town of Ypres as a ruined memorial (see www. cwgc.org/ypres/content.asp?id=38&menu=subsub). Fortunately for the inhabitants, once he had gone, the town was slowly rebuilt as a copy of its former self – the houses, shops, churches and offices being built from old plans, photographs and the memories of people. The centre of the town is now an almost exact copy of how it was before 1914. Virtually the only thing that had survived more or less intact were the fortified walls of the town, built to Vauban's plans for defence against very different artillery, several hundred years before.

The Battle of Passchendaele or, more formally, the Third Battle of Ypres, took place between July and November 1917. The word 'Passchendaele' itself became a very emotive word in the English language for several generations, through to the grandchildren of those who fought there, providing evidence of the nature of cultural memory, i.e. that it has a relatively short emotional life. Now, the word does not convey the emotions to younger generations that it once had.

The site of the battlefield, extending several miles to the south, east and north of the town of Ypres in southwest Belgium, was fought over throughout the First World War. In 1914 it was the scene of bitter fighting as the Allies and the Germans were involved in their race to the sea. It helped to establish where the front lines were going to stay for most of the war. By 1917, the soldiers who fought at the Third Battle were fighting over ground that was already scarred from shellfire and contained the bodies of many thousands of troops of both sides.

The British, defending the salient around Ypres where there had been little movement for nearly 3 years, planned to strike through the German lines, cut off the occupied Belgian ports, and take Antwerp in the north of Belgium. It was an ambitious plan and, as with so many ambitious plans in this war, it was doomed to failure. In the end, the British managed to take a few square miles of territory, the biggest advantage being the Passchendaele Ridge itself, from where German artillery observers had been targeting the British troops since the end of 1914.

The precursor to the main battle took place in April, when nineteen mines, dug by ex-coal miners, were exploded under the German lines along the Messines Ridge, causing havoc among the German troops. The Allies quickly took the ridge, but advanced no further. Twenty-one mines had been laid. One blew up in the 1950s; the other is still underground somewhere, still charged with explosives, no doubt unstable after so many years in the ground.

Charles Hunt was an ordinary Private with the Queen's Royal West Surrey Regiment. He came from Belper, Derbyshire, and had two sisters and a large extended family. There was nothing special about him, except to his family; he was just one of millions of men who joined up and fought for their country between 1914 and 1918. In July 1917 he was behind the lines somewhere near Ypres, perhaps spending time at Poperinghe, a favourite town for soldiers who had a few days off, as there was an ample supply of beer and girls, the two things a soldier most needs before he heads into the fight – and if he returns from the fight. In late July his battalion moved up to the line near Hill 60, situated to the southeast of Ypres, just off the Menin Road. There is a memorial there today, as at most of the important sites. The battalion took part in the advance on the second day, 1 August 1917. Charles Hunt advanced up the hill through Sanctuary Wood, so called because in the early days of the war men could rest from battle among the trees, but now it was in no man's land – not a place of rest, but a place of broken trees, filthy craters and intense danger, where many men took their permanent rest around that time; Charles Hunt was one of them.

Charles was killed in that first advance. We assume and hope that his death was a quick one, because his body was never found. We do not know whether he died from being too close to an exploding shell and his body being torn to pieces, or whether he died some horrific slow death, with his body gradually submerging under piles of earth and mud. Unless he becomes one of the many soldiers' bodies now being dug up by WWI archaeologists, we will never know.

Not knowing how their loved one died was always difficult for relatives and friends. That is why the concept of the Unknown Soldier came about. The Unknown Soldier was selected from all the unidentifiable bodies of all the battlefields. No-one could tell who it was, and so it became the symbol for all grieving families who did not have a grave to visit.

Charles Hunt's name is inscribed on the Menin Gate, along with nearly 60,000 others, all missing in action around Ypres. As there was not enough space on the Menin Gate for the missing, those who were missing after 1917 were inscribed on plaques on the walls of the nearby

Tyne Cot Cemetery, the largest on the battlefield, situated on the slopes at the top of which is Passchendaele village, the main aim of the battle of 1917 – finally reached after many months of fighting, and of which nothing remained. The village now is completely rebuilt.

Visiting the Ypres area for the first time, you experience emotional numbness at the sight of so many cemeteries containing the graves of so many young men. The British graves are all of white Portland stone, and the graves are all well tended, situated on land that has been donated to the UK forever. It may help to imagine each stone as a man, returning to the parade ground, to get a feeling for the numbers involved.

A tour of a battlefield when you are exploring the experiences of a single soldier is, in many ways, more satisfying than visiting without such a focus. While an understanding of the 'grand plan' is developed, you learn little of the experiences of war. Focusing on a specific individual and walking the battlefield as though seeing it through his eyes provides a personal perspective that gives a greater psychological understanding. Before going to the site of the battle, read about what happened to the person, or to the person's battalion – if, as I did, you have little personal information about the individual. Look at maps, try and trace the route the person took so that when you are there you can follow that route – and not the routes specified by any tourist agency. Get the personal perspective.

Once at the battlefield it is important to visit the key sites and the museums so that you can see the personal items carried by the soldiers, the weapons used, but also the very personal things – the letters, the tin openers, the copies of newspapers, and the pictures of girlfriends. Again, it personalises the experience and allows you to get inside the head of the soldier. Personally, I do not like the modernisation of museums in the Ypres area (and elsewhere). They distract from the experience. You can look at a computer screen and see fancy animations and films anywhere, but you can rarely see the individual items, the rusting guns, the uniforms, the personal equipment. The museums in the Ypres area vary from a few piles of rusting junk to ultra-modern high-tech installations. The preservation of memory for the First World War is undergoing massive change; as the generations who knew veterans die, then the events become history, not memories handed down through generations, something which ceases usually at the second generation.

The tour

Ypres itself is a good place to base the visit, though there are villages all around where you can get good accommodation. The shape of the battlefield makes Ypres the central focus. Take a good map of the area, and mark it with the key sites of interest. This two-day tour uses both walking and driving. There is no attempt to explore the whole battlefield, as it is a personal tour, though I would recommend you drive around the whole area just to get a sense of the size of the battlefield, to see the perspectives of other soldiers, and to explore the monuments and museums in other areas. The first day is spent around the area in which Charles Hunt fought, and the second covers some of the key sites of the battlefield.

Day 1: searching for Charles Hunt

Start in the centre of Ypres, by the Cloth Hall, rebuilt between the 1920s and 1960s from the rubble that was all that remained after the First World War, and walk out of the town by the Menin Gate, the route taken by many thousands of men marching to the battle. We will return to the Menin Gate later. For now, you cannot avoid seeing some of the thousands of names of the missing, and the magnificence of the memorial. A few hundred yards further on, turn right on the Menin Road. You walk through the outskirts of Ypres, passing a British cemetery on the right. It is often informative to visit the cemeteries you pass, and look at the names and regiments. Most men were buried near to where they fell, so cemeteries say a lot about the battles that took place. To get some idea of the scale of death, imagine the men standing again. Look also at the personal inscriptions at the bottom of many gravestones, the only personal touch allowed to the families. While many have standard phrases relating to religion, many have more personal touches.

The roundabout you approach when leaving Ypres is Hellfire Corner. A small monument indicates the furthest advance of the Germans in 1918. Here the troops were subjected to enemy shellfire. The German guns were trained on the corner, so large camouflage sheets were put up along the road to hide the troop movements from the German spotters on the small hills to the east and the south. Stay on the Menin Road – you will pass another cemetery on your right. The German frontline trenches were situated across the hill in front in July 1917; while the hill is not high, the Germans could see the British positions and movements very clearly, and the British, Charles Hunt included, had to advance up the hill into the German machine guns. It must have been very different to the peaceful rural scene now. To the right of the road you can see Sanctuary Wood, where you are heading shortly. Straight ahead, there are the white headstones of Crater Cemetery, the stones of those who died advancing up the hill.

Take the road to the right indicating Hill 60. You pass another, large, cemetery on the right. You are then at the edge of Sanctuary Wood. A little way further along is Hill 60 Museum, which is well worth a visit. Inside is an array of stereoscopes, machines that are set up with hundreds of three-dimensional photographs of the war. Many are quite gruesome, men and horses dead. This gives a good impression of the battlefield of the time. The museum also has many artefacts from the war – many displayed well, and others piled up rusting. Outside there is an area of 'original' trenches, some of which have been reconstructed, including tunnelled areas. There are even some tree trunks remaining which had been destroyed by shellfire. The trenches were British.

On leaving the museum, Hill 60 is on the right. Again, there are memorials to see. Charles Hunt was positioned around here before the battle started on 31 July. He would have seen the first troops advancing up through the ruins of Sanctuary Wood towards the chateau at the top of the hill occupied by the Germans. No doubt he, like most others, was terrified of what was to come, but the soldiers supported each other.

The next day Charles's battalion advanced across the line of that taken by the troops the previous day. Standing on Hill 60, they advanced through Sanctuary Wood towards what is now Crater Cemetery. Now walk up the path to the south of Sanctuary Wood. This opens out onto a track, and then a road. Turn left. Look around and get an impression. The slope you have just come up saw the deaths of many men. When you are at the top you have reached the German lines, though very little now remains. After a couple of hundred yards there is a track which heads into Sanctuary Wood. Go down this and into the wood. When I first walked in this wood alone I started to imagine the ghosts of the thousands of men who had died here. Then I realised that these men were fighting for my country and would be protective. The path leads straight down through the wood to a track, where you turn right and head up to the Menin Road. But while in the wood, it is worth exploring. It is in places like this that you often get the best feel for a battleground, a place that is relatively untouched and which still has traces of the lines of trenches if you look carefully. But be careful, not every ditch is a trench! It is also in places like this that you find relics of the war: bullets, shellcases and, sometimes, intact shells complete with detonator and explosive! If you do find a shell – and they are quite common – don't touch, but report it to the police for disposal. I have found intact shells up to 3 feet long, and they still look frightening. There was so much ordnance fired in these battles, and so much of it was ineffective, i.e. it didn't explode. There are still many tons to be found. And no doubt more deaths. I found a large piece of shellcase just outside the wood, splintered and twisted by its explosion. While it almost certainly didn't kill Charles Hunt, there is some comfort in thinking that it did, instantly.

Across the road there is a hotel, in the grounds of which are a number of mine craters, now filled with water and forming a decorative feature in the garden. For a small sum you can enter the area and explore. There are other artefacts and the remains of a German trench, one that was blown up by the mines that made these craters.

Turn right onto the Menin Road and walk down to Crater Cemetery, so called because it was built on the site of a large crater, the shape of which can still be seen at the top end of the cemetery. This is a large cemetery, containing around 6,000 men. From here you can see why they died. You are standing near the German front line, from where they shot down onto the advancing British troops. It is here that I like to think Charles Hunt is buried, one of the 2,000 or so unknown graves. I have no idea whether he is here, but this view illustrates our need for a site of memory – to use Nora's phrase, a place to mourn.

After visiting the cemetery, go to the museum across the road. It contains a large number of artefacts, well displayed, and even partially labelled. There is a good collection of shells of many sizes. There is also a café.

After the museum, head back down the Menin Road towards the British lines and Ypres. When you start to go uphill there is a crossroads. Turn left and follow the road to the next village, Gommecourt. At the end of the road there is another cemetery, on the site of an old tile factory. Turn left (south) down the road and after a few hundred yards turn right onto a small road which leads to the lake. The nearest part of the lake is called Hellblast Corner, and was the area where Charles Hunt's battalion formed up before heading into the front line. Walk by the lake (either side) and head back to Ypres. By the roundabout with a large tap you can either go straight on, then turn left and follow the walls back to the Menin Gate, though you can enter the town through an earlier path, or you can turn left and enter by the Lille Gate, but we will be returning this way tomorrow.

Before 8 p.m. you should be standing in the Menin Gate, probably with hundreds of other people. Just before the hour the road is closed to traffic, then several firemen of the town march up and play the 'Last Post'. It is a very moving ceremony, and has been carried out every evening since the Menin Gate was finished in 1926 – apart from the years of occupation, 1940–4.

Ypres has a number of interesting restaurants and bars, and the local beers are varied and flavourful. By the end of the day you may be in need of several beers and a good talk about what you have seen.

Day 2: museums, memorials and cemeteries

The first part of the day involves visiting two sites away from Ypres, with the afternoon spent in the town. Drive to Hill 62. When I first visited this site there was an old café across the road, basically a shed full of bits and pieces from the war. Now there is a smart modern cafe and the artefacts have gone to an Ypres museum. Hill 62 is of interest because the area was left largely as it was in 1918. It is a mass of shell holes, mounds and a virtually intact British pillbox. The site demonstrates the value of actually walking a battlefield in a way different to that experienced yesterday, which was on a large scale, where most of the trenches and sites have to be imagined. It is not difficult to imagine Hill 62 as a battlefield. Though it is now covered with grass, trees and brambles, take that away and the shape is intact.

After Hill 62 drive to the Tyne Cot cemetery (named by the Northumberland Fusiliers after a barn they called Tyne Cottage which stood near a level crossing). If you choose your route carefully you can take in other sites of interest from the battle. Tyne Cot Cemetery is on the slopes of Passchendaele Ridge, not a high hill, but fought over for the last weeks of the battle. Passchendaele village is at the top of the hill, the final point reached during the battle. You will see that very few miles were gained for the loss of so many troops over several months. The way you enter the cemetery depends on your view regarding memory. The old entrance, at the bottom of the hill – the bottom of the Passchendaele Ridge – is the best. You enter the cemetery and immediately get an impression of the size. This is the largest cemetery on the battlefield, and the largest cemetery cared for by the Commonwealth War Graves Commission. Not only does it contain nearly 12,000 graves, it also has many panels of names of nearly 35,000 soldiers for whom there is no known grave. In the end the Menin Gate was not big enough to contain all the names of those lost without a grave.

You can enter the Tyne Cot Cemetery from the top, through the new entrance opened by Queen Elizabeth. This entrance typifies the new way of memorialising the war, with a modernist building and various displays. Personally I see this as a distraction from the cemetery, but we all commemorate in different ways. We will return to this topic below.

After the cemetery, go to the town of Zonnebeke, where there is an interesting museum in the chateau. At the entrance to the park there are old concrete sentry boxes. The museum itself has a range of good displays, but the best part is the dugout. This is a reconstruction of a WWI dugout, complete with various rooms fulfilling a number of functions, from hospitals to officers' quarters.

Return to Ypres. There are many walks and places to visit in Ypres. Just wandering aimlessly around the town you will get a feel for the architecture. The centre of the town does feel a little frozen in time due to it being rebuilt in the pre-war style. The Cloth Hall is a magnificent building, ruined by war and rebuilt over 50 years. The main museum is in here, but take time to look at the building itself. Parts of the original walls remain, but only the very lower parts. The museum itself is modern, and this is where I have reservations. When I visited, there was a group of schoolchildren going around, but few of them were looking at the exhibits, the artefacts of war. Most of them spent their time pressing buttons for the computer demonstrations, something which they might as well have stayed at home to do via the Internet. The modernisation of museums, while there is an attempt to create a particular narrative of war, distracts from the contemplation of the museum pieces themselves. This does seem to reflect a trend towards accepting shorter attention spans and not enabling visitors to learn about the war.

Walk down to the Lille Gate. Here there is a peaceful little cemetery built as part of the town walls, where you can sit and contemplate, and look out across the moat towards the south towards Hill 62 and the Messines Ridge. Just by the Lille Gate is a bar and museum. Both are excellent. They are run by a Belgian enthusiast, who is very happy to discuss his museum project with visitors.[1] The museum is at the back of the bar. It contains many artefacts from the war, and the benefit is that the owner is always thinking of new ways to display them. One memorable display has the visitor at the foot of the stairs of a dugout, and a soldier who has been shot and has fallen halfway down the stairs.

After you have been in the museum, have a drink in the bar. They have a special brew to commemorate the war – and you can buy a beer jug to remember your visit.

Creating your own battlefield tour

As you will have seen from the above, the concepts of narrative and social discourse are very important for a battlefield tour. If you just turn

---

[1] I recently visited Ypres (December 2009) and unfortunately the owner had died, aged only forty-six. Currently, his wife is still running the bar and the museum is still open, but not being developed.

up to where a battle took place, and wander round looking at the memorials and the museums, you will get a feel for the battle that took place, but if you want to get into the heart of the battle then you need to do preliminary reading about the battle, and perhaps find something out about specific individuals who fought there, not necessarily the generals and commanders, about whom many people will have written, but about some of the ordinary soldiers who fought – about their experiences, thoughts and feelings regarding the battle. The people who fought in the First and Second World Wars left numerous accounts of their experiences – some published as books, some available as diaries on the Internet, and many at archives such as that of the Imperial War Museum in London, which has recorded the experiences and memories of many participants.

When learning about a particular individual, or even about a particular unit, it is valuable to follow in the footsteps of where he fought, get a feel for the territory, and see where he was positioned and where the enemy was positioned. Where possible, retrace his movements. If you are aware of the names of the dead – perhaps a relative, perhaps a friend of the person whose story you are following – visit the grave. It can be more moving to find a single grave than to take in the enormity of so many dead. If it is the Commonwealth War Graves Commission, then there will be a book that lists the dead in a box at the cemetery entrance. This book can provide interesting information about the dead: where they were from, and their parents' names, which gives it a personal quality. There may be other personal elements. When visiting a cemetery near Amiens, my father was sitting at the entrance to the cemetery, looking through the book, when he came across the name of a family he knew from his village, the Elliots, whose son was buried there. This was an enormous coincidence in the circumstances; he had no idea where this soldier was buried. He just had a recollection from when he was a child of the family who had the missing son.

But why, you may ask, is this chapter in the book? What has it to do with narrative and social discourse? It is here to show how our understanding of war, how our memories of war, how the history of war, can be better understood if your interest is made personal. I have trodden on many battlefields, from the English and US Civil Wars, to the First and Second World Wars, to Bosnia, and each time I have gained a better understanding of the battle, a more personal understanding of what it means to soldiers who fight.

14   Conclusions and future directions

This brief chapter draws together the material that has been examined through the book, identifies some key themes relating to memory, war and trauma, and proposes a framework for future research. In the end the purpose of research in this field has to be helping those who have suffered psychologically due to war or other traumatic events. This book has not looked at psychological therapies in any detail, because that has not been the purpose of the book, but it is hoped that clinicians and therapists will find valuable lessons for therapeutic practice within these pages. We do now understand a great deal about war and the psychological impact war can have on people. The introduction of PTSD in 1980 provided a useful impetus for research, and there are now well over 20,000 academic papers published on this topic. While they do, of course, vary in quality, overall it has meant that we have a much better grasp of the key issues surrounding war trauma.

What have we learned?

This book has demonstrated, I hope, that a good understanding of memory, war and trauma requires more than psychological research. War is a topic that affects most people in one way or another, whether as active participants, a family member of someone in the armed forces, students of history or someone exposed to the media.

Interdisciplinarity

Throughout the book the discussions have been largely about the importance of interdisciplinarity. This is currently a trendy word in academia, and trendy is not necessarily either interesting or pertinent, but within the area of war trauma interdisciplinarity is invaluable. As we have seen, we cannot fully understand the nature and effects of war trauma without drawing on the expertise of researchers in a number of disciplines, including not only psychology but also sociology, history, political science and literature. And it is not just academics who are making the contribution – it is novelists, poets and biographers, people who think about and write about war. Without their contribution, most of us would know little about war.

In order to understand an individual's memories of war and the impact they have on behaviour, we have to look beyond the individual to wider society, social constructs, politics and history. What I hope has been made clear in this book is that we gain a more coherent and complete understanding of war trauma through a thorough study of these different areas. The chapter on literature, with the focus on Remarque's *All Quiet on the Western Front*, was an attempt to show how literature can contribute to a psychological understanding when the literature itself is seen as data. Remarque (1929) experienced the trenches of the Western Front first hand, and so was in a good position to write about what they were like, drawing on the freedom of a novelist to arrange and present complex ideas about the impact of war experience on people. The book is not only a psychological account; it is also presenting an account of the culture in WWI Germany.

Literature is a rich source of narrative psychological understanding, and psychologists should be encouraged to read more. Good novelists are also good psychologists, as characters have to be strong and well rounded. The interactions between the characters in a good novel are necessarily psychologically insightful; they are telling the story of the human condition. Psychologists who sneer at the psychological insights from literature are missing an important point about science: science is not about the methods used; it is about increasing systematic knowledge and understanding about one's subject. The experimental method might be very helpful at helping us to gain insight, but so is reading Dostoevsky.

Narrative

The key argument within the book has been the centrality of narrative to the human condition. Without narrative we are nothing. Without narrative we cannot understand either the personal or the social world. It has been argued here – and elsewhere – that humans are essentially storytellers, and we have a whole range of stories that we use, stories that we tell our families, stories for our friends, stories for our professional lives and stories we tell ourselves. One of the wonderful things about being a person is that we can manipulate our memories more or less at will – though often such manipulations are implicit or unconscious. Depending on the audience, we can remember certain events about the past and conveniently forget or omit others, depending on the impression we want to make on other people. Sometimes these narratives are explicit – we deliberately present a certain image of ourselves, for instance in a job interview or when trying to chat up a member of the opposite sex. At other times we unconsciously project an image of ourselves to other people, and the narrative is more implicit. As we get to know people our narratives develop and change according to the relationship we have with the person. The social one is nearly always involved, as a narrative needs an audience. The only exceptions, and they may not be exceptions, are the narratives we tell ourselves about ourselves, but again, how we wish to project ourselves will still, in the end, feed our social narratives.

In one sense being traumatised, being unable to form a narrative, reduces someone to something less than a person because the traumatised person cannot tell the story of their experiences. This is disorientating and depressing for the person because they cannot make sense of what happened to them. It is important that we, as professionals, find ways of helping people to recover the stories of their lives. We develop and use narratives in different ways, and this should be acknowledged for war veterans. Cognitive behaviour therapy is not for everyone; it suits people who can be helped to resolve their trauma. For many people, the sophisticated use of language and thinking skills that is required is not available. The Normandy veteran who writes poems to resolve his traumatic thoughts may not necessarily desire that the narrative of the poem is read by anyone, but the poem is certainly a narrative. The veteran who does not have the cognitive skills or motivation to write may not be able to find an appropriate audience – social support – to enable the narrative to be expressed.

Social discourse

Narratives are not only developed through an internal focus on memories and the ways these are structured; they are developed, as we have seen, through interpersonal interaction and through internalising and interacting with social discourses. Narratives do not develop in isolation. If we are to understand why people think as they do, we have to look around them at the world in which they live. 'No man is an island' is very true for us all. The way we think, what we believe, how we express emotions, all depend on our culture. This has important implications for memory, war and trauma, as memories are constructions, and such constructions depend – as Bartlett (1932) showed with 'The War of the Ghosts' – on the society in which we live. A person traumatised by war is traumatised via the culture in which he lives, and any treatment or therapy for trauma must take account of that.

Universality and cultural specificity

Throughout the book there has been a theme of how psychologists should attempt to differentiate universal and cultural aspects of thought and behaviour. With respect to war trauma, we know that people in different societies react in different ways to traumatic events – that PTSD may not be relevant to non-Western, or even non-United States, societies. But we are also aware that some of the symptoms are universal. The difficulty is that we do not yet understand which elements are universal. It is proposed here that the narrative is the key universal element, the need or drive to make sense of the world that is at the heart of what it is to be human. Traumatic events shake and break our understanding of what the world means, and resolving trauma is about learning to integrate the traumatic memories into the world view.

The two coping styles, avoidance and processing, are universal ways of dealing with problems. Nearly everyone makes use of both strategies, but perhaps the majority use avoidance for most of the time. The work of Horowitz and Creamer is seminal in developing our understanding of how processing and avoidance interact and provides us with the fundamental underpinnings of the trauma response. Social support is also a universal; while different cultures may use social support in different ways, people in all societies depend on each other.

The cultural elements are concerned with the nature of social support, the contents of memory, specific coping styles and the specific means of resolving traumatic stress. These have been little studied, and need a great deal of further work. Unfortunately most research has made the assumption that PTSD is a universal phenomenon, and focused on that, instead of finding ways to separate out the universal and cultural factors. Coping, though there may be universal styles of processing and avoidance, takes different forms. Research with Iranian and Iraqi veterans of the Iran–Iraq War shows that these veterans are more likely to use religion as an important means of dealing with their problems than people in the West. The centrality of religion suggests a fatalism on the part of the veteran, who fought the jihad for god, and puts his faith in god to always do what is right. These veterans tend not to have the individualistic view of many in the West, but an ideal of the collective, where the individual matters less.

History and memory

Memory and history do not conflict in the way that Pierre Nora has proposed, but they have a chronological and psychological development from one to the other. As the people who lived through a particular period die, memories become the past and then the collective memories are reinterpreted into history (then some events and objects of the past are translated into heritage and become enshrined and unchanging, but that is not central to the current discussion). In this way, we see how memories fade, not just through the individuals who experienced significant events, but also through their children and grandchildren who have their own versions of the memories of those times, partly because they grew up with hearing about the events, partly because parently behaviour may have been altered by living through the events, and partly through the surrounding culture, which remains affected by significant events for many years.

This can be linked to memorialisation and commemoration. We memorialise to remember, but memorials are stone. Commemorations make memorials human, and enable us to recall the past. With regard to the World Wars, until now such commemorations have been attended by participants and their families; now most participants are dead or very old. If such commemorations are going to be helpful, they need to also look forward. One thing humans have been very bad at is learning from the past. Each generation repeats the mistakes of the previous one. If we listen to our elders it is to eventually ignore them. For instance, in the Balkans there have been major wars for most generations for many hundreds of years. (Ivo Ilich, 1916, 1994 – *The Bridge Over the Drina* – illustrates this very well.)

We are perhaps at a turning point in our understanding of the role of commemoration, and may be moving from a position of looking back to looking forward with the past at the forefront. The National Memorial Arboretum at Alrewas, near Lichfield, is not only a site containing many memorials commemorating past battles and armed forces units; it has an explicitly educational focus, and it is also a meeting place for veterans' groups. We may well be, in the Western world, undergoing a fundamental revision of the ways in which we interpret history and memory. We are now approaching the point when everyone who experienced the World Wars is dead. Will we continue to have a need to commemorate these wars in the ways we have done in the past? What sense is there in such commemorations for people who did not live through the wars? If commemoration of war is going to continue, then it is likely that it will start to take different forms. The educative function mentioned above is likely to be critical here, and will necessarily bring together people from a range of disciplines who are in a position to teach younger people about war, memory and history. It will certainly not be the sole responsibility of historians; it will become the preserve of others such as psychologists, cultural theorists and sociologists. Furthermore, the ceremonies at the Cenotaph and elsewhere may also change. Many people feel that a strongly religious service is inappropriate, as is a service that is seen as nationalistic. The Germans lost millions of people in the war; so did the Russians and the Japanese. In an increasingly globalised world, a smaller world, we need to recognise the losses faced by all the participants in war, to stop glorifying our victories and instead focus on the human suffering caused by war.

Treatment

While treatment has not been a key focus of this book, it is hoped that the contents will be useful for clinicians of various perspectives when dealing with war trauma. It is clear that something more than clinical skills is needed for a war veteran. The clinician must have an understanding of the historical period of the war – the battles and politics involved – which all add towards an empathic understanding of the person's experiences. Beyond that, the clinician should have an understanding of the role of narrative and social discourse, both as part of normal psychological life and as a key part of the way in which a person thinks and acts as a response to a traumatic event. Explicitly or implicitly, narrative development must play a key role in the resolution of traumatic memories.

Beyond memory, war and trauma

I hope that the insights gained from developing a broader understanding of war trauma will encourage others to look at how psychologists can increase their understanding of different topics by drawing on understanding from other disciplines and from the world around. Memory itself is such a big topic that its study should not just be in the hands of people who work in psychological laboratories. Memory is not about learning lists of numbers; it has a huge social and cultural function, and whenever there are technological or other changes in society, we should be looking at how the nature of memory changes. When printing was invented, it meant that people no longer had to have epic poets to remember the history of society; the information was written in books. Now that the Internet has arrived, perhaps we no longer need to remember which books contain which information; we just use a search engine. These changes have an impact on memory, and they are social and cultural events.

Developing the narrative method

It is clear that we should incorporate narrative more centrally as part of our psychological theories, but we also need to develop narrative method further. Narrative is not well developed within psychology, but it is well developed in linguistics and other areas. The work of Karen Burnell in Chapter 9 showed that we can use narrative in a sophisticated and yet psychologically meaningful manner. There is an urgent need to develop these methods further and to find ways in which we can draw together narrative and other methods, including quantitative approaches. We have to develop theory and method together to identify and code narrative constructions, identify the significant elements of narrative, and use these to determine and predict a person's recovery from trauma.

Future directions

This is an exciting time to be interested in war trauma research. The area has matured over the last couple of decades, drawing on the theoretical work of psychologists who have displayed an interest in the area for more than a century. There is a sense that an integrative understanding of the processes – biological, neurological, behavioural, cognitive, psychodynamic, humanist, social and cultural – is now possible. It is possible because war trauma presents a practical problem that has to be dealt with, and once professionals get their hands on a practical problem, they will find the means of dealing with it irrespective of personal perspective; so the cognitivist clinician makes use of behavioural understanding, the humanist uses cognitive behaviour therapy, and the psychodynamic practitioner recognises that there are occasions when a traumatised person needs drug therapy. The more open-minded therapists take this eclectic approach, drawing on the expertise developed over many years by practitioners in other perspectives.

This then leaves the scientist with a job to do, integrating the work of these multifaceted perspectives and learning to understand how they fit together. And in order to do this the scientist must draw on a range of methods. The experimentalist must now apply qualitative techniques, and the qualitative practitioner must learn the benefits of quantification. But this is all within psychology. We are now at the start of something bigger. Within academia there is now a push for interdisciplinary work, for academics within one discipline to draw on the skills and expertise of academics in other disciplines who have very different theories, methods and even language. The work on war trauma is open to this interdisciplinarity. As already discussed, if we want to fully understand the interrelated concepts of memory, war and trauma, we must look to other disciplines: to history, sociology, art and literature.

For me, the key paradigm shift in psychology is the turn to narrative described by Bruner. This shift, though far from complete, is having a profound effect on psychological theory and method. It is early days yet, but the area of narrative is changing the nature of the discipline of psychology. From the experimental cognitive science of the post-war period, psychology has undergone profound change, and much of it is political. Cognitive experimentalism has given way to neuroscience, which is obtaining the necessary funding to develop a more sophisticated understanding of the neurological underpinnings of psychological theory. Traditional experimental social psychology has given way to a more sophisticated set of approaches – largely qualitative and partly drawn from other social sciences. There is a clear rift between these two elements of psychology, though a full understanding of the mind and behaviour requires both.

Narrative offers a means of integration, a way to bring these two extremes of psychology together. Accepting the need for a narrative understanding of memory, war and trauma means that we must draw on neuropsychological understanding, as well as on traditional cognitive and social theories. As mentioned earlier, we are, in psychology, only just beginning to make use of narrative approaches, but these approaches are, and will be, fruitful. At the moment our understanding of the neurological underpinnings of narrative is negligible. The limited methods used by neuroscientists, plus the problems associated with defining the components of narrative, make it very difficult to understand the brain mechanisms associated with narrative. It is likely that this understanding will grow as we address practical problems such as war trauma.

The advent of narrative and other new methods within psychology will enable us to approach our research questions from a cultural as well as a brain science perspective. The majority of psychological theory has been established in the West, using western methods and western perspectives, with assumptions made about the universality of such processes. In fields such as trauma, we are starting to acknowledge the range of responses that people have, and how these responses are not just the result of universal psychological processes, but also that they depend in part on the cultural background of the researcher, the participant, and the body of work the researcher draws on to derive their research questions and methods. Even the term 'western' is a misnomer, as it generally refers to Anglo-Saxon psychology, not even accounting for the varying philosophies and perspectives within Europe – perspectives that have much to offer in the understanding of war trauma.

We may also be at the point where we are going to change the nature of commemoration. Throughout the twentieth century, commemoration related to the World Wars. Once the participants are dead, and the memories of these wars fades into the past and into the history books, we will have to question why and how we use commemoration. What is the purpose of 11 November? Why do we continue to parade in the streets? Is it appropriate to make these events militaristic? I do not have the answers to these questions, but it is certain that there will be changes and, as discussed above, the changes will have to take account of what it is that we want to suggest to the younger generations about war and remembering war. Up to now, commemoration of the World Wars has been a way of letting veterans know that we remember what they did, and that the difficult and traumatic memories they might have are not forgotten. This, in itself, has been of personal benefit to thousands of veterans. Once these people are dead, can commemoration take on a new role and be educative?

Of course, we still have people dying in what, to us outsiders, are smaller wars, but to the participants are just as important as any war of the past. People are endangered, wounded, maimed and killed. Friends are lost and hardships endured, and still in the cause of the nation, or 'the greater good'. The difference is that these wars are irrelevant to most people in the UK. They are minor sideshows that make for pub arguments and good TV, but they do not affect most of us. Why should we commemorate the dead of these smaller wars? We will not commemorate them in the same way as those of the World Wars simply because they do not affect us all. There is no total war. Nevertheless, these participants should not be forgotten, and their actions on behalf of the nation should not be forgotten, but if we are to remember them, it has to be in a different context to the current ceremonies.

Finally, this book has been concerned with memory, war and trauma, specifically with the effects of war on veterans and on others who take part. Instead of just focusing on the psychological problems that veterans face – the PTSD, anxiety and depression, the alcohol and drug abuse, and the problems relating to families and work – I have tried to take a much broader perspective and show how veterans live in a social context and have narratives about their experiences that derive, at least in part, from that social context. I have tried to show, without providing any specific techniques, how clinicians may benefit from drawing on this broader perspective in their treatment of war veterans. Wars can deeply affect societies, and it is important, if we are to understand how we remember wars, to take into account the broader perspective, to show how memory works in the social and collective senses, and how memories are transmitted and changed through generations. I hope this book has given the reader pause for thought, as it has swept through this broad range of subjects, areas that are at once disparate and brought together by the study of memory, war and trauma.

References

Adler, A. 1958. *Individual Psychology*. London, Harper Perennial

Aldwin, C. M., Levinson, M. R. and Spiro, A. 1994. 'Vulnerability and resilience to combat exposure: can stress have lifelong effects?', *Psychology and Aging* 9: 34–44

Amdur, R. L. and Liberzon, I. 2001. 'The structure of posttraumatic stress disorder symptoms in combat veterans: a confirmatory factor analysis of the impact of event scale', *Journal of Anxiety Disorders* 15: 345–57

American Psychiatric Association (APA). 1952. *Diagnostic & Statistical Manual of Mental Disorders*. Washington, DC: APA

American Psychiatric Association (APA). 1968. *Diagnostic & Statistical Manual of Mental Disorders*, 2nd edn. Washington, DC: APA

American Psychiatric Association (APA). 1980. *Diagnostic & Statistical Manual of Mental Disorders*, 3rd edn. Washington, DC: APA

American Psychiatric Association (APA). 1987. *Diagnostic & Statistical Manual of Mental Disorders*, 3rd edn (revised). Washington, DC: APA

American Psychiatric Association (APA). 1994. *Diagnostic & Statistical Manual of Mental Disorders*, 4th edn. Washington, DC: APA

American Psychiatric Association (APA). 2000. *Diagnostic and statistical manual of mental disorders DSM-IV-TR*, 4th edn. Washington, DC: APA

Anderson, C., Jeffrey, M. and Pai, M. N. 1944. 'Psychiatric casualties from the Normandy beachhead – first thoughts on 100 cases', *The Lancet* 2: 218–21

Androutsopoulou, A., Thanopoulou, K., Economou, E. and Bafti, T. 2004. 'Forming criteria for assessing the coherence of clients' life stories: a narrative study', *Journal of Family Therapy* 26: 384–406

Anthony, J. L., Lonigan, C. J. and Hecht, S. A. 1999. 'Dimensionality of posttraumatic stress disorder symptoms in children exposed to disaster: results from confirmatory factor analyses', *Journal of Abnormal Psychology* 108: 326–36

Atkinson, P. 1997. 'Narrative turn or blind alley?', *Qualitative Health Research* 7(3): 325–44

Atkinson, P. and Silverman, D. 1997. 'Kundera's *"Immortality"*: the interview society and the invention of self', *Qualitative Inquiry* 3: 304–25

Baars, J. 1997. 'Conflicting trends in the Netherlands', *The Gerontologist* 40: 302–4

Babington, A. 1983. *For the Sake of Example: Capital Courts-Martial 1914–1920*. London: Cooper

Baddeley, A. and Wilson, B. 2002. 'Prose recall and amnesia: implications for the structure of working memory', *Trends in Cognitive Sciences* 4: 417–23

Baerger, D. R. and McAdams, D. P. 1999. 'Life story coherence and its relation to psychological well-being', *Narrative Inquiry* 9: 69–96

Baker, S. L. 1975. 'Military psychiatry', in Freedman, A. M., Kaplan, H. I. and B. J. Sadock (eds.) *Comprehensive Textbook of Psychiatry*, vol. II, p. 2355. Baltimore: Williams & Wilkins

Bamberg, M. and McCabe, A. 1998. 'Editorial', *Narrative Inquiry* 8(1): iii–v

Barclay, C. R. and Smith, T. S. 1992. 'Autobiographical remembering: creating personal culture', in Conway, M. A., Rubin, D. C., Spinnler, H. and Wagenaar, W. A. (eds.) *Theoretical Perspectives on Autobiographical Memory*. Dordrecht: Kluwer Academic Publishers

Barker, C. R. and Last, R. W. 1979. *Erich Maria Remarque*. London: Oswald Wolff

Barrett, T. W. and Mizes, J. S. 1988. 'Combat level and social support in the development of posttraumatic stress disorder in Vietnam veterans', *Behavior Modification* 12: 100–115

Bartlett, F. C. 1932. *Remembering: A Study in Experimental and Social Psychology.* Cambridge University Press

Benowitz, L. I., Moya, K. L. and Levine, D. N. 1990. 'Impaired verbal reasoning and constructional apraxia in subjects with right hemisphere damage', *Neuropsychologia* 28: 23–41

Bertaux, D. 1995. A response to Thierry Kochuyt's 'Biographic and empiricist illusions: a reply to recent criticism'. *Biography and Society Newsletter*, 2–6. Research Committee 38: International Sociological Association

Binneveld, J. M. W. 1997. *From Shell Shock to Combat Stress: A Comparative History of Military Psychiatry.* Amsterdam University Press

Bolton, D. and Hill, J. 1996. *Mind, Meaning and Mental Disorder.* Oxford University Press

Bonne, O., Brandes, D., Gilboa, A. *et al.* 2001. 'Longitudinal MRI study of hippocampal volume in trauma survivors with PTSD', *The American Journal of Psychiatry* 158: 1248–51

Bornat, J., Dimmock, B., Jones, D. and Peace, S. 2000. 'Researching the implications of family change for older people: the contribution of a life-history approach', in Bornat, J., Chamberlayne, P. and Wengraf, T. (eds.) *The Turn to Biographical Methods in Social Science*. London: Taylor & Francis/Routledge

Bradshaw, S. L., Ohlde, C. D. and Horne, J. B. 1991. 'The love of war: Vietnam and the traumatised veteran', *Bulletin of the Menninger Clinic* 55: 96–103

Bramsen, L. and van der Ploeg, H. M. 1999. 'Fifty years later: the long term psychological adjustment of aging World War II survivors', *Acta Psychiatrica Scandinavica* 100: 350–8

Braun, A. R., Guillemin, A., Hosey, L. and Varga, M. 2001. 'The neural organisation of discourse: an H_2150-PET study of narrative production in English and American sign language', *Brain* 124: 2028–44

Bremner, J. D. 1998. 'Neuroimaging of posttraumatic stress disorder', *Psychiatric Annals* 28: 445–50

Bremner, J. D. 2005. *Does Stress Damage the Brain? Understanding Trauma-Related Disorders from a Mind–Body Perspective*. New York: Norton

Bremner, J. D. and Brett, E. 1997. 'Trauma-related dissociative states and long-term psychopathology in posttraumatic stress disorder', *Journal of Traumatic Stress* 10: 37–50

Bremner, J. D., Krystal, J. H., Southwick, S. M. and Charney, D. S. 1995. 'Functional neuroanatomical correlates of the effects of stress on memory', *Journal of Traumatic Stress* 8(4): 527–53

Bremner, J. D., Vermetten, E., Schmahl, C., Vaccarino, V., Vythilingam, M., Afzal, N., Grillon, C. and Charney, D. S. 2005. 'Positron emission tomographic imaging of neural correlates of a fear acquisition and extinction paradigm in women with childhood sexual-abuse-related post-traumatic stress disorder', *Psychological Medicine* 35: 791–806

Brewer, W. F. 1992. 'The theoretical and empirical status of the flashbulb memory hypothesis', in Winograd, E. and Neisser, U.(eds.) *Affect and Accuracy in Recall: Studies of 'Flashbulb' Memories* (vol. 4: Emory Symposia in Cognition), pp. 247–305. New York: Cambridge University Press

Brewin, C. R. and Holmes, E. A. 2003. 'Psychological theories of posttraumatic stress disorder', *Clinical Psychology Review* 23: 339–76

Brewin, C. R., Dalgleish, T. and Joseph, S. 1996. 'A dual representation theory of post-traumatic stress disorder', *Psychological Review*, 103: 670–86

Brewin, C. R., Andrews, B. and Rose, S. 2000. 'Fear, helplessness and horror in posttraumatic stress disorder: investigating DSM-IV criterion A2 in victims of violent crime', *Journal of Traumatic Stress* 13: 499–509

British Psychological Society (BPS). 1995. *Recovered Memories: Report of the BPS Working Party*. Leicester: BPS

British Psychological Society 2006. *Code of Conduct and Ethical Guidelines*. Accessed from: www.bps.org.uk/the-society/code-of-conduct/code-of-conduct_home.cfm, 7 June 2009

Bruner, J. 1986. *Actual Minds, Possible Worlds*. Harvard University Press

Bruner, J. 1990. *Acts of Meaning*. Harvard University Press

Bryant, R. A. and Harvey, A. H. 1997. 'Attentional bias in posttraumatic stress disorder', *Journal of Traumatic Stress* 10: 635–44

Buckley, T. C. and Kaloupek, D. G. 2001. 'A meta-analytic examination of basal cardiovascular activity in posttraumatic stress disorder', *Psychosomatic Medicine* 63: 585–94

Buckley, T. C., Blanchard, E. B. and Hickling, E. J. 1998. 'A confirmatory factor analysis of posttraumatic stress symptoms', *Behaviour Research and Therapy* 36: 1091–9

Burnell, K. and Jones, R. 2005. *Private/Public Commemoration of the Falklands War: Mutually Exclusive, or Joint Endeavours?* University of Southampton: Postgraduate Forum Conference, 'Interdisciplinarity'

Burnell, K., Coleman, P. and Hunt, N. 2006. 'Falklands War veterans: perceptions of social support and the reconciliation of traumatic memories', *Aging and Mental Health* 10(3): 282–9

Burnell, K., Hunt, N. and Coleman, P. 2007. 'Using narrative analysis to investigate the role of social support in the reconciliation of traumatic war memories', *Health Psychology Update* 15(3)

Burnell, K., Coleman, P. and Hunt, N. (2010). 'World War Two veterans, social support and narrative coherence', *Aging & Society* 30: 57–78

Butler, R. 1963. 'The life review: an interpretation of reminiscence in the aged', *Psychiatry* 26: 65–76

Calhoun, L. G. and Tedeschi, R. G. (eds.) 2006. *Handbook of Posttraumatic Growth: Research and Practice.* New York: Lawrence Erlbaum Associates

Cannon, W. 1929. *Bodily Changes in Pain, Hunger, Fear and Rage.* London: Appleton

Carlton, C. 1991. 'The impact of the fighting', in Morrill J. (ed.) *The Impact of the English Civil War.* London: Collins and Brown

Chemtob, C., Roitblat, H. L., Hamada, R. S., Carlson, J. G. and Twentyman, C. T. 1988. 'A cognitive-action theory of post-traumatic stress disorder', *Journal of Anxiety Disorders* 2: 253–75

Childs, D. 2008. *Growing Remembrance: The Story of the National Memorial Arboretum.* London: Pen & Sword Military

Christianson, S. A. 1992. 'Emotional stress and eyewitness testimony: a critical review', *Psychological Bulletin* 112: 284–309

Cobley, E. 1994. 'Cultural transformation: review of L. Hanley, *Writing War: Fiction, Gender, and Memory*', *Canadian Literature* 14: 154–6

Coleman, P. G. 1999. 'Creating a life story: the task of reconciliation', *The Gerontologist* 39: 133–9

Coleman, P. 2005. 'Uses of reminiscence: functions and benefits', *Aging and Mental Health* 9(4): 291–4

Connerton, P. 2008. 'Seven types of forgetting', *Memory Studies* 1(1): 59–71

Cook, J. M. 2001. 'Post-traumatic stress in older adults', *PTSD Research Quarterly* 12(3): 1–3

Creamer, M. 1995. 'A cognitive processing formulation of posttrauma reactions', in Kleber, R. J., Figley, C. R. and Gersons, B. P. R. (eds.) *Beyond Trauma: Cultural and Societal Dynamics*, pp. 55–73. New York: Plenum Press

Creamer, M., Burgess, P. and Pattison, P. 1992. 'Reaction to trauma: a cognitive processing model', *Journal of Abnormal Psychology* 101: 452–9

Crossley, M. L. 2000. *Introducing Narrative Psychology: Self, Trauma, and the Construction of Meaning.* Buckingham: Open University Press

Da Costa, J. M. 1871. 'On irritable heart: a clinical study of a form of functional cardiac disorder and its consequences', *The American Journal of the Medical Science* 61: 17–52

Dale, H. and Hunt, N. 2008. 'The perceived need for spiritual and religious treatment options in chronically ill individuals', *Journal of Health Psychology* 13(5): 712–18

Daly, R. J. 1983. 'Samuel Pepys and post-traumatic stress disorder', *British Journal of Psychiatry* 143: 64–8

Davidson, J. R. T., Kudler, H., Smith, R., Mahorney, S., Lipper, S., Hammett, E., Saunders, W. and Cavenar, J. O. 1990. 'Treatment of post-traumatic stress disorder with amitryptilene and placebo', *Archives of General Psvchiatrv* 47: 259–66

Davis, C. G. and Lehman, D. R. 1995. 'Counterfactual thinking and coping with traumatic life events', in Roese, N. J. and Olson J. M. (eds.) *What Might Have Been: The Social Psychology of Counterfactual Thinking*, pp. 353–74. Mahwah, NJ: Lawrence Erlbaum Associates

DeDous, J. F., Romanski, I. and Xagoraris, A. 1989. Indelibility of sub-cortical emotional memories, *Journal of Cognitive Neuroscience* 1: 238–43

Derderian, R. L. 2002. 'Algeria as a lieu de mémoire: ethnic minority memory and national identity in contemporary France', *Radical History Review* 83: 28–43

De Silva, P. 2006. 'The tsunami and its aftermath: explorations of a Buddhist perspective', *International Review of Psychiatry* 18(3): 281–7

Dollard, J. and Miller, N. 1950. *Personality and Psychotherapy: An Analysis in Terms of Learning, Thinking and Culture*. New York: McGraw-Hill

Durkheim, E. 1947. *The Elementary Forms of the Religious Life*. Glencoe, IL: The Free Press

Eberly, R. E. and Engdahl, B. E. 1991. 'Prevalence of somatic and psychiatric disorders among former prisoners of war', *Hospital & Community Psychiatry* 42: 807–13

Eco, U. 1992. *Interpretation and Overinterpretation*. Cambridge University Press

Ehlers, A., Maercker, A. and Boos, A. 2000. 'PTSD following political imprisonment: the role of mental defeat, alienation, and permanent change', *Journal of Abnormal Psychology* 109: 45–55

Ehrlich, P. 1988. 'Treatment issues in the psychotherapy of Holocaust survivors', in Wilson, J., Harel, Z. and Kahana, B. (eds.) *Human Adaptation to Severe Stress: From the Holocaust to Vietnam*. New York: Plenum Press

Einhorn, B. 2001. 'Gender, nation, landscape and identity in narratives of exile and return', *Women's Studies International Forum* 23: 701–13

Elder, G. H. and Clipp, E. C. 1989. 'Combat experience and emotional health: impairment and resilience in later life', *Journal of Personality* 57: 311–41

Ellenberger, H. F. 1970. *The Discovery of the Unconscious*. New York: Basic Books

Emery, P. F. and Emery, O. B. 1989. 'Psychoanalytic considerations on post-traumatic stress disorder', *Journal of Contemporary Psychotherapy* 19(4): 39–53

Erichsen, J. 1866. *On Railway Spine and other Injuries*. London: Walton and Maberly

Erikson, E. H. 1982. *The Life Cycle Completed*. New York: Norton

Falger, P. R. J., op den Velde, W., Hovens, J. E., Schouten, E. G. W., de Groen, J. H. M. and van Duijn, H. 1992. 'Current posttraumatic stress disorder and cardiovascular risk factors in Dutch resistance veterans from World War Two', *Psychotherapy and Psychosomatics* 57: 164–71

Favorini, A. 2003. 'History, collective memory, and Aeschylus' the Persians', *Theatre Journal* 55(1): 99–111

Figley, C. (ed.) 2005. *Compassion Fatigue: Coping with Secondary Traumatic Stress Disorder in Those Who Treat the Traumatised*. New York: Brunner/Mazel

Fletcher, P. C., Happe, F., Frith, U., Baker, S. C., Dolan, R. J. and Frackowiak, R. S. J. *et al.* 1995. 'Other minds in the brain: a functional imaging study of "theory of mind" in story comprehension', *Cognition* 57: 109–28

Foa, E. B. and Riggs, D. S. 1993. 'Post-traumatic stress disorder in rape victims', in Oldham, J., Riba, M. B. and Tasman, A. (eds.) *American Psychiatric Press Review of Psychiatry*, vol. 12, pp. 273–303. Washington, DC: American Psychiatric Press

Foa, E. B. and Rothbaum, B. O. 1998. *Treating the Trauma of Rape: Cognitive Behavioural Therapy for PTSD*. New York: Guilford Press

Foa, E. B., Steketee, G. and Rothbaum, B. O. 1989. 'Behavioural/cognitive conceptualisations of post-traumatic stress disorder', *Behavior Therapy* 20: 155–76

Foa, E. B., Riggs, D. S. and Gershuny, B. S. 1995. 'Arousal, numbing, and intrusion: symptom structure of PTSD following assault', *The American Journal of Psychiatry* 152: 116–20

Fontana, A. and Rosenheck, R. 1998. 'Psychological benefits and liabilities of traumatic exposure in the war zone', *Journal of Traumatic Stress* 11: 485–505

Foy, M. R., Stanton, M. E., Levine, S. and Thompson, R. F. 1987. 'Behavioural stress impairs long-term potentiation in rodent hippocampus', *Behavioral and Neural Biology* 48: 138–49

Frankl, V. E. 1963/1984. *Man's Search for Meaning*. New York: Pocket Books

Frankl, V. E. 1969. *The Will to Meaning: Foundations and Applications of Logotherapy*. New York: World Publishing Company

Frans, O., Rimmo, P. A., Aberg, L. and Fredrikson, M. 2005. 'Trauma exposure and post-traumatic stress disorder in the general population', *Acta Psychiatrica Scandinavica* 111: 291–9

Fransella, F., Bell, R. and Bannister, D. 2004. *A Manual for Repertory Grid Technique*, 2nd edn. West Sussex: John Wiley

Freeman, M. 1993. *Rewriting the Self: History, Memory, Narrative*. London: Routledge

Freud, S. 1921. 'Introduction to psychoanalysis and the war neuroses', in Strachey, J. (ed.) *Standard Edition of the Complete Psychological Works of Sigmund Freud*, vol. 17. London: Hogarth Press

Fromholt, P., Larsen, P. and Larsen, S. F. 1995. 'Effects of late-onset depression and recovery on autobiographical memory', *Journals of Gerontology Series B: Psychological Sciences and Social Sciences* 50(2): 74–81

Fuster, J. M., Bodner, M. and Kroger, J. K. 2000. 'Cross-modal and cross-temporal association in neurons of the frontal cortex', *Nature* 405: 347–51

Garcia, J. and Koelling, R. A. 1966. 'The relation of cue to consequence in avoidance learning', *Psychonomic Science* 4: 123–4

Gardner, R. A. 1997. 'The embedment-in-the-brain circuitry phenomenon: implications for psychoanalytic treatment', *The Journal of the American Academy of Psychoanalysis* 25: 161–76

Geary, P. 1994. *Phantoms of Remembrance: Memory and Oblivion at the End of the First Millennium*. Princeton University Press

Gergen, K. and Gergen, M. M. 1988 'Narrative and the self as relationship', *Advances in Experimental Social Psychology* 21: 17–56

Goenjian, A. K., Najarian, L. M., Pynoos, R. S., Steinberg, A. M., Manoukian, G., Tavosian, A. and Fairbanks, L. A. 1994. 'Posttraumatic stress disorder in elderly and younger adults after the 1988 earthquake in Armenia', *The American Journal of Psychiatry* 151: 895–901

Goldberg, D. 1978. *Manual of the General Health Questionnaire.* Windsor: National Foundation for Educational Research

Graesser, A. C., McNamara, D. S., Louwerse, M. M. and Cai, Z. 2004. 'Coh-Metrix: analysis of text on cohesion and language', *Behavior Research Methods, Instruments, & Computers* 36: 193–202

Graham, B. and Shirlow, P. 2002. 'The Battle of the Somme in Ulster memory and identity', *Political Geography* 21: 881–904

Greening, T. 1990. 'PTSD from the perspective of existential-humanistic psychology', *Journal of Traumatic Stress* 3(2): 323–6

Guidano, V. 1995. 'Self-observation in constructivist psychotherapy', in Neimeyer, R. A. and Mahoney, M. J. (eds.) *Constructivism in Psychotherapy,* pp. 155–168. Washington, DC: American Psychological Association

Habermas, T. and Bluck, S. 2000. 'Getting a life: the emergence of the life story in adolescence', *Psychological Bulletin* 126: 748–69

Halbwachs, M. 1992. *On Collective Memory.* London: University of Chicago Press. Originally published as *Les Cadres Sociaux de la Mémoire* (1952), Presses Universitaires de France

Hanley, L. 1991. *Writing War: Fiction, Gender and Memory.* University of Massachusetts Press

Hargreaves, G. R. 1939. 'Psychological casualties in war', *British Medical Journal* 2: 1161

Harvey, A. G., Bryant, R. A. and Rapee, R. M. 1996. 'Preconscious processing of threat in posttraumatic stress disorder', *Cognitive Therapy and Research* 20: 613–23

Hassan, J. 1997. 'From victim to survivor: the possibility of healing in ageing survivors of the Nazi Holocaust', in Hunt, L., Marshall, M. and Rowlings, C. (eds.) *Past Trauma in Late Life: European Perspectives on Therapeutic Work with Older People.* London: Jessica Kingsley

Herman, J. L. 1992. *Trauma and Recovery.* London: Pandora

Hesnard, A. 1914. 'Mental and nervous symptoms following naval disasters' [Les troubles nervoux et psychiques consecutifs aux catastrophes navale], *Revue de Psychiatrie de l'Université d'Ottawa* 18: 139–51

Hibberd, D. 1992. *Wilfred Owen: The Last Year.* London: Constable

Hinchman, L. and Hinchman, S. (eds.) 1997. *Memory, Identity, Community: The Idea of Narrative in the Human Sciences.* Albany, New York: SUNY Press

Hobsbawm, E. and Ranger, T. 1983. *The Invention of Tradition.* Cambridge University Press

Holman, E. A. and Silver, R. C. 1998. 'Getting "Stuck" in the past: temporal orientation and coping with trauma', *Journal of Personality and Social Psychology* 74: 1146–63

Horowitz, M. J. 1986. *Stress Response Syndromes,* 2nd edn. Northvale, NJ: Jason Aronson

Horowitz, M. J., Wilner, N. and Alvarez, W. 1979. 'Impact of Event Scale: a measure of subjective stress', *Psychosomatic Medicine* 41(3): 209–18

Hough, M. S. 1990. 'Narrative comprehension in adults with right and left hemisphere brain damage: theme organisation', *Brain and Language* 38: 253–77

Hunt, N. 1996. 'The long term psychological consequences of war experience,' Ph.D. thesis

Hunt, N. 1997. 'Trauma of war', *The Psychologist* 10(8): 357–60

Hunt, N. 1999. '*All Quiet on the Western Front* and understanding of psychological trauma', *Narrative Inquiry* 1: 207–12

Hunt, N. 2004. 'The contribution of *All Quiet on the Western Front* to our understanding of psychological trauma', *European Psychiatry* 19: 489–93

Hunt, N. 2008a. 'The long term effects of war experience', *Aging and Mental Health* 11(2): 156–8

Hunt, N. 2008b. 'Health consequences of war and political violence', in Kurtz, L. (ed.) *Encyclopaedia of Violence, Peace and Conflict*, 2nd edn. Oxford: Elsevier Press

Hunt, N. and Gekenyi, M. 2003. 'Comparing refugees and non-refugees: the Bosnian experience', *Journal of Anxiety Disorders* 19(6): 717–23

Hunt, N. and McHale, S. 2008. 'Memory and meaning: individual and social aspects of memory narratives', *Journal of Loss & Trauma* 13(1): 42–58

Hunt, N. and Robbins, I. 1998. 'Telling stories of the war: ageing veterans coping with their memories through narrative', *The Oral History Review* 26(2): 57–64

Hunt, N. and Robbins, I. 2001a. 'The long-term consequences of war: the experience of World War II', *Aging and Mental Health* 5(2): 183–90

Hunt, N. and Robbins, I. 2001b. 'World War II veterans, social support, and veterans' associations', *Aging and Mental Health* 5(2): 175–82

Hunt, L., Marshall, M. and Rowlings, C. 1997. *Past Trauma in Late Life: European Perspectives on Therapeutic Work with Older People*. London: Jessica Kingsley

Hutton, P. H. 1993. *History as an Art of Memory*. University Press of New England

Ilich, I. 1916/1994. *The Bridge Over the Drina*. London: Harvill Press

James, W. 1890/2007. *Principles of Psychology*. New York: Cosimo

Janet, P. 1925. *Psychological Healing: A Historical and Clinical Study*, vol. 1. London: Allen & Unwin

Janoff-Bulman, R. 1992. *Shattered Assumptions: Towards a New Psychology of Trauma*. New York: Free Press

Jelicic, M. and Bonke, B. 2001. 'Memory impairments following chronic stress? A critical review', *European Psychiatry* 15: 225–32

Jones, E. 2004. 'Doctors and trauma in the First World War: the response of British military psychiatrists', in Gray, P. and Oliver, K. (eds.) *The Memory of Catastrophe*. Manchester University Press

Keegan, J. 1976. *Who's Who in Military History*. London: William Morrow

Judah, T. 2000. *The Serbs: History, Myth and the Destruction of Yugoslavia*. Yale University Press

Kamierska, K. 2002. 'Narratives on World War II in Poland: when a life story is a family history', *The History of the Family* 7: 281–305

Kang, H., Dalager, N., Mahan, C. and Ishii, E. 2005. 'The role of sexual assault on the risk of PTSD among Gulf War veterans', *Annals of Epidemiology* 15: 191–5

Kenyon, G. M. and Randall, W. L. 1999. 'Introduction: Narrative Gerontology', *Journal of Aging Studies* 13: 1–15

Kessler, R. C., Sonnega, A., Bromet, E. *et al.* 1995. 'Posttraumatic stress disorder in the National Comorbidity Survey', *Archives of General Psychiatry* 52: 1048–60

Kihlstrom, J. F. 2002. 'No need for repression', *Trends in Cognitive Sciences* 6: 12

Kihlstrom, J. F., Beer, J. S. and Klein, S. B. 2002. 'Self and identity as memory', in Leary, M. R. and Tangney, J. (eds.) *Handbook of Self and Identity*, pp. 68–90. New York: Guilford Press

Kilshaw, S. 2004. 'Friendly fire: the construction of Gulf War Syndrome narratives', *Anthropology & Medicine* 11(2): 149–60

Kirschenbaum, L. A. 2004. 'Commemorations of the siege of Leningrad: a catastrophe in memory and myth', in Gray, P. and Oliver, K. (eds.) *The Memory of Catastrophe*. Manchester University Press

Knapp, A. B. 1988. *The History and Culture of Ancient Western Asia and Egypt.* Thomson Learning

Knox, D. 2006. 'The sacralised landscapes of Glencoe: from massacre to mass tourism, and back again', *International Journal of Tourism Research* 8: 185–97

Koss, M. P., Figuerado, A. J., Bell, I., Tharan, M. and Tromp, S. 1996. 'Traumatic memory characteristics: a cross-validated mediational model of response to rape among employed women', *Journal of Abnormal Psychology* 105: 421–31

Krook, D. 1969. *The Elements of Tragedy.* Yale University Press

Kubany, E. S. 1994. 'A cognitive model of guilt typology in combat-related PTSD', *Journal of Traumatic Stress* 7: 3–19

Lang, P. J. 1979. 'A bio-information theory of emotional imagery', *Journal of Psychophysiology* 16: 495–512

LeDoux, J. 1995. 'Emotion: clues from the brain', *Annual Review of Psychiatry* 46: 209–35

Lennon, J. J. and Foley, M. 2000. *Dark Tourism: The Attraction of Death and Disaster.* Thomson Learning

Levine, S. and Ursin, H. 1991. 'What is stress?', in Brown, M. R., Koob, G. F. and Rivier, C. (eds.) *Neurobiology and Neuroendocrinology of Stress*, pp. 3–21. New York: Marcel Dekker

Lev-Wiesel, R. and Amir, M. 2001. 'Secondary traumatic stress, psychological distress, sharing of traumatic reminiscences and marital quality among spouses of Holocaust child survivors', *Journal of Marital and Family Therapy* 27(4): 297–308

Lev-Wiesel, R. and Amir, M. 2006. 'Growing out of the ashes: posttraumatic growth among Holocaust child survivors – is it possible?', in Calhoun, L. G. and Tedeschi, R. G. (eds.) *Handbook of Posttraumatic Growth: Research and Practice*, pp. 248–63. New York: Lawrence Erlbaum

Linde, C. 1993. *Life Stories: The Creation of Coherence.* Oxford University Press

Lindemann, E. 1944. 'Symptomatology and management of acute grief', *The American Journal of Psychiatry* 101: 141–8

Linley, P. A. and Joseph, S. 2004a. 'Positive change following trauma and adversity: a review', *Journal of Traumatic Stress* 17(1): 11–21

Linley, A. and Joseph, S. (eds.) 2004b. *Positive Psychology in Practice*. London: John Wiley

Linley, P. A. and Joseph, S. 2006. 'The positive and negative effects of disaster work: a preliminary investigation', *Journal of Loss & Trauma* 11(3): 229–45

Lipgar, R. M. and Pines, M. 2003. *Building on Bion Roots: Origin and Contexts of Bion's Contributions to Theory and Practice*. London: Jessica Kingsley

MacIntyre, A. 1984. *After virtue*, 2nd edn. University of Notre Dame Press

Maercker, A., Herrle, J. and Grimm, I. 1999. 'Dresdener Bombennachtsopfer 50 Jahre danach: Eine Untersuchung patho- und salutogenetischer Variablen' [Dresden bombing night victims 50 years later: a study of patho- and soluto-genic variables], *Zeitschrift für Gerontopsychologie und -psychiatrie* 12: 157–67

Maguire, E. A., Frith, U. and Morris, G. M. 1999. 'The functional neuroanatomy of comprehension and memory: the importance of prior knowledge', *Brain* 122: 1839–50

March, J. S. 1990. 'The nosology of posttraumatic stress disorder', *Journal of Anxiety Disorders* 4: 61–82

Marr, R. A. 2004. 'The neuropsychology of narrative: story comprehension, story production and the interrelation', *Neuropsychologia* 42: 1414–34

Martin, J. R. 2003. 'Cohesion and texture', in Schiffrin, D., Tannen, D. and Hamilton, H. E. (eds.) *The Handbook of Discourse Analysis*. London: Blackwell

Maslow, A. H. 1954. *Motivation and Personality*. New York: Harper

Mason, J. W. 1975. 'A historical view of the stress field, part II', *Journal of Human Stress* 1: 6–12

Mayes, R. and Horowitz, A. V. 2005. 'DSM-III and the revolution in the classification of mental illness', *Journal of the History of the Behavioral Sciences* 41(3): 249–67

McAdams, D. P. 2001. 'The psychology of life stories', *Review of General Psychology* 66: 1125–46

McAdams, D. P. 2006. 'The problem of narrative coherence', *Journal of Constructivist Psychology* 19: 109–25

McCauley, J., Kern, D. E., Kolodner, K. *et al.* 1997. 'Clinical characteristics of women with a history of childhood abuse: unhealed wounds', *Journal of the American Medical Association* 277: 1362–8

McEwen, B. S. and Magarinos, M. 1997. 'Stress effects on morphology and function of the hippocampus', *Annals of the New York Academy of Sciences* 821: 271–84

McFarlane, A. C. 1992. 'Avoidance and intrusion in posttraumatic stress disorder', *Journal of Nervous and Mental Disease* 180: 439–45

McWilliams, L. A., Cox, B. J. and Asmundson, G. J. G. 2005. 'Symptom structure of posttraumatic stress disorder in a nationally representative sample', *Journal of Anxiety Disorders* 19: 596–601

Meichenbaum, D. 2006. 'Resilience and posttraumatic growth: a constructive narrative perspective', in Calhoun, L. G. and Tedeschi, R. G. (eds.) *Handbook of Posttraumatic Growth: Research and Practice*. London: Lawrence Erlbaum

Menchú, R. 1983. *I Rigoberta Menchú: An Indian Woman in Guatemala*. Brooklyn, NY: Verso

Michaels, A. J., Michaels, C. E., Moon, C. H., Smith, J. S., Zimmerman, M. A. and Taheri, P. A. 1999. 'Posttraumatic stress disorders after injury: impact on general health outcome and early risk assessment', *Journal of Trauma* 47: 460–7

Mishler, E. 1986. *Research Interviewing: Context and Narrative*. Harvard University Press

Mishler, E. G. 1995. 'Models of narrative analysis: a typology', *Journal of Narrative and Life History* 5: 87–123

Moskovitz, S. 1983. *Love Despite Hate*. New York: Norton

Mulder, R. T., Beautrais, A. L., Joyce, P. R. and Fergusson, D. M. 1998. 'Relationship between dissociation, childhood sexual abuse, childhood physical abuse, and mental illness in a general population sample', *The American Journal of Psychiatry* 155: 806–11

Murray, J., Ehlers, A. and Mayou, R. 2002. 'Dissociation and post-traumatic stress disorder: two prospective studies of motor vehicle accident survivors', *British Journal of Psychiatry* 180: 363–8

Neimeyer, R. A. 2005. 'Widowhood, grief and the quest for meaning: a narrative perspective on resilience', in Carr, D., Nesse, R. M. and Wortman, C. B. (eds.) *Late Life Widowhood in the United States*, pp. 68–80. New York: Springer

Neimeyer, R. A. 2006a. *Meaning Reconstruction and the Experience of Loss*. Washington, DC: American Psychological Association

Neimeyer, R. A. 2006b. 'Re-storying loss: fostering growth in the posttraumatic narrative', in Calhoun, L. G. and Tedeschi, R. G. (eds.) *Handbook of Posttraumatic Growth: Research and Practice*. London: Lawrence Erlbaum

Neimeyer, R. A. and Levitt, H. 2001. 'Coping and coherence: a narrative perspective', in Snyder, D. (ed.) *Coping with Stress: Effective People and Processes*, pp. 47–67. Oxford University Press

Nemeroff, C. B., Bremner, J. D., Foa, E. B., Mayberg, H. S., North, C. S. and Stein, M. B. 2006. 'Posttraumatic stress disorder: a state-of-the-science review', *Journal of Psychiatric Research* 40: 1–21

Nemeroff, C. B., Entsuah, R., Benattia, I., Demitrack, M., Sloan, D. M. and Thase, M. E. 2008. 'Comprehensive Analysis of Remission (COMPARE) with Venlafaxine versus SSRIs', *Biological Psychiatry* 63: 424–34

Ness, G. J. and Macaskill, N. 2003. 'Preventing PTSD: the value of inner resourcefulness and a sense of personal control of a situation. Is it a matter of problem-solving or anxiety management?', *Behavioural and Cognitive Psychotherapy* 31(4): 463–6

NICE. 1995. Guidelines for PTSD: www.nice.org.uk/guidance/CG26

Nora, P. 1989. 'Between Memory and History: Les Lieux de Mémoire', *Representations* 26: 7–25

Notestine, C. F., Stein, M. B., Kennedy, C. M., Archibald, S. L. and Jernigan, T. L. 2002. 'Brain morphometry in female victims of intimate partner violence with and without posttraumatic stress disorder', *Biological Psychiatry* 51: 1089–101

Novoa, O. P. and Ardila, A. 1987. 'Linguistic abilities in patients with prefrontal damage', *Brain and Language* 30: 206–25

Nutt, D. J. and Malazia, A. L. 2004. 'Structural and functional brain changes in posttraumatic stress disorder', *Journal of Clinical Psychiatry* 65(suppl 1): 11–17

O'Brien, T. 1994. *Civil Defence*. London: HMSO

O'Kearney, R. and Perrott, K. 2006. 'Trauma narratives in posttraumatic stress disorder: a review', *Journal of Traumatic Stress* 19(1): 81–93

Olick 2008. 'Collective memory: a memoire and prospect', *Memory Studies* 1(1): 23–9

Orr, S. P., Metzger, L. J., Lasko, N. B., Macklin, M. L., Peri, T. and Pitman, R. K. 2000. 'De novo conditioning in trauma-exposed individuals with and without posttraumatic stress disorder', *Journal of Abnormal Psychology* 109: 290–8

Pals, J. L. 2006. 'Narrative identity processing of difficult life experiences: pathways of personality development and positive self-transformation in adulthood', *Journal of Personality* 74(4): 1079–109

Park, C. L., Cohen, L. H. and Murch, R. 1996. 'Assessment and prediction of stress related growth', *Journal of Personality* 64: 71–105

Pennebaker, J. W. 1997. 'Writing about emotional experiences as a therapeutic process', *Psychological Science* 8: 162–9

Pennebaker, J. W. and Graybeal, A. 2001. 'Patterns of natural language use: disclosure, personality and social integration', *Current Directions in Psychological Science* 10: 90–3

Pitman, R. K. 2001. 'Investigating the pathogenesis of posttraumatic stress disorder with neuroimaging', *Journal of Clinical Psychiatry* 62: 47–54

Posner, M. I. 1993. 'Interaction of arousal and selection in the posterior attention network', in Baddeley, A. and Weiskrantz, L. (eds.) *Attention: Selection, Awareness and Control. A Tribute to Donald Broadbent*, pp. 390–405. Oxford University Press

Quinlan, M. 2005a. *Remembrance*. Hertford: Authors OnLine

Quinlan, M. 2005b. *British War Memorials*. Hertford: Authors OnLine

Rachman, S. 1980. 'Emotional processing', *Behaviour Research and Therapy* 18: 51–60

Reid, J. J. 2000. *Crisis of the Ottoman Empire*. Wiesbaden, Germany: Franz Steiner Verlag

Remarque, E. M. 1929. *All Quiet on the Western Front*. London: Triad Books

Riessman, C. K. 2000. 'Analysis of personal narratives', in Gubrium, J. F. and Holstein, J. A. (eds.) *Handbook of Interviewing*. London: Sage

Rivers, W. H. R. 1922. *Conflict and Dream*. Cambridge University Press

Robbins, I. 1997. 'Understanding and treating the long term consequences of war trauma', in Hunt, L., Marshall, M. and Rowlings, C. (eds.) *Past Trauma*

in Late Life: European Perspectives on Therapeutic Work with Older People.
London: Jessica Kingsley

Robbins I. 2007. 'The war on terror: the road from Belmarsh to Guantanamo
Bay', in Roberts, R. (ed.) *Just War: Psychology and Terrorism.* Ross-on-Wye:
PCCS Books

Rogers, C. 1980. *A Way of Being.* Houghton Mifflin

Rosen, E. 1960. *Witchcraft in England, 1558–1618.* University of Massachusetts
Press

Rosen, G. M. and Lilienfeld, S. O. 2008. 'Posttraumatic stress disorder: an
empirical evaluation of core assumptions', *Clinical Psychology Review*
28: 837–68

Rosen, G. M., Spitzer, R. L. and McHugh, P. R. 2008. 'Problems with the
post-traumatic stress disorder diagnosis and its future in DSM-V', *British
Journal of Psychiatry* 192: 3–4

Rosner, R. and Powell, S. 2006. 'Posttraumatic growth after war', in Calhoun,
L.G. and Tedeschi, R.G. (eds.) *Handbook of Posttraumatic Growth: Research
and Practice*, pp. 197–213. New York: Lawrence Erlbaum

Ross, D. (ed.) 1994. *Modernist Impulses in the Human Sciences, 1870–1930.*
Baltimore, MD: Johns Hopkins University Press

Salmon, T. W. 1921. 'Some problems of disabled ex-service men three years after
the armistice', *Mental Hygiene* 6: 271–86

Sargant, W. 1967. *The Unquiet Mind.* London: Heinemann

Sargant, W. and Slater, E. 1944/1963. *An Introduction to Physical Methods of
Treatment in Psychiatry.* London: Livingstone

Sawyer, K. 2003. 'Coherence in discourse: suggestions for future work', *Human
Development* 46: 189–93

Schauer, M., Neuner, F. and Elbert, T. 2005. *Narrative Exposure Therapy:
A Short-Term Intervention for Traumatic Stress Disorders after War, Terror, or
Torture.* Göttingen, Germany: Hogrefe & Huber

Schreiber, N., Wentura, D. and Bilsky, W. 2001. 'What else could we have done?
Creating false answers in child witnesses by inviting speculation', *Journal of
Applied Psychology* 86(3): 525–32

Sebald, W. G. 2003. *On the Natural History of Destruction.* London: Random
House

Sel, R. 1997. 'Dissociation as complex adaptation', *Medical Hypotheses* 48: 205–8

Selye, H. 1956. *The Stress of Life.* New York: McGraw-Hill

Shalev, A. Y., Freedman, S., Peri, T., Brandes, D., Sahar, T., Orr, S. P.
and Pitman, R. K. 1998. 'Prospective study of posttraumatic stress
disorder and depression following trauma', *The American Journal of
Psychiatry* 155: 630–7

Shay, J. 1991. 'Learning about combat stress from Homer's Iliad', *Journal of
Traumatic Stress* 4(4): 561–79

Shay, J. 1994. *Achilles in Vietnam: Combat Trauma and the Undoing of Character.*
New York: Atheneum/Macmillan

Sigal, J. J. 1998. 'Long term effects of the Holocaust: empirical evidence for
resilience in the first, second and third generation', *The Psychoanalytic
Review* 85(4): 579–85

Simms, L. J., Watson, D. and Doebbeling, B. N. 2002. 'Confirmatory factor analyses of posttraumatic stress symptoms in deployed and nondeployed veterans of the Gulf War', *Journal of Abnormal Psychology* 111: 637–47

Singer, J. A. and Rexhaj, B. 2006. 'Narrative coherence and psychotherapy: a commentary', *Journal of Constructivist Psychology* 19(12): 209–17

Smith, J., Larkin, M. and Flowers, P. 2009. *Interpretative Phenomenological Analysis: Theory, Method and Research*. London: Sage

Southwick, S. M., Bremner, J. D., Rasmusson, A., Morgan, C. A., Arnsten, A. and Charney, D. S. 1999. 'Role of norepinephrine in the pathophysiology and treatment of posttraumatic stress disorder', *Biological Psychiatry* 46: 442–4

Speed, N., Engdahl, B., Schwarz, J. and Eberly, R. 1989. 'Posttraumatic stress disorder as a consequence of the POW experience', *Journal of Nervous and Mental Disease* 177(3): 147–53

Spiro, A., Schnurr, P. P. and Aldwin, C. M. 1994. 'Combat-related post-traumatic stress disorder symptoms in older men', *Psychology and Aging* 9: 17–26

Squire, L. R. 1992. 'Memory and the hippocampus: a synthesis from findings with rats, monkeys, and humans', *Psychological Review* 99: 195–231

Squire, C. (ed.) 2000. *Culture in Psychology*. London: Routledge

Stam, R. 2007. 'PTSD and stress sensitisation: a tale of brain and body part 1: human studies', *Neuroscience & Biobehavioral Reviews* 31: 530–57

Stamp, G. 2006. *Memorial to the Missing of the Somme*. London: Profile

Stein, N. and Glenn, C. 1979. 'An analysis of story comprehension in elementary schoolchildren', in Freedle, R. D. (ed.) *Advances in Discourse Processes*, vol. 2. Norwood, NJ: Ablex

Stewart, B. S. 1969. 'The cult of the royal martyr', *Church History: Studies in Christianity and Culture* 38: 175–87

Stoyle, M. 2004. 'Remembering the Civil Wars', in Gray, P. and Oliver, K. (eds.) *The Memory of Catastrophe*, pp. 19–30. Manchester University Press

Strauss, A. and Corbin, J. 1998. *Basics of Qualitative Research*. London: Sage

Strecker, E. A. and Appel, K. E. 1964. *Psychiatry in Modern Warfare*. New York: MacMillan

Tajfel, H. 1981. 'Social stereotypes and social groups', in Turner, J. C. and Giles, H. (eds.) *Intergroup Behaviour*, pp. 144–67. Oxford: Blackwell

Tedeschi, R. G. and Calhoun, L. G. 1995. *Trauma and Transformation: Growing in the Aftermath of Suffering*. Thousand Oaks, CA: Sage

Tedeschi, R. G. and Calhoun, L. 1996. 'The Posttraumatic Growth Inventory: measuring the positive legacy of trauma', *Journal of Traumatic Stress*, 9: 455–71

Tedeschi, R. G., Park, C. L. and Calhoun, L. G. (eds.) 1998. *Posttraumatic Growth: Positive Changes in the Aftermath of Crisis*. Mahwah, NJ: Lawrence Erlbaum

Terr, L. 1990. *Too Scared to Cry: Psychic Trauma in Childhood*. New York: Basic Books

Thelen, D. 1990. *Memory and American History*. Indiana University Press

Trandel, D. V. and McNally, R. J. 1987. 'Perception of threat cues in post-traumatic stress disorder: semantic processing without awareness?', *Behaviour Research and Therapy* 25: 449–76

Trimble, M. 1985. 'Post traumatic stress disorder: the history of a concept', in Figley, C. R. (ed.) *Trauma and Its Wake.* New York: Brunner/Mazel

Turner, R. J. and Marino, F. 1994. 'Social support and social structure: a descriptive epidemiology', *Journal of Health and Social Behavior* 35(3): 193–212

van der Hart, O. and Horst, R. 1989. 'The dissociation theory of Pierre Janet', *Journal of Traumatic Stress* 2: 397–412

van der Kolk, B. A. and Fisler, R. 1995. 'Dissociation and the fragmentary nature of traumatic memories: overview and exploratory study', *Journal of Traumatic Stress* 8(4): 505–25

van der Kolk, B. A. and van der Hart, O. 1991. 'The intrusive past: the flexibility of memory and the engraving of trauma', *American Imago* 48: 425–54

Vermetten, E., Vythilingam, M., Southwick, S. M., Charney, D. S. and Bremner, J. D. 2003. 'Long-term treatment with paroxetine increases verbal declarative memory and hippocampal volume in posttraumatic stress disorder', *Biological Psychiatry* 54: 693–702

Watson, P. 1978. *War on the Mind.* London: Hutchinson

Waugh, M. J. 1997. 'Keeping the Home Fires Burning', *The Psychologist* 10(8): 361–3

Weine, S. M., Becker, D. F., McGlashan, T. H., Laub, D., Lazrove, S., Vojvoda, D. and Hyman, L. 1995. 'Psychiatric consequences of "ethnic cleansing": clinical assessments and trauma testimonies of newly resettled Bosnian refugees', *The American Journal of Psychiatry* 152: 536–42

Wilkomirski, B. 1995. *Fragments: Memoires of a Childhood 1939–48.* London: Picador

Williams, L. M., Kemp, A. H., Felmingham, K., Barton, M., Olivieri, G., Peduto, A., Gordon, E. and Bryant, R. 2006. 'Trauma modulates amygdala and medial prefrontal responses to consciously attended fear', *NeuroImage* 29: 347–57

Wilson, J. P. 1994. 'The historical evolution of PTSD diagnostic criteria: from Freud to DSM-IV', *Journal of Traumatic Stress* 7(4): 681–98

Wilson, R. A. 2005. 'Collective memory, group minds and the extended mind thesis', *Cognitive Processing* 6(4): 227–36

Wolfe, J. 1995. 'Trauma, traumatic memory, and research: where do we go from here?', *Journal of Traumatic Stress* 8(4): 717–27

Wrye, H. K. 1994. 'Narrative scripts: composing a life with ambition and desire', *The American Journal of Psychoanalysis* 54: 127–41

Yalom, I. D. 1983. *Existential Psychotherapy.* New York: Basic Books

Yehuda, R. and McFarlane, A. C. 1995. 'Conflict between current knowledge about posttraumatic stress disorder and its original conceptual basis', *The American Journal of Psychiatry* 152: 1705–13

Yehuda, R., Kahana, B., Schmeidler, J., Southwick, S. M., Wilson, S. and Giller, E. L. 1995. 'Impact of cumulative lifetime trauma and recent stress on current post-traumatic stress disorder symptoms in Holocaust survivors', *The American Journal of Psychiatry* 152: 1815–18

Yehuda, R., Golier, J., Tischler, L., Stavitsky, K. and Harvey, P. 2005. 'Learning and memory in aging combat veterans with PTSD', *Journal of Clinical and Experimental Neuropsychology* 27: 504–15

Yehuda, R., Golier, J. A., Tischler, L., Harvey, P. D., Newmark, R., Yang, R. K. *et al.* 2006. 'Hippocampal volume in aging combat veterans with and without PTSD: relation to risk and resilience factors', *Journal of Psychiatric Research* 41: 435

Zerubavel, E. 1997. *Social Mindscapes: An Invitation to Cognitive Sociology.* Harvard University Press

Zoellner, L. A., Alvarez-Conrad, J. and Foa, E. B. 2002. 'Peritraumatic dissociative experiences, trauma narratives and trauma pathology', *Journal of Traumatic Stress* 15(1): 49–57

Index